Stanley KUBRICK

a guide to references and resources

A
Reference
Publication
in
Film

Ronald Gottesman
Editor

Stanley
KUBRICK

a guide to
references and resources

WALLACE COYLE

G.K.HALL &CO.
70 LINCOLN STREET, BOSTON, MASS.

Library of Congress Cataloging in Publication Data

Coyle, Wallace.
Stanley Kubrick, a guide to references and resources.

(A Reference publication in film)
Includes indexes.
1. Kubrick, Stanley. I. Title. II. Series: Reference publication in film.
PN1998.A3K7367 791.43'0233'0924 80-20649
ISBN 0-8161-8058-X

This publication is printed on permanent/durable acid-free paper
MANUFACTURED IN THE UNITED STATES OF AMERICA

for
Mary

Contents

Preface

On the basis of only ten feature length films, Stanley Kubrick ranks as one of the world's greatest living directors. His seemingly limitless capabilities as writer, producer, set designer, cinematographer, and special effects coordinator are enlarged with each new film he releases. Judged by both his fellow directors and professional film critics, Kubrick's place in the history of the modern cinema seems assured on the evidence of at least three films that have become classics in their own right: *Dr. Strangelove, Or How I Learned to Stop Worrying and Love the Bomb* (1964), *2001: A Space Odyssey* (1968), and *A Clockwork Orange* (1971). Beyond these singular achievements, Kubrick has produced and directed some of the most controversial films ever made. As a pioneer in the area of special effects design and cinematography, Kubrick embodies individual talents and abilities that are often associated with an entire technical staff of experts in the modern film industry. Because so much has been written about Kubrick, including three full-length books by Alexander Walker, Norman Kagan, and Gene Phillips, it seems reasonable at this point to examine Kubrick's career in the film industry and the wide diversity of critical response that his films have engendered. Because Kubrick is such an individualistic director and because his work is so very different from that of his American contemporaries, he deserves the consideration of every serious student of film. This study is the first attempt to assemble all the diverse critical assessments of Stanley Kubrick's career as a film director.

The biographical sketch of Kubrick (section I) attempts to bring together all the details of his early life and development as a film director. Since there is no definitive biography of Kubrick, this account is based on published facts about his life that have appeared in interviews and articles, and on the detailed information in Alexander Walker's book *Stanley Kubrick Directs* (1971). Because Walker is a personal friend of Kubrick's and had access to him in writing his book, his information has been considered the most accurate of all published material on Kubrick's life. I have tried to show how much Kubrick was a self-made director who taught himself many of the basic techniques and ideas about film making. Unlike the traditional image of a Hollywood director working his way up in the "system," Kubrick did his apprentice work as a still photographer for *Look* magazine, learning the basics of still photography and the art of working with people.

His subsequent career illustrates how much of a free hand Kubrick has enjoyed in making his films, controlling all aspects of their production with an independence that is rare among American and British film directors.

The critical survey of Kubrick's work (section II) tries to suggest some of the thematic and cinematic qualities of his film productions. My purpose here is to examine some of the major ideas and techniques that Kubrick has incorporated in many of his films without attempting to impose a critical straitjacket on the interpretation of them. I have tried to reflect the breadth and depth of Kubrick's diversity by analyzing each of his feature films in terms of the film itself and of some of the major critical reactions to it.

The scope of the critical reaction to Kubrick's films is, in itself, one of the best indications of the extent to which his films have been influential in the development of the modern cinema. I have also tried to indicate the unusual response that films like *2001: A Space Odyssey* and *A Clockwork Orange* have elicited from critics concerned with the psychological, social, and moral effects of these films on the movie-going audience. I have suggested that many of Kubrick's films explore the plight of alientated man in a society or systematized world devoid of human feeling. Finally, I have examined how much Kubrick is the total director in his control of all aspects of production, including script selection, casting, special effects design, and final editing. Since one could easily devote a whole volume to Kubrick's technical abilities as a cinematographer, editor, and special effects coordinator, I have limited my discussion in this area to some of the more important contributions he has made here. I have included additional references to the many articles written about Kubrick's technical expertise in section IV.

In compiling the list of film synopses and credits (section III), I have relied on the material in Walker (*Stanley Kubrick Directs*) and Phillips (*Stanley Kubrick: A Film Odyssey*), the relevant issues of *Filmfacts,* and prints of each of Kubrick's films with the exception of *Fear and Desire.* Because *Fear and Desire* is no longer available for viewing, I have relied on the summary of the plot in Norman Kagan's book, *The Cinema of Stanley Kubrick* (pp. 9-17). For each of the films, I have tried to be as detailed as possible and have included all available information about their production and distribution. I have also included all information relating to the music used in Kubrick's films along with individual titles and composers. Summarizing the narrative action of *2001: A Space Odyssey* presented a special problem of dealing with a film that depends so much on visual experience rather than traditional dramatic plot. I have dealt with this by suggesting some of the important scenic effects in an essentially visual spectacular. Finally, I have included all of the information available for Kubrick's latest film, *The Shining,* scheduled for release by Warner Brothers in 1980.

In Writings About Stanley Kubrick (section IV) I have included all books, articles, dissertations, and theses written about him from 1953 to 1979. I have presented a brief summary of each item and have often included direct quotations from the articles or books to summarize the content. Since Kubrick is an American director living in England, I have tried to show the extent of his international reputation by listing as many foreign publications and reviews as possible. Each entry in a foreign language contains a brief summary of the content and a notation of the language of the article.

In Writings and Other Film-Related Activity (section V) I have included all articles written by Kubrick and the credits for the film *One-Eyed Jacks,* the only film Kubrick worked on as a director for only a short time.

I have provided a list of Archival Sources (section VI) for further research on Kubrick and his films. Included here are all items relating to the location of materials such as scripts, press books, stills, prints, and posters pertaining to the Kubrick films. Information on the use of these materials, hours of operation, curators/librarians, and any restrictions is also provided, along with complete address information. Finally, I have included a list of Film Distributors (section VII) for Kubrick's feature films, with the address of each film company. The indexes consist of a Film Title Index in which each of Kubrick's films is entered, and an Author Index for each item in sections III–VI.

Acknowledgments

A project of this size involves the support and cooperation of a number of individuals, institutions, and private organizations. I am very happy to acknowledge the cooperation of the distributors of Stanley Kubrick's films for making copies of the films available to me for my research on this book: Ms. Rhonda Bloom of Films Incorporated; Mr. Robert Burriss of Warner Brothers, Non-Theatrical Division; Mr. Donald Krim of United Artists–16; and Swank Films Inc. In addition, I would like to thank the following institutions for research support and assistance: Boston Public Library; Boston University Library; Brandeis University Library; Theater Arts Library of the University of California at Los Angeles; University Film Study Center, Cambridge, Massachusetts; the Motion Picture, Broadcasting, and Recorded Sound Division of the Library of Congress; The Museum of Modern Art Film Study Division; the Wisconsin Center for Film and Theater Research; the Billy Rose Theater Collection of the New York Public Library at Lincoln Center; Emerson College; Northeastern University Inter-Library Loan Department; the Inter-Library Loan Department of Denison College; and the British Film Institute in London.

All scholars working on Stanley Kubrick are indebted to the fine critical studies by Alexander Walker, Gene D. Phillips, and Norman Kagan, and I would like to acknowledge my own particular debt to their important contributions in the field. In addition, I would like to thank many scholars, critics, librarians, and other friends who have been so very helpful to me in locating materials on Kubrick: Gene D. Phillips, Marvin D'Lugo, T. J. Ross, John Harrington, Carol Cantor, Gene Walz, Jeffrey Chown, Terry Turner-Ladner, Gary Goshgarian, Robert Parker, Audree Malkin, Laura M. Duncan, Victor Howes, Barbara J. Humphrys, Charles Silver, Maxine Fleckner, and Paul Myers. This book could not have been finished without the support and assistance of all of my colleagues in the Department of English at Northeastern University, especially, Gerald Griffin, Guy Rotella, Timothy Donovan, Samuel Morse, Franklin Norvish, Stanley Trachtenberg, M. X. Lesser and, most of all, Lloyd Skiffington.

Completion of this volume was made possible in part by a grant from the Faculty Development Fund at Northeastern University, Office of the Provost. For their continued assistance and support, I would like to thank Walter Jones, Harry Allan,

John Curry, and Kenneth G. Ryder, President of Northeastern University. None of my efforts in screening Kubrick's films would have been possible without the complete cooperation of Dr. Mina Ghattas, Carol Poulliotte, and Ross Kershaw of the Office of Learning Resources at Northeastern University. I am grateful to the Department of English for granting released time from my teaching duties to complete work on this book during the academic year 1977-78.

On a personal note, I would like to thank my father, and Billy, Eddie, and Cathy, who gave needed encouragement to see this project through to completion. My dedication of this volume to my wife is, indeed, "Too little payment for so great a debt."

I Biographical Background

Stanley Kubrick was born in the Bronx, New York, on 26 July 1928, to Jacques L. Kubrick, a doctor, and Gertrude (Perveler) Kubrick. Kubrick has one sister, Barbara, now Mrs. Robert Kroner. As a child, Kubrick was fascinated by the extensive collection of books in his father's library and was attracted to stories and novels at an early age. During his years at P. S. 90 in the Bronx, Kubrick spent many of his after-school hours attending movies at local theaters such as the Loew's Paradise Theater. His fascination with film and fiction was the outgrowth of these early childhood experiences. He became interested in photography as a hobby and was presented with his first camera on this thirteenth birthday.

During his schooling at William Howard Taft High School, Kubrick was an indifferent student and attained low grades in many of his subjects, including English. As the high school newspaper photographer, Kubrick had the opportunity to expand his interest in photographic techniques and found it to be an interesting and challenging hobby. His earliest experiment in still photography was a series of pictures of his high school English teacher, Aaron Traister, reading selected passages from *Hamlet.* During his junior year at Taft, Kubrick (at age 16) sold his first photograph to *Look* magazine for $25. The photograph depicted the grief-stricken reaction of a newsstand dealer reading the headlines of Franklin D. Roosevelt's death.

Following his graduation from Taft High School in 1945, Kubrick attended evening classes at the City College of the City University of New York, but left in his freshman year to accept a full time position as an apprentice photographer for *Look.* Under the direction of Helen O'Brian, Picture Editor for *Look,* Kubrick traveled around the world on assignments in Portugal, Sarasota, Florida, and an extended campaign trip with Senator Robert Taft in Ohio. During this period at *Look,* his fellow workers recalled that he would carry his photographic equipment in a paper bag to avoid being considered a tourist in New York City. At age nineteen, Kubrick married Toba Metz, a Taft High School classmate.

Kubrick and his friend Alex Singer became interested in the short documentary films that were used as "fillers" at the local movie houses in New York. Kubrick decided that he could make a film like them for about half the cost and decided to try his hand at the project. Kubrick began spending all of his free evenings at the

Museum of Modern Art film screenings of the classic directors' works. He was especially attracted to the film techniques of some of the most famous directors including Pudovkin, Eisenstein, Max Ophuls, and Orson Welles. These were to be the most important influences on his work as a director. Kubrick (at age 22) purchased his first 35mm Eyemo camera and began work on his first short film, *Day of the Fight.*

With the help of Singer, and $800 of his own money, Kubrick produced *Day of the Fight* (1950). The film was based on a *Look* picture story that he had done on the middleweight boxer, Walter Cartier, and dealt with the last few hours before Cartier entered the ring for his fight. The completed film, including a musical soundtrack (by Gerald Fried), cost Kubrick $3800. The short was purchased by RKO Pathe News for $4000 and opened at the Paramount Theater in New York City. After seeing his first film, Kubrick decided to quit his job at *Look* and make his career as a film director.

With the success of Kubrick's first short feature, RKO agreed to finance $1500 for a second short feature, *Flying Padre,* a study of the Reverend Fred Stadtmueller of Mosquero, New Mexico. The film depicted the day to day life of a priest who flies to the various points in his parish by Piper Cub airplane. After this film was completed, Kubrick was determined to make his own feature length film. He began studying the films of Max Ophuls and Orson Welles and read Pudovkin's *Film Technique.* In addition, he spent all of his free time attending screenings of the old classic films in the New York movie houses and at the Museum of Modern Art. This was to be the extent of his formal education in the art of the cinema.

Along with a high school classmate, Howard O. Sackler (author of *The Great White Hope*), Kubrick put together the screenplay for his first feature film, *Fear and Desire.* With $10,000 borrowed from his father and uncle, Martin Perveler, Kubrick began shooting the film on location in the San Gabriel Mountains outside Los Angeles. This experience in directing, editing, and producing his own film taught Kubrick many of the important basic steps in producing a feature film, particularly the all-important technical details dealing with editing and marketing. With his wife, Toba, Kubrick hired some day laborers and, with two other friends, completed the filming of *Fear and Desire* at a total cost of $50,000. Kubrick described the theme of *Fear and Desire* in a letter to Joseph Burstyn:

> Its structure: allegorical. Its conception: poetic. A drama of 'man' lost in a hostile world—deprived of material and spiritual foundations—seeking his way to an understanding of himself, and of life around him. He is further imperiled on his Odyssey by an unseen but deadly enemy that surrounds him; but an enemy who, upon scrutiny, seems to be almost shaped from the same mold .... It will, probably, mean many things to different people, and it ought to.[1]

The film included some heavy symbolism and, although it was well photographed, none of the major film distributors was interested in buying it. The popular distributor of art films, Joseph Burstyn, agreed to release the film and it opened at the

Guild Theater in New York City on 29 March 1953. While the favorable reception of *Fear and Desire* was not widespread, the positive comments on Kubrick's cinematography were enough to encourage him to make a second feature film. In addition, Kubrick earned his professional cinematographer's union card for his work on filming *Fear and Desire.*

After his divorce from Toba (Metz) Kubrick in 1952 and his marriage the same year to Ruth Sobotka, a dancer with Balanchine's City Center ballet company, Kubrick began work on *Killer's Kiss.* It cost $40,000 to make and was partially financed by one of Kubrick's relatives, Morris Bousel, a pharmacist. The film was made on location at the Laurel Boxing Arena in New Jersey, a dance hall in Brooklyn, and a mannequin factory in the Bronx. When Kubrick finished the film, he was able to sell it to United Artists Corporation for $75,000 and the film was released in September 1955. In addition, United Artists agreed to finance Kubrick in making low budget films at $100,000 apiece.

Upon completing *Killer's Kiss,* Kubrick met James B. Harris, the son of the owner of Flamingo Films, a distributor of television films. With Kubrick's interest in making films, and the financial backing of Harris, this meeting was to be instrumental in the development of Kubrick's career as a film director. The two men formed Harris-Kubrick Productions, a company dedicated to making quality films on a modest budget. In 1955, Harris bought the screen rights for Lionel White's novel *Clean Break.* After signing Sterling Hayden to play the lead role, Harris and Kubrick began filming with a $200,000 advance from United Artists. The balance of the cost, $120,000, was contributed by Harris and the film was released in April 1956. For a low budget film, *The Killing* was very well received with a particularly good notice in *Variety.*

Attracted by the critical attention to *The Killing,* Kubrick and Harris were invited by Dore Schary, the production head at MGM, to examine properties that MGM had purchased as potential screenplays. Harris and Kubrick received a forty-week contract from Schary and spent half of this time looking over projects in Hollywood. Earlier, Kubrick had read Humphrey Cobb's 1935 novel, *Paths of Glory,* and thought that it might make a good film. The novel had been rejected by all the major Hollywood studies including MGM. Due to a staff change at MGM, Dore Schary was replaced, and Kubrick and Harris left the studio with their own completed script for the film. Kubrick sent the script to Kirk Douglas, who agreed to star in the film after approving changes and additional dialogue by Calder Willingham.

Kubrick packed his crew and materials and moved to Munich, Germany, to begin shooting at the United Artists' Geiselgasteig Studios. Much of the work involved in shooting the film required realistic recreation of the trench warfare of World War I and the simulation of land mines and artillery fire. Kubrick met the challenge with a detailed plan for filming the battle scenes which included numerous "takes" to get the scenes in the trenches exactly right. The film cost $850,000 to make and was released on Christmas Day, 1957. Since this was Kubrick's first film with a major Hollywood star, the debut of *Paths of Glory* attracted a great deal of critical attention and praise from many of the major American and European film critics.

Besides publicizing Kubrick as one of the most promising of the new independent directors in Hollywood, *Paths of Glory* marked the emergence of Kubrick as a financially "marketable" director. His careful attention to film techniques and editing responsibilities earned him the respect of professional cinematographers and actors alike. Both Adolphe Menjou and Kirk Douglas (co-stars in the film) praised Kubrick's abilities as a director. His reputation as a perfectionist in the trade began with this film and was to be a trademark associated with Kubrick's films from *Paths of Glory* to the present. The best example of Kubrick's dedication to his craft and his commitment to the *auteur* concept of complete control over the film art was a statement that Kubrick made to Harris after filming *Paths of Glory*:

> "There are certain things about filmmaking that are difficult, but you've got to remember that you have to live with a film for the rest of your life. If there's some shortcoming in a film that was brought about by your failure to face a problem—you didn't want to hurt somebody's feelings or you wanted to avoid conflict—it's still your film to live with the rest of your life."[2]

Kubrick's concern with this philosophy of composition has been the hallmark of his films ever since.

Following his third marriage in April 1958 to Suzanne Christiane Harlan (the German-born actress who appears at the end of *Paths of Glory*), Kubrick returned to Hollywood to seek additional feature film projects. He completed a screenplay entitled "The Burning Secret" (from a novel of the same name by Stefan Zweig), along with Calder Willingham, but the project was never completed by MGM and was subsequently shelved. Kubrick then turned his energies to working with Marlon Brando as director of the film *One-Eyed Jacks.* After a period of about six months, it was obvious to the two collaborators that they were not happy with the direction of the project, and they parted on 19 November 1958. Kubrick received $100,000 for his work on the film (which was later directed by Brando himself). Brando's comments on Kubrick are very interesting in that they show what one strong individualist thought of another:

> "Stanley is unusually perceptive and delicately attuned to people. He has an adroit intellect and is a creative thinker, not a repeater, not a fact gatherer. He digests what he learns and brings to a project an original point of view and a reserved passion."[3]

Soon after this breakup, Kubrick received an emergency call from his friend, Kirk Douglas, on location in Madrid filming *Spartacus.* Douglas urged Kubrick to take over the direction of the film after the original director, Anthony Mann, had walked off the set after three days of filming. Kubrick accepted the offer, went to Spain for the filming of the battle scenes, and returned to California for the studio scenes at Universal Pictures. At the age of thirty, Kubrick found himself making a multi-million dollar film with a cast of major acting professionals. He has described his role in the filming of *Spartacus* as simply that of another hired hand without any direct control over the script and other production decisions. Because Kirk Douglas was the Executive Producer, Kubrick's role was even further diminished in his direction of the epic. This was the only film that Kubrick has made to date in which he did not have complete control over selection of script, actors, editing, and production decisions. His experience with *Spartacus* convinced him to make all of these major decisions before seeking financial backing for his future films. While *Spartacus* did receive some favorable comments, most critics found the story plodding and underdeveloped. The best comments on the film focused on Kubrick's use of the widescreen process and his cinematography. Kubrick has never referred to the film as his own and in recent years has disowned any credit for it.

During the time that Kubrick spent on the production of *Spartacus,* he and Harris acquired the film rights to *Lolita* at a cost of $150,000. The author, Vladimir Nabokov, met with Kubrick and agreed to write a screenplay for the film at Kubrick's request. Meanwhile, Harris and Kubrick began a nationwide talent search for the teenage girl to be selected to play Lolita. This search resulted in the casting of Sue Lyon to play in the film along with Peter Sellers, James Mason, and Shelley Winters. Since the pressure of production censorship hung over the film, Kubrick moved the production to England and began shooting the film.

The critical reaction to *Lolita,* released in April 1962, was both outrage and applause. Many critics felt that Kubrick had done an injustice to the novel in taking such liberties with the plot and characters. Others felt that, given the real limitations of the cinema at the time in portraying the erotic elements of the novel, Kubrick had done a good job in altering the direction of the filmed version. *Lolita* also marked the end of Kubrick's partnership with Harris, who had decided to go into directing films on his own. Kubrick and Harris have remained friends since this breakup.

Throughout the early sixties, Kubrick had become interested in the increasing tension of the nuclear arms race and the threat of the hydrogen bomb to mankind. Kubrick had decided to remain in England after *Lolita* and began to spend a great deal of his time reading about the arms race in popular and technical publications including *British Aviation.* As an outgrowth of this interest, he requested additional help from the office of the Institute for Strategic Studies, and its director, Alaistair Buchan, suggested Peter George's novel, *Red Alert,* for Kubrick's reading. Attracted by the suspenseful plot and theme of the novel, Kubrick began thinking of its potential as a film. As he and Terry Southern developed the ideas for the film, he became more and more aware of the fundamental absurdity of the situations in the book. This reading, research, and adaptation of *Red Alert* resulted in Kubrick's next film, *Dr. Strangelove, Or How I Learned To Stop Worrying and Love the Bomb.*

Once Kubrick developed his ideas on the film, he decided to make it a black comedy about the arms race and the potential threat of the hydrogen bomb. Kubrick remarked:

> "The real image doesn't cut the mustard, doesn't transcend. I'm now interested in taking a story, fantastic and improbable, and trying to get to the bottom of it, to make it seem not only real, but inevitable."[4]

This concept of making *Dr. Strangelove* not only real but inevitable became the keynote of his production work. Kubrick assembled volumes of information about the arms race, including as much technical data as he could get hold of. After casting Peter Sellers, George C. Scott, and Sterling Hayden in the film, Kubrick began shooting *Strangelove* at the Shepperton Studios in London. The film was released in New York City on 3 December 1963.

If anyone had any doubts about Kubrick's abilities as a technical craftsman and superb director prior to this, *Dr. Strangelove* removed them. The reception of the film was outstanding and many film critics received volumes of mail attacking or defending Kubrick's satire. *Dr. Strangelove* received more critical acclaim than any other film Kubrick had directed to date. It was named one of the Ten Best Films of 1964 by the prestigious New York Film Critics. By 1964, Kubrick had taken an important step forward in writing, directing, and producing one of the most devastating satires on the futility of nuclear warfare and the limitations of mankind in creating "monsters" he could not control.

Following the critical acclaim of *Dr. Strangelove,* Stanley Kubrick immersed himself in three and a half years of meticulous research, experimentation, and production for what many critics believe to be the greatest science fiction film ever made, *2001: A Space Odyssey.* Kubrick's training in the pre-production aspects of his projects–reading, research, and planning–was to serve him well in undertaking the production of one of the most unusual films ever conceived and produced in modern cinema. Kubrick and Arthur C. Clarke wrote the screenplay for *2001: A Space Odyssey,* which was based on Clarke's short story *The Sentinel.* Calling on the combined resources of dozens of private research agencies, scientists, universities, and government organizations, Kubrick amassed a complete library of information and plans related to the problems of future space travel and the subject of extra-terrestrial life. He converted his Boreham Wood studio (outside London) into a warehouse of materials needed for the production of the epic film.

On 22 February 1965, MGM Studios announced that they were financing the cost of a film tentatively entitled *Journey Beyond the Stars,* directed by Stanley Kubrick. Beyond the traditional problems associated with film production, *2001: A Space Odyssey* (as the film was finally called), involved the added burden of the creation and filming of 205 special effects sequences that were designed and supervised by Kubrick himself. The problems were not even imagined by officials at MGM when they allotted about five million dollars for the production cost. After more than three years of production, filming, and editing, Kubrick released *2001: A Space Odyssey* on 1 April 1968. The final cost for the film was $10,500,000.

The critical reaction to the film was very favorable, although some critics wondered what the film was all about. After its initial tour, the film was withdrawn and later released to record-breaking audiences throughout the United States.

Today, the film remains one of the most popular films ever made and is in continual demand at colleges and universities throughout the country. While many stockholders at MGM were worried about its financial return, Kubrick seems to have justified their faith by recent reports that the film grossed over $98 million in one year alone for just domestic sales. This film will remain one of the most daring and dramatic contributions that Stanley Kubrick has made to the modern history of cinema.

Between the completion of *2001: A Space Odyssey* and the announcement of *A Clockwork Orange,* Kubrick had researched and planned a film called *Napoleon,* which was to be an exhaustive study of the French leader's life. The project fascinated Kubrick and, although he has temporarily shelved the idea (because of Hollywood reluctance to finance an epic spectacle after the 1971 film *Waterloo* with Rod Steiger), he hopes to return to it sometime in the future.

After reading Anthony Burgess's novel *A Clockwork Orange,* Kubrick re-read it and decided to explore the possibilities of making a film of it. After meeting with Burgess and discussing his plans, Kubrick purchased the screen rights and began planning for the production. Next, Kubrick met with Malcolm McDowell, the star of the film, and mapped out his ideas for the filming. Beginning in September 1970, Kubrick started shooting on location in London and at the studios. He completed the film in March 1971, and *A Clockwork Orange* was released on 20 December 1971. The reaction to the film was voluminous and violent. Many critics refused to see the film as anything more than blatant pornography, and a visual glorification of sex and violence. Beyond this group, several notable critics including Vincent Canby, Judith Crist, and Penelope Gilliatt praised Kubrick as the master of satiric cinema who had brilliantly adapted Burgess's novel.

A Clockwork Orange received the New York Film Critics Award as the Best Film of 1971 and Kubrick was voted the Best Director of the year. Despite some of the initial negative reviews, Kubrick's film has remained extremely popular with audiences in both the United States and Europe. Recently, *A Clockwork Orange* broke some of the all-time attendance records in Spain, and 16mm releases of the film continue to be the most popular of any films at colleges and universities throughout the United States.

The tremendous financial success of *Dr. Strangelove, 2001: A Space Odyssey,* and *A Clockwork Orange* guaranteed that Kubrick could maintain the *auteur*'s freedom and control over all aspects of film production. Recently, Kubrick has also received a percentage of all profits from his films, something that adds to his artistic freedom in getting the best from his actors and the best financial backing from the studio. After providing views of the immediate future (*A Clockwork Orange*) and the distant future (*2001: A Space Odyssey*), Kubrick decided to journey to the past for his most recent film, a nineteenth-century view of an eighteenth-century hero, *Barry Lyndon.*

The subject of Kubrick's latest film is the novel by William Makepeace Thackeray entitled *The Luck of Barry Lyndon, Esq.* (1844), dealing with the rise and fall of an Irish hero in the world of eighteenth-century manners and mores.

Kubrick selected Ryan O'Neal and Marisa Berenson to play the lead roles and began on-location shooting in Ireland during the spring of 1974. Always conscious of the costly interruptions of his shooting schedule by the curious public, Kubrick imposed strict security measures in making *Barry Lyndon.* No one was allowed on any of the sets without his permission and all information about the story, the actors, and the filming was kept out of the press until the film was finished, edited, and ready for release.

The epic scope of *Barry Lyndon* presented enormous cinematic problems in creating and recording on film a world of decorum, manners, and delicate detail. Kubrick's problems were further compounded by the need to create period costumes, weapons, sets, and lighting effects for indoor and outdoor scenes. For the director who created *2001: A Space Odyssey,* the problems were simply other challenges to be met and overcome. Kubrick's dazzling photography (including the use of special lenses for candlelight sequences) distinguises this film as one of the truly fine masterpieces of the modern cinema. So accurate is Kubrick's reproduction of the eighteenth century, that one critic has pointed out the similarity of Kubrick's film sequences to Hogarth and Constable paintings. *Barry Lyndon* required an enormous budget, location shooting in Ireland and England, and the total re-creation of a lifestyle that was completely alien to the twentieth century. *Barry Lyndon* looks backward to Kubrick's technical experience with *Spartacus,* his thematic concerns in *Paths of Glory,* and the visual splendor of *2001: A Space Odyssey.*

When *Barry Lyndon* was released in December 1975, the critical reaction was extremely negative. While all of the major critics praised Kubrick's abilities with cameras, costumes, and color, most of them found serious problems with the story and the poor development of characters. Another problem that bothered the critics in the early reviews of *Barry Lyndon* was the lack of motivation and resolution in the plot. *Barry Lyndon* was nominated for a number of awards and received an Academy Award for Best Costuming in a Film for 1975. After a brief first run, *Barry Lyndon* was withdrawn from distribution and has only recently appeared in a 16mm version.

For the past year and a half, Stanley Kubrick has been working on a production of Stephen King's novel, *The Shining.* The film stars Jack Nicholson and it was shot on location in England and at Kubrick's studios at Boreham Wood. Plans are now underway to release the film in 1980.

Today, Kubrick remains one of the most innovative and creative directors in modern cinema. To understand Kubrick one must understand his philosophy of composition. His film projects begin with the idea of adapting a novel or short story (nine of his eleven feature films have been adapted from novels), and exhaustive study and research of all aspects of the original work. Because Kubrick desires artistic control over all aspects of his films, he spends an enormous amount of time in the pre-production planning of each of his films: script selection and writing, actor selection, set design, cinematography, special effects coordination, on-location site selection, and selection of all technical and artistic production staff. As a dedicated craftsman, Kubrick dislikes wasting the time and talents of actors and technical staff who work for him. Because of this commitment he plans his shooting schedules and production work to make the best use of his time and the studio's budget. His work on *2001: A Space Odyssey* brought a great deal of publicity to his fanatic work schedule and his dedication to the art of film in every detail. In a highly competitive film industry, Kubrick has gained the reputation of an ultimate perfectionist unwilling to accept second best.

As the dedicated film director, Kubrick has maintained a rather distant, impersonal relationship with the public, speaking only through his films. Since the filming of *Lolita* in 1962, Kubrick has resided in Boreham Wood, just outside London, with his wife, Christiane (a professional artist), and his three daughters, Katharine (age 24), Anya (age 18), and Vivian (age 17). Kubrick's large manor house is a combination home library, workshop, and office with the studios nearby. He very rarely travels out of England (having a mortal fear of planes) and then only to deal with problems related to the release of his films in America. In addition to being a voracious reader of all types of literature, Kubrick is an avid chess fan. His lifelong fascination with the game may offer an insight into his own attitude toward film making:

> "If chess has any relationship to filmmaking, it would be in the way it helps you develop patience and discipline in choosing between alternatives at a time when impulse decision seems very attractive. Otherwise it is necessary to have perfect intuition—and this is something very dangerous for an artist to rely on."[5]

At age fifty-two, Kubrick is the ultimate craftsman, deeply committed and methodical, an artistic and commercial success in the modern cinema.

NOTES

1. Norman Kagan, *The Cinema of Stanley Kubrick* (New York: Grove Press, 1972).
2. Paul D. Zimmerman, "Kubrick's Brilliant Vision," *Newsweek,* 79, no. 1 (3 January), pp. 28-33.
3. Jeremy Bernstein, "Profiles: How About A Little Game?" *New Yorker,* 42 (12 November), pp. 70-73.
4. Norman Kagan, *The Cinema of Stanley Kubrick,* p. 73.
5. Stanley Kubrick as quoted in Alexander Walker, *Stanley Kubrick Directs* (New York: Harcourt Brace Jovanovich, 1971), p. 271.

II Critical Survey of the Oeuvre

One of the most difficult tasks facing any writer in discussing the films of Stanley Kubrick is the attempt to place an umbrella of selected themes or common ideas over the diverse and unique productions that have characterized Kubrick's twenty-five year career. The problem is compounded because of the range of subject matter and the varied style of Kubrick's ten feature films. Unlike many traditional film directors, Kubrick has not made a career of producing repeated efforts in one genre, nor has he been involved with limited directorial control over studio-bought scripts that he has not selected himself. While it is relatively easy to show the development of Kubrick as a director from his earliest documentary short *Day of the Fight* (1951) to his most recent film *The Shining* (1980), it is not so easy to discuss these films as a group demonstrating recurring themes and techniques. Kubrick's films in both their form and content defy easy categorization.

From the start of his career as an amateur film maker, Kubrick has been very much the ideal of the *auteur* director, insisting on control over script selection, film editing, set design, cinematography, production, and direction. In this sense, each of Kubrick's films represents his evolving development only as a director of a particular film at a particular time. The diversity of his films, from *Lolita, Spartacus,* and *Dr. Strangelove,* to *2001: A Space Odyssey* and *Barry Lyndon,* has represented ever widening circles of challenge in both form and content for this unique director. In Kubrick's films, form and content are so integrated that many film critics have found it difficult, if not impossible, to discuss either of these aspects in isolation. If McLuhan's phrase, "the medium is the message," is useful here, Alexander Walker's caution (in *Stanley Kubrick Directs*) that in Kubrick's case one would "prefer to say that the medium is the metaphor," seems even more useful.[1]

Keeping these premises in mind, we may look at four critical concepts that have characterized the form and content of Stanely Kubrick's films: (1) the thematic exploration of alienated man in confrontation with a society or system that he can only partially understand, accept, or control; (2) the dramatic exploitation of the visual language of film including extensive use of composition, juxtaposition, visual irony, *mise en scene,* contrast, color, and meticulous editing; (3) particular attention to the ironic and satiric statement in film dialogue, acting, and narration;

(4) the integrated use of popular and classical music to add thematic dimensions to the development of plots, characters, and ideas.

With the exception of Kubrick's earliest short documentaries (*Day of the Fight, The Flying Padre,* and *The Seafarers*), all of his feature length films have dealt with the confrontation of alienated man with a society or system that he can only partially understand, accept, or control. Some of the major themes in his films have been concerned with the working out of this confrontation to some sort of resolution either in the destruction, defeat, or death of individuals at the hands of the system or social forces. From *Fear and Desire* (1953) to *The Shining* (1980), many of Kubrick's heroes are forced to confront a situation in which they have become involved, and in which they ultimately become the victim or scapegoat. This is true of the struggle of the four soldiers in *Fear and Desire,* Davy Gordon in conflict with Vince Rapallo's gang in *Killer's Kiss,* Johnny Clay in the execution of the perfect racetrack robbery in *The Killing,* Colonel Dax in the court martial confrontation in *Paths of Glory,* the failure of the slave revolt in *Spartacus,* Humbert's developing conflicts with Charlotte, Lolita, and Quilty in *Lolita,* the absurdist struggle of man against machine in *Dr. Strangelove, Or How I Learned to Stop Worrying and Love the Bomb,* the confrontation of man, machine, and monolith in *2001: A Space Odyssey,* and finally, the struggle of Redmond Barry against the world of society and gentlemen in *Barry Lyndon.*

In Kubrick's satiric vision, he often places his characters in a dilemma and then stands back to allow the viewer to watch the outcome unencumbered by editorial comment. While the viewer is often aware of the futility of the struggle involved in the story, Kubrick retains the master's control over the unpredictable endings and often ironic conclusions of his films. Many of Kubrick's characters are "heroic" in their alienation from society, either as servants or victims of pressures they can only partially control or survive. Thus, main figures like Davy Gordon, Colonel Dax, Spartacus, Alex, Dave Bowman, and Lionel Mandrake become engulfed in a system that they rebel against in order to try to insure their own survival. Still other figures like Johnny Clay, Humbert Humbert, and Redmond Barry attempt to impose their own controls on a system that they only partially understand and are ultimately defeated by. The latter group is often seen as illustrating an attempt by the individual to impose his will on a larger group/society unwilling to accept or acknowledge a challenge to its own control. While many of Kubrick's critics dwell upon his pessimistic treatment of man, the attractive (and often overlooked) dimensions of his plots are the struggles of individuals against these forces, against these threats to human endurance and survival. If Kubrick's heroes do not ultimately prevail, their struggle to endure is often both abominable and admirable.

The second concept that has characterized Stanley Kubrick's films is his exploitation of the visual language of film. From his earliest feature film, *Fear and Desire,* critics and audiences have been aware of how well Kubrick says things visually in his films. There is a certain tightening of form and a concern with the telling aspect in each shot and sequence that harken back to Kubrick's initiation as a still photographer for *Look* Magazine. This experience with *Look* taught Kubrick the vital importance of the visual image and the careful selection of every frame and every angle in the final editing process. In addition to the extensive use of *mise en scene,* color, costume, and design, Kubrick has concentrated on the critically important task of personally editing and re-editing every shot and sequence in his feature films, resulting in a precise correlation between visual and verbal language. His concern for the exact shot, precise camera angle, and lighting has led to his reputation among professional cinematographers as the ultimate craftsman.

Unlike many popular film directors, Kubrick's use of visual effects is not simply designed as a gimmick to attract audiences to his films. His use of composition and editing are crucial to the tracking shots of *Paths of Glory* (1957), the ever tightening centers of action in *Dr. Strangelove,* the visual experience of the space-time relationship in *2001,* and the extensive thematic use of sets and colors in both *A Clockwork Orange* and *Barry Lyndon.* Kubrick has capitalized on the thing that film as a medium of communication does best: saying things visually. Beyond the aesthetic importance of Kubrick's visual excellence, he has pioneered changes in the technical field of cinematography, particularly in his last three features: *2001: A Space Odyssey, A Clockwork Orange,* and *Barry Lyndon.* In these most recent films, especially *2001,* Kubrick has perfected the extensive use of special effects sequences, lighting, wide angle photography, elaborate sets, special lenses and recording devices, and almost surrealistic color photography.

A third characteristic of Kubrick's films has been the central importance of the ironic and satiric statement in his dialogue. Even though Kubrick has adapted all but two of his films from literary works, he has exercised great care in developing all of his film scripts with particular attention to correlating what is being said and seen on the screen. From *Paths of Glory* to *Barry Lyndon* there are abundant examples of the ways in which Kubrick develops character, conflict, and situation through the selective use of verbal language. Kubrick's films are often characterized by the ironies between what a character is saying and what the audience is seeing on the screen at the same time. Films as diverse as *Lolita* and *Dr. Strangelove* underscore the specialized attention that Kubrick brings to dialogue in not allowing himself to repeat something verbally that can be said better visually or vice versa. One of the heaviest demands that Kubrick places on his viewers is the ability to keep up with the verbal and visual satire of films like *Dr. Strangelove, A Clockwork Orange,* and *2001: A Space Odyssey,* i.e., the ability to absorb, rather rapidly, the full impact of what the director is saying about the characters and situations on the screen. In addition, Kubrick explores the critical importance of understatement in film dialogue by his careful attention to editing and soundtrack recording. Even in a film like *2001* (which contains 46 minutes of dialogue in a three hour film), Kubrick exercises great care in what he allows us to hear of human and machine communication: what we hear answers fewer questions for us than what we see.

Finally, Kubrick makes unusual and often innovative use of popular and classical music selections as an integral part of the development of theme and situation in his films. Few viewers will forget the ironic strains of "Try a Little Tenderness" as the overture or "We'll Meet Again" as the finale to *Dr. Strangelove, Or How I*

Learned to Stop Worrying and Love the Bomb, or the particular appropriateness of the "Blue Danube Walz" or "Thus Spake Zarathustra" in *2001: A Space Odyssey,* and "Singing in the Rain" at the beginning and ending of *A Clockwork Orange.* As in his visual taste, so also in his musical taste, Kubrick is the master of the satiric thrust, the careful selection of just what the audience will be hearing on the soundtrack while watching a particular sequence on the screen. Kubrick is vitally concerned with directing audience attention to the visual sequence and his use of popular and classical music is a means to this end. In addition to the obvious function of music as a transition device from one major sequence to another in *2001: A Space Odyssey* and *Barry Lyndon,* Kubrick often uses music to identify a particular setting or mood ("When Johnny Comes Marching Home Again" in the B-52 sequences in *Dr. Strangelove*), or a particular melancholy tone (throughout *Lolita*; Irish scenes in *Barry Lyndon*), or to underscore an important theme (*Paths of Glory* scene with German barmaid singing) that can be presented best with the music and the simple panning of the camera over a sea of faces. Kubrick also uses familiar music in rather unfamiliar places (Overture to *William Tell* in *A Clockwork Orange*) or, as pointed out previously, in situations where he wishes to call attention to the irony of an incident or character (e.g., the music used in the endings to all of his films, especially, *Dr. Strangelove, 2001,* and *A Clockwork Orange*). While *2001* popularized Strauss's "Thus Spake Zarathustra" beyond anyone's expectations, it is important to remember the essential cinematic function of this selection and others in Kubrick's films. Certainly, a volume could (and perhaps should) be devoted to Kubrick's selection of music and his thematic use of music in contemporary cinema.

Each of these four concepts suggests some of the important characteristics of the films of Stanley Kubrick. In addition, they point to many of the innovations that Kubrick has explored in his film career and helps explain his present position as one of the foremost film directors in the world. These concepts are meant to be suggestive of the total vision of Kubrick's cinema and the extent to which they apply to each of his feature films. The following examination of each of his feature films will help demonstrate his development as a film director and the distinctive contributions he has made to professional cinema.

1 EARLY WORK AND FEAR AND DESIRE (1953)

Kubrick's earliest films, all short documentaries, *Day of the Fight, The Flying Padre,* and *The Seafarers,* demonstrate his meticulous concern for detail in shot selection and editing. In each of these films Kubrick shows his still photographer's expertise in composing each sequence to achieve a special effect. Presenting a day in the life of a professional boxer, Walter Cartier, from the moment he gets out of bed to the time he retires at the end of the day, Kubrick uses several types of shots including a view of the lights above the boxing ring to present typical happenings in non-traditional ways. Another documentary short, *The Flying Padre,* covers a day in the life of a Catholic priest as he visits his parish by Piper Cub airplane in New Mexico. Both of these early films attracted little critical attention, but provided Kubrick with the interest and desire to make his first full length feature film.

Critical reaction to Kubrick's first feature film, *Fear and Desire* (1953), was neither very favorable, nor widespread. Of the few local notices, published in the *New York Times, The New Yorker,* and *Variety,* most were critical of the acting, story line, and direction. What did achieve some notice was the quality of the cinematography (done by Kubrick), considering the shoestring budget on which the film was made. Images of the soldiers in the forest and the way in which Kubrick caught the ideas of death in the soldiers' faces were indicative of a film that had better cinematography than plot interest. Many film critics felt that Kubrick had belabored the theme of disliking war and that this, the poor script, and only one professional actor were its chief problems. More important than the film itself was the experience that *Fear and Desire* gave Kubrick in the mechanics of making a full length feature film, in serving as his own director, editor, script writer (with Howard O. Sackler), and cinematographer. This experience not only demonstrated that he could make a feature film but also showed Kubrick the vital role of the production tasks associated with assembling the final version of the film for release. Interestingly enough, since *Fear and Desire* (with the exception of *Spartacus*), Kubrick has insisted on and obtained script selection, final editing, and production rights on all of his films.

2 **KILLER'S KISS** (1955)

In *Killer's Kiss,* Kubrick explores a number of unique ideas in a rather melodramatic way. The viewer is conscious of darkness, evil, and gloominess throughout the film and, with the exception of the opening and closing sequences in Pennsylvania Station, New York, most of the action takes place in darkened corridors, rooms, and streets. The mood of the film seems more striking than any of the acting or action sequences of the film and that mood (reminiscent of the *film noir*) is developed with Kubrick's conscious attention to the uses of light and darkness as contrasting symbols in the story. Characters seem more stereotyped than developed and spend much of their time storytelling their way through the film. For example, Davy Gordon begins the story with a flashback that takes us to the girl (Gloria) he meets. She tells her story in another flashback and then we return to Davy and the reconciliation (at Pennsylvania Station) at the conclusion of the film. Though the film borders on melodrama, Kubrick exhibits a number of different developments beyond *Fear and Desire* as both director and cinematographer.

Kubrick's development of the heavy-handed Vince Rapallo culminates in the well directed and well photographed fight to the death in the mannequin factory. Throughout the film, light and darkness are used to contrast the worlds of goodness and evil: on the streets of Broadway, in the dance hall, and in the dockside chase scene. All of these scenes accentuate the world of criminals and the mob Gordon is combating. The chase scene at the end of the film is very realistic and well paced.

Finally, the viewer is taken into the mind of the hero, Davy Gordon, and all of our subsequent reactions to the events in the film are colored by Davy's presentation of the action beforehand. Although the audience knows the outcome from the start (since Davy has survived to tell the story), Kubrick does focus on the cornered individual who is forced to stand and fight. Davy fights a much more important battle with Rapallo than the one in the ring. As in many of Kubrick's later films, the individual finds himself in a position in which, for one reason or another, the traditional rules of behavior are removed and he is left to his own devices for survival. Rather than being caught by the system, Davy rises above it and confronts it on the gangster's terms and turf. Kubrick directs our attention to the results of Gordon's battle with Rapallo. The technique in this early Kubrick film (similar to the violence and evil of *A Clockwork Orange*) raises an otherwise melodramatic chase story to an interesting visual experience by focusing on the low scenes of Broadway life, the "nightmare" vision Davy has, and the final fight scene already mentioned.

Critical reaction to *Killer's Kiss* was largely negative because of the poor handling of the script and the rather melodramatic depiction of the boy-saves-girl-in-the-nick-of-time type of story. Gavin Lambert in *Sight and Sound* saw both the problems and the potential of the film director in calling Kubrick "a maturing and distinctive personality." Subsequent studies and analyses of the film have retained the opinion that it is a good first effort and helpful in seeing where Kubrick was headed in his film career.

3 THE KILLING (1956)

In his next film, *The Killing*, Kubrick achieves an expertise as director that presages his first commercially successful major film, *Paths of Glory* (1957), and closes out Kubrick's career as an amateur film maker. In both form and content, *The Killing* demonstrates Kubrick's evolution as a director in three very important ways: (1) his use of multiple points of view in a film (similar to his work in *Dr. Strangelove*), (2) his control of the intensity of action and the pace of the film, (3) his significant development of both major and minor characters. Each of these techniques is critical to the success of the film and notable as a technique Kubrick would capitalize on in his later films.

What strikes the viewer at the outset of *The Killing*, and, for that matter, throughout the film, is the precise control Kubrick exercises over the material and the narrative points of view in the film. How the story is told here is as critical to the success of the film as what is being told. Using a narrator to develop and explain the action and relationships, Kubrick accomplishes a great deal of plot development quickly. While the narrator stands outside the action of the film, the viewer is brought into the action by the separate stories of the various characters' motivations in robbing the racetrack. Each participant in the robbery is seen as an individual before we see him in a group. We have our own viewpoints to consider along with the straightforward (objective) narrator's point of view. Kubrick uses this device to manipulate and control his plot, as well as to develop a stopwatch countdown to the robbery itself. At several critical points, the narrator's intervention accomplishes the needed narrative link to provide explanations of certain actions and responses, such as the predetermined action to be taken in case of any slip-up at the robbers' meeting point. This use of multiple narrative points of view also contributes to the development of suspense and the building up of action to the surprise ending. As the film develops, we are given numerous details about the precise timing involved in the robbery and a suggestion of the fatal flaw in the plan that will bring about the denouement. George, the least likely character, is the weak link in the chain of dedicated and precise criminals intent on pulling off the "perfect crime." Ironically, he is also the character intent on seeking revenge.

Related to the use of multiple points of view is the intensity and compression of time and action in the film. Through the use of a repeated time sequence, the viewer is given the exact action of each character during the same time period. Kubrick adds an almost documentary realism by allowing us to see both each individual's actions and the group working together in the success of the robbery. Kubrick's effective editing draws our attention to the passage of time needed to accomplish the robbery. Fully three-quarters of the film is concerned with the planning and execution of the robbery and the meticulous attention that goes into each man's preparation. As a final irony, Kubrick adds the surprise ending where all of the careful planning is undercut by chance happenings.

Finally, Kubrick elicits outstanding character portrayals in this film. In particular, the acting of Elisha Cook and Sterling Hayden adds much to the realism of the plot. Tight control of script and editing round out these portrayals of low-life characters that are similar in some ways to *Killer's Kiss.* Kubrick had proven his ability as a director by showing off some very good acting in an otherwise low budget film.

Critical reaction to *The Killing* was generally favorable, with important notices appearing in *Variety, Sight and Sound,* and the *New York Times.* Almost all the critics were impressed with Kubrick's handling of lighting techniques and cinematography. Since this was Kubrick's first feature length film with a known Hollywood actor (Sterling Hayden), the film attracted additional critical attention from those writers who saw good acting performances as an added plus to a traditional box office standby, the gangster film. *Variety* praised the film for its economic value as a co-feature in both first run and rerun houses. More important, *The Killing* attracted the critical attention of Kirk Douglas, who was to be instrumental in financing and starring in Kubrick's next feature film, *Paths of Glory.*

4 PATHS OF GLORY (1957)

With *Paths of Glory* (1957), Stanley Kubrick established himself as one of the most promising directors in Hollywood. After the release of *The Killing,* Kubrick and Harris ventured to Hollywood to look over properties at MGM, where they decided on Humphrey Cobb's World War I novel. Both visually and verbally, *Paths of Glory* is one of the most significant antiwar statements in the history of the America cinema, comparable in many ways to Renoir's *Grand Illusion.*

Through Colonel Dax, the main figure in the film, the viewer watches the rules of war operating on officer and line soldier alike. Kubrick exposes us to the absurdities of war and the crises of men under pressure both on the battlefield and off. His superb direction resulted in outstanding performances by Kirk Douglas, Adolphe Menjou, and George MacCready as the three main characters in conflict with one another. In addition to the acting, one is aware of Kubrick's masterful attention to visual detail: the attack on the Ant Hill, the tracking shots in the trenches, the line soldiers suffering from battle fatigue, the Napoleonic grace of the chateau setting of the court martial, and the harshly realistic execution scene. Both biting and incisive, Kubrick's satire on the inhumanity of war and men in war is brilliant. Few viewers will ever forget the appeal of Dax to basic human instincts or the rapid cut to the convicted soldiers' last meal.

Kubrick's precise dialogue is another masterful stroke. The contrast between General Broulard's view of war and that of Colonel Dax is drawn in three separate confrontations that illustrate their diametrically opposite views on killing, war, and duty. Dax stands for a soldier's concept of duty and the bravery of an officer defending men against ultimate annihilation on and off the battlefield. Broulard symbolizes the view of victory at any cost. Kubrick's attention to the development of conflict and character is best illustrated in the "kangaroo type" court martial where Dax is called upon to defend his soldiers on trial for their lives. In *Paths of Glory,* Kubrick continually confronts us with the choices man has to make at every turn: to get killed or die in an attack staged for the generals, to lie or to defend the hypocrisy of the General Staff, to choose victory over human compassion and respect for life itself. The ending of the film remains Kubrick's most profound presentation of the basic humanity in mankind even at its worst. Panning over a sea of faces, Kubrick probes the minds and hearts of combat-sickened soldiers expressing the human compassion for a German girl who stands for the numerous victims of war's atrocities. Kubrick's unflinching camera work provides the final conclusion to the bitterness and tragedy of war in 92 minutes of incredible realism.

The reception of *Paths of Glory* ranged from outright rejection by the French government (and a seventeen-year ban on showing the film in France) to extensive praise from some of the major American and European film critics. Both the acting and cinematography elicited a great deal of praise and publicity that made Kubrick's name well known as one of the most promising of the new Hollywood breed of independent directors. Since its original release in 1957, *Paths of Glory* has retained the interest of audiences who see it as a serious philosophic examination of war and the inhumanity of man at his worst.

5 SPARTACUS (1960)

After completing the filming of *Paths of Glory*, Kubrick returned to Hollywood, where he was asked to take over the direction of a new film starring Kirk Douglas. The good points about *Spartacus* are the early scenes in the gladiator school and the impressive epic battle scenes. The story centers about the epic hero Spartacus (from the Howard Fast novel) and his relations with his family and fellow slaves. Unlike many traditional epic films (*Hercules, The Ten Commandments, Ben Hur*), Spartacus deals with the private life of the hero, interspersed with extensive battle scenes and the accompanying pageantry. The viewer is often aware of the vast panoramic screen and the large cast, with little dialogue and many underdeveloped characters throughout.

Although the film offers many leading actors and actresses (Lawrence Olivier, Kirk Douglas, Charles Laughton, Peter Ustinov, Jean Simmons, and Tony Curtis), it contains too much martial noise and music that detract from the obvious need of character development and motivation. The relationship between Spartacus and Verania is delegated to two very short scenes showing their meeting and marriage. Kubrick exposes us to the spectacle of war but, because of the directorial influence of Kirk Douglas and Dalton Trumbo, he never probes deeply into the events behind the battles. The resulting film is cinematically appealing but artistically a failure.

Spartacus received a large number of mixed reviews with many critics seeing it as another "toga saga" unredeemed by any other strong attractive qualities. Many critics felt that a great deal of money had been spent with very poor results. Bosley Crowther summed up his feelings about the film in a *New York Times* review where he lamented the fact that so much time was spent in the film worrying about the plight of Spartacus's wife in post-war Rome and why so little time was spent on the fate of 10,000 executed Christians. In summary, *Spartacus* offered a number of positive points in Kubrick's favor: (1) realistic battle scenes, (2) careful attention to cinematography, including extensive use of wide angle lenses and panoramic shots, (3) good acting but not enough development of individualized roles, and (4) practical experience for Kubrick in directing and producing a multi-million dollar epic film. Several critics concluded that Stanley Kubrick had done an excellent job considering the extensive control and editing decisions that Kirk Douglas (Executive Producer) and Dalton Trumbo (Producer) had over the finished product. Kubrick made a firm decision after finishing *Spartacus* never again to direct a film in which he did not have complete control over production, direction, and editing.

6 LOLITA (1962)

Kubrick's next film, *Lolita* (1962), is an important milestone in his career as a film director because it offers a number of very difficult production problems, both in adapting a controversial novel and in making a film in 1962 dealing with the sensitive relationship between the central character, Humbert Humbert, and a young nymphet. As a concession to such organizations as the Legion of Decency, Kubrick had to make certain changes in the film version of *Lolita* that definitely altered the essential direction of the book (and screenplay) by Vladimir Nabokov. In essence, Kubrick was to become deeply involved in the direction, screenplay, and production of a unique and (for the 60s) controversial film.

Many readers felt that it would be difficult, if not impossible, to transfer Nabokov's novel to the silver screen because of the style of the novel and the heavy reliance on the use of interior monologues. Kubrick responded to the challenge by saying:

> People have asked me how it is possible to make a film out of *Lolita* when so much of the quality of the book depends on Nabokov's prose style. But to take the prose style as any more than just a part of a great book is simply misunderstanding just what a great book is. Of course, the quality of the writing is one of the elements that make a novel great. But this quality is a result of the writer's obsession with his subject, with a theme and a concept and a view of life and an understanding of character. Style is what an artist uses to fascinate the beholder in order to convey to him his feelings and emotions and thoughts. These are what have to be dramatized, not the style. The dramatizing has to find a style of its own, as it will do if it really grasps the content. And in doing this it will bring out another side of that structure which has gone into the novel. It may or may not be as good as the novel; sometimes it may in certain ways be even better.[2]

In fact, Kubrick did bring out another aspect of the structure of the novel: the element of black comedy. Rather than diminishing the effect of the film, this treatment of the satiric element in Nabokov's novel added to the success of *Lolita* as a film. The result is a film depicting the dramatic conflict between Quilty, Lolita, and Humbert. Since Kubrick could not explore the sexual relationship between Humbert and Lolita with complete artistic freedom, he chose to direct the viewer's attention to the satiric dimenions of small-town American life as seen through the eyes (and narration) of Humbert Humbert. The success of the film version of *Lolita* depends on at least three elements: (1) the acting of Peter Sellers as Clare Quilty, (2) the clever use of dialogue, (3) the detailed development of Humbert as a tragic figure. Each of these aspects deserves separate consideration.

Although Nabokov received sole credit for the screenplay in the film *Lolita*, Kubrick was responsible for the additional dialogue in the film that contributed to developing the character of Clare Quilty (Peter Sellers). Kubrick also added many of the scenes in the film, including the opening ping-pong game between Quilty and Humbert, which emphasizes the triangle between Lolita, Humbert, and Quilty. By opening the action with the death of Quilty and the flashback to four years before, Kubrick achieves a sustained interest in the development of Humbert and his relationship with Lolita. Quilty appears throughout the film and acts as a thematic commentary on Humbert's infatuation with Lolita. He also serves as an interesting sounding board for Kubrick's and Nabokov's satiric comments on various institutions in American life—the school psychologist, the center of attention in Ramsdale, the romantic attachment to Charlotte, the cause of Lolita's departure from Humbert, and the final demise of Quilty at the hands of Humbert. Sellers's performance is superb in each of these roles and he adds a sense of counterpoint and black humor to the depiction of Humbert's obsession with Lolita.

The use of witty dialogue and clever double-entendre adds yet another important dimension to the success of *Lolita* as a satire. Kubrick is at his best here and never seems to miss the opportunity to add a verbal pun or play on words to fit the situation. Always conscious of the essential visual dimension of film, Kubrick concentrates our attention on the various symbols throughout the film and their potential significance to character revelation and plot development. Several examples come to mind: the dialogue between Charlotte and Humbert in negotiating for the room (with bikini-clad Lolita in the foreground, "What made you decide, Mr. Humbert? Was it the view?"), the drive-in movie scene, the chess game and Charlotte's comment as Lolita passes by, "You took my queen!", or the classic confrontation between Humbert and the mourners following Charlotte's death (as he sits in the bathtub), "You mustn't thing of doing anything rash!" Each of these comic scenes adds much to the satiric dimension of the film by alternating comic and tragic aspects of the story (including Humbert's trip to "Camp Climax for Girls" to pick up Lolita for the trip back home and the news of her mother's death).

Finally, Kubrick's casting of James Mason in the role of Humbert Humbert adds a great deal to the film version of *Lolita.* Mason offers a charming performance, displaying an initial infatuation with Lolita that eventually leads to the poignant reunion scene at the end of the film. His attraction to Lolita and the commentary of the journal add just enough satiric comment to show the audience how much and how fast he falls in love with her. Again, Kubrick's use of the flashback helps to explain Humbert's actions at the end of the film, which harken back to the opening confused sequence with Quilty. Perhaps Mason seems even more believable in the role in contrast to the extremes of Charlotte (Shelley Winters) and Quilty (Peter Sellers).

Critical reaction to *Lolita* was largely negative. Since the publicity ad for the film asked "How did they ever make a film of *Lolita*?", many critics expected more than the film delivered. While most critics praised the acting of Mason and Sellers, they found difficulty with the direction and purpose of the film. Other writers found the film a bastardization of the Nabokov novel and set about showing how much better the novel was. Their comments suggested that Kubrick was not doing anything terribly original and that the film adaptation failed even to suggest the complexity of Nabokov's characters. As Kubrick has observed since the release of *Lolita,* he would certainly have made a different film in the current atmosphere of greater artistic freedom and the absence of the censorship of the 1960s.

Kubrick's next four films marked distinct contributions to the modern cinema in four very different ways. *Dr. Strangelove, 2001: A Space Odyssey, A Clockwork Orange,* and *Barry Lyndon,* offer specific views of the plight of mankind in the present, the distant future, the near future, and the distant past. In each production Kubrick has extended his ability and reputation as an innovative and daring director. Each of these films is very different from Kubrick's earlier work because each offers a satiric vision of man's inability to cope with a world gone wrong. Each film seems to reiterate Kubrick's questioning of the ability of mankind to control his destiny. Finally, all of these films raise serious philosophical questions concerning mankind's ability to save itself in a world that it continually tries to over-control. In these last four films, Kubrick has produced masterpieces that are truly one of a kind in the modern cinema, films that explore the nature of life, death, violence, and the limits of human endurance.

7 DR. STRANGELOVE, OR HOW I LEARNED TO STOP WORRYING AND LOVE THE BOMB (1964)

With the release of *Dr. Strangelove,* Kubrick's position as one of the most gifted and innovative directors in American cinema was assured. The film is a satiric analysis of what would happen if control of the hydrogen bomb got into the wrong hands–the hands and mind of a psychotic Air Force general. This is the dramatic situation that the film sets out to explore. Through characteristic Kubrick techniques–visual irony, satiric dialogue, concise editing, the use of thematic background music, and the superb development of character and action–he produced the ultimate antiwar satire complete with total destruction of the world. From the opening plane refueling sequence against the background of "Try a Little Tenderness" to the closing mushroom clouds of nuclear annihilation (with "We'll Meet Again" on the soundtrack), Kubrick is the undisputed master of how to attack and ridicule every aspect of the military and mankind.

From a director's point of view, *Dr. Strangelove* is an excellent example of an almost flawless film. With the tight, precise control over three areas of action–the cockpit of the B-52, the War Room, and the control room at Burpleson Air Force Base–Kubrick begins our countdown to destruction. As the story develops, the interrelationship between character, plot, and theme becomes obvious: mankind is on a collision course of its own making. Man's destiny becomes synonymous with the race to undo what man has done to himself. Kubrick is conscious of the unities of time, place, and action in the film and these unifying elements are essential to his ultimate success in *Strangelove.* Kubrick explores three related themes here: (1) the theme of man vs. machine and the destruction of the world at the hands of man's scientific wonders, (2) the theme of making war, not love, where humans are emotionless, sterile, and literally in love with war and the machines of war-making, (3) the theme of man vs. man in the race for one-upmanship between the Russians and the Americans. Each of these themes is integrally related to the other and to the "resolution" of the problem in Dr. Strangelove's behavior.

Dr. Strangelove is unlike any other satire on the military in both intention and achievement. Kubrick explores all of the possible ramifications of such a problem occurring and traces the outcome of each sequence of disasters. The viewer witnesses the extermination of the entire human race at the hands of machine-men gone mad. Kubrick takes aim at all of the mythic Hollywood images of the romantic war heroes from *Sergeant York* to *Thirty Seconds Over Tokyo, Twelve O'Clock High,* and *From Here to Eternity,* and replaces them with an insane Air Force general, a foppish American president, a degenerate Russian premier, and a host of subordinate beings at the mercy of the Doomsday device. Throughout all of this, Kubrick keeps showing us the absurdity of mankind cornered by its own stupidity. We do, indeed, learn to stop worrying (about the bomb) and to love the bomb as a deliverance from all of this!

Dr. Strangelove generated more popular interest than any of Kubrick's earlier films and we have yet to see the last article analyzing this controversial film. This is not at all surprising considering the content of the original reviews in such prestigious pages as *The New York Times, Time* Magazine, *The Village Voice, Saturday Review, Newsweek, New Republic, Commonweal,* and *Commentary.* Most reviewers saw Kubrick's *Dr. Strangelove* as either brilliant black comedy or a satiric put-down in bad taste. Perhaps the most useful and developed analysis was the review by Robert Brustein in *The New York Review of Books*: "Kubrick has flushed a monster from its psychic lair—the universal fear of nuclear accident—and then proceeded to feed and nourish it, letting it perform its worst before your eyes. The consequence of this spectacle is . . . a temporary purgation; to witness the end of the world as a comic event is, indeed, to stop worrying and love the bomb."[3] Brustein went on to discuss the form of Kubrick's film as Juvenalian satire and to distinguish the qualities of *Strangelove* that make it one of the most "courageous" films ever made.

Despite the rather wide diversity of critical opinion, most observers agreed that Kubrick had done a commendable job of dealing with a subject that was difficult to come to grips with in cinematic terms. Comparisons were made to *Fail Safe* and *The Bedford Incident* as contemporary films dealing with a serious treatment of the same subject. Among the positive reviews, critics prasied the controlled development of theme, plot, and conflict in the film, as well as the acting ability of Peter Sellers, George C. Scott, and Sterling Hayden. Recent studies of the film have attested to its enduring qualities and the cinematic expertise of the director. Its popularity in 16mm versions today attests to the importance of *Strangelove* as a film that went beyond the "bomb shelter fever" of the sixties.

8 **2001: A SPACE ODYSSEY** (1968)

Quite apart from its obvious landmark in Kubrick's career as a film director, *2001: A Space Odyssey* represents a major contribution to the development of film as a medium of expression. The film deals with man's first contact with extraterrestrial life and, although major segments of the film take place in the year 2001, the scope of the film spans the lifetime of man from the prehistoric age to the distant future. The best place to begin an analysis of the film is with Stanley Kubrick's own comment on the purpose and scope of *2001: A Space Odyssey*:

> I tried to create a visual experience, one that by-passes verbalized pigeonholing and directly penetrates the subconscious with an emotional and philosophical content . . . . I intended the film to be an intensely subjective experience that reaches the viewer at an inner level of consciousness, just as music does . . . . You're free to speculate as you wish about the philosophical and allegorical meaning of the film. . . .[4]

Kubrick's own comment on the essential "visual experience" of *2001: A Space Odyssey* is the most critical concept to keep in mind in understanding this unique film. Unlike any other Kubrick film (and for that matter *any* other film) *2001* explores the place of man in the vast space-time relationship of the distant past, the future, and a time/space/world beyond man's understanding. In the process Kubrick raises a number of deep philosophical issues related to the quest for knowledge and the limitations of man's understanding of himself and his creations.

Using the appearance of a black monolith to link the four central sequences of the film, Kubrick sets out on a modern odyssey to explore the question of man's progress through time, his quest for knowledge, and the search for an understanding of life and death that has dominated man's curiosity from the dawn of time. The main action of the film (sequences 2, 3, and 4) deals with the investigation of a powerful signal beamed from the planet Jupiter (monolith) and the resulting missions sent from earth to trace and document the origin of the strange signal. This is the basis of the plot; yet most of the film focuses on the visual dimensions of the space/time relationship with a bare minimum of narrative plot (only 46 minutes of dialogue in a film almost three hours long). Kubrick fully utilizes the spectacular visual qualities of film to explain his message here. The result is a film that asks many questions about the physical place of man in the universe and the metaphysical questions of his origins, evolution, and ultimate destiny.

Arthur C. Clarke, Kubrick's co-writer on *2001: A Space Odyssey,* offers one of the most clearly stated ideas on the theme of the film:

> It's about concern with man's hierarchy in the universe which is probably pretty low . . . . We set out with the deliberate intention of creating a myth. The Odyssean parallel was in our minds from the beginning, long before the film's title was chosen.[5]

Of the many themes suggested by Kubrick and Clarke in the film, four seem to stand out: (1) the quest for knowledge and understanding through man's history and future explorations of the last frontiers of space and time, (2) the conflict in human values between man and the machines he has created that end by controlling him and his fate (as in the machine world of *Dr. Strangelove* gone mad with ability to exterminate man), (3) the exploration of the third and fourth dimensions of time/space on a two-dimensional screen, (4) the myth of man's origins, the creation/death/rebirth myths, and the metaphysical speculations of man's understanding of himself and his universe. All of these themes suggest some of the broader outlines of questions Kubrick alludes to in his film, yet, they also suggest some of the distinct limitations of talking about a cinematic experience that depends so heavily on very non-traditional form and content.

As might be expected, there has been more critical reaction to Kubrick's *2001: A Space Odyssey* than to any film he has made to date. This is not surprising because the film has opened so many new avenues for speculation and critical appreciation. Essentially, critical response to the film can be grouped in four large areas: (1) the popular reviews of the film when it first came out, (2) technical analysis of the 205 special effects sequences in the film and the cinematography of Kubrick, (3) thematic studies of the meaning of the film and the explanation of its numerous symbols, and (4) studies of the film as an example of the science fiction film genre.

Many distinguished film critics were simply baffled by *2001: A Space Odyssey* when it first appeared in 1968. All of the major film critics in the popular *New York Times, Saturday Review, Newsweek, Commentary,* and *New Yorker* were deeply impressed by the visual dimensions of the film and the seemingly unbelievable presentation of space and time that Kubrick explored in the film. But many of these same critics felt (as John Simon) that it was a "shaggy god story" with little or no plot and unresolved questions throughout. Many of these early reviews spent a great deal of time talking about visual effects because they were unsure or totally unaware of what the film was about. This created a demand by both audiences and critics for further explanations from Kubrick and Clarke. In a rare interview, Kubrick talked about the reaction to the film, its visual dimension, and the increasing popularity of the film with young audiences (many of whom identified with the time ride sequence and the effects of hallucinogenic drugs).

Other critics were frankly skeptical about the intention and achievement of the film and could not decide whether Kubrick had created an outstanding film or one that was stylistically breathtaking but thematically flawed. Still other critics found the visual quality and special effects to be the only saving graces in a long, boring film. Finally, some critics saw Kubrick's film as being largely experimental and avant garde, one that, while demonstrating outstanding cinematography, did nothing to advance Kubrick's career or the art of the science fiction film.

The remaining articles on Kubrick's film have dwelt on many specialized aspects of the production, thematic meaning, and place of the film in the science fiction film genre. The technical articles have explored and explained most of the visual qualities of the film including the special effects sequences, use of color, use of music, use of special lenses and cameras, and the detailed research that went into documenting and reproducing the effects of space travel. In addition, numerous articles have appeared to explain the various psychological, sociological, theological, historical, and philosophical meanings of the monolith and the theme of the film. Finally, more recent critics have tried to place the film within the larger context of the science fiction film genre by showing how much it is both similar to and a radical departure from many of the more traditional formulas within it. At this point, more than ten years after its original release, it is clear that we have not seen the last analysis of this most controversial and innovative film.

9 A CLOCKWORK ORANGE (1972)

One of the greatest problems that critics and audiences alike have had in seeing *A Clockwork Orange* as the masterpiece that it is, is the limitation of judging the film apart from the charges of its being pornographic. This problem has severely limited critics from fairly judging Kubrick's singular achievement in adapting Anthony Burgess's novel of the society of the immediate future. Once one understands the thematic implications of Kubrick's film, *A Clockwork Orange* becomes a savagely bitter satire of man and society that moves far beyond the preoccupation with sex and violence that has unduly concerned so many of its detractors. In *A Clockwork Orange,* Kubrick achieves a scathing indictment of a futuristic society as complex as his attack on man and the military in *Dr. Strangelove.* But *Clockwork* substitutes violence and brutality for the humor and absurdity of *Dr. Strangelove,* and in the process explores the treatment of the individual at the hands of an almost Orwellian society.

If Kubrick devotes intense visual concentration to the studied violence and sadistic brutality of Alex and his cohorts at the beginning of *A Clockwork Orange,* it is to contrast that behavior with the equally dehumanizing behavior of the society that attempts to reform Alex with the Ludovico treatment of rehabilitation, which reduces him to an animal without free choice in his behavior. Part of the critical success of the film is the result of Kubrick's ability to make the viewer both physically and mentally repulsed by Alex's attacks on innocent victims, and his subsequent punishment at the hands of a society that programs individuals to respond to the dictates of its will. The experience of viewing *A Clockwork Orange* is analogous to the conditioning Alex undergoes, i.e., both Alex and the viewer are "conditioned" by *film* to react against aggression and violence. In Kubrick's vision, the cure for Alex is worse than the disease; in the viewer's vision Alex goes from being the enemy of society to its lobotomized victim.

The inhumanity of the individuals in *A Clockwork Orange* is not limited to Alex and his gang (or to the very violent opening scenes) but is institutionalized and legalized by those members of the government who are interested in the political value that Alex has to the advancement of their cause. In the same manner that we see Alex's victims become pawns at the hands of the thugs, we see Alex become a pawn of the ministry, a clockwork orange at the mercy of "reformers" intent on the preservation of a public image at any cost. The climactic scene with Alex in the hospital, greeted by the Prime Minister while Beethoven blares in the background, is the high point of Kubrick's satiric attack on the hypocrisy of the state. The film closes with Alex back to his old behavior under the cheering applause of Victorian society and his final comment, "I was cured alright." If Kubrick's film works for us (the viewers), we are also cured "alright" to believe that man's worst enemy is his collective self (society) and the standardization/regulation of the individual in the name of progress.

In both form and content, *A Clockwork Orange* resembles the worlds of *Dr. Strangelove* and *2001: A Space Odyssey* in portraying the individual, alienated person at the mercy of human monsters. Like the machines of *Strangelove* and *Space Odyssey,* the society of *A Clockwork Orange* becomes a machine-like system intent on programming man for systematic destruction. It is interesting to see how Kubrick uses music in all three films to underline the essential dramatic irony of the situation in which man is caught. In *Clockwork,* for example, Beethoven becomes the delight and destruction of Alex, offering another illlustration of how much Kubrick integrates the visual and verbal qualities of his cinematic art.

The critical reaction to Kubrick's *A Clockwork Orange* can be neatly divided into two very different categories. A large number of critics reacted to the excessive violence in the film and its explicit treatment of sexual deviance. For most of these critics *Clockwork* was an outright exploitation film intent on arousing the prurient instincts of the audience, and therefore had no redeeming social or artistic value. It is interesting to see how many of its detractors used the film as an occasion to attack Kubrick's own morals and his ultimate intentions as a film director. Much of this criticism became an overt attack on the dangers inherent in allowing such a film to be released (similar to recent reactions to *The Warriors*) and the sounding board for how movies have lowered the standards of society's morals. The extent of this negative criticism brought a counterattack from Kubrick in the pages of the *New York Times* defending the right of a director to present ideas in his films without advocating them as a way of life.

A second, more rational, reaction to the film attempted to examine the theme and development of Kubrick's ideas and to suggest the excellence of the film. These critics examined more of the plot and the development of Alex as a character victimized by a state system. More recent studies of the film have praised Kubrick's technical expertise (color, cinematography, set design, music, and costumes) and his two-part structure in developing the rise-fall-rehabilitation of Alex. Several of these studies have compared Kubrick's vision with that of Swift, Orwell, and Huxley in illustrating his satiric ability. Finally, more acute insights have been offered about the nature of violence in the film and how much the film explores the psychological and sociological causes of the individual's behavior in a mechanized, almost sterilized, society of the near future. These critics have attempted to judge Kubrick's film in relation to his earlier work and as a logical extension of his concern with the place of modern man in an increasingly dehumanized world.

10 BARRY LYNDON (1975)

Kubrick's most recent film, *Barry Lyndon* (1975), traces the rise and fall of an eighteenth-century Irishman intent on achieving social status and mobility by any means within his grasp or cunning. The film is based on William Makepeace Thackeray's novel *The Luck of Barry Lyndon.* It is another "epic" film in both scope and direction, and as such offers numerous examples of Kubrick's abilities as a cinematographer, special effects designer, and screen writer. But unlike other epic films, Kubrick's goes to the heart of the story by focusing on the individual in relation to his background rather than focusing on the heroic exploits of an individual to the exclusion of his cultural milieu. *Barry Lyndon* is an unusual film that combines the visual spectacle of *2001: A Space Odyssey* with the satiric insight of *A Clockwork Orange* in seeing the individual as a victim of a society he aspires to become part of but that ultimately defeats him. It is a film that spends much of its time establishing setting, background, and situation in order to allow the viewer to measure the hero, Barry Lyndon, against the manners and mores of the eighteenth century.

The structure of *Barry Lyndon* resembles that of a mock epic where the hero is continually defeated and ultimately victimized by the system he hopes to conquer. In the film, love leads to frustration, jealousy, and cuckolding. The rules of society's aristocratic class work against, rather than for, the hero. In the process of the hero's exploits, the viewer is constantly asked to examine Barry's individual actions against a larger framework in which he is constantly diminished by his environment. So much of this film depends on the ability of the viewer to see the minuscule role of man in the larger system that controls him and his destiny that Kubrick spends a great deal of time re-creating the world of the eighteenth century so that we may judge Barry by the actions of the period itself.

One of the most interesting features of *Barry Lyndon* has to do with the rules and code of conduct that govern everything from gambling to dueling to waging war and love. The film depends heavily on establishing the period, the decoration, and decorum of the drawing rooms of eighteenth-century Europe, complete with elaborate costumes and almost Hogarthian sets. Man's conduct is measured by his status in society and the proper rules by which war is fought, love is made, and honor is defended. Kubrick shows the mockery of human values that are subordinated to the ritualistic duels that legalize the killing and maiming of the individual. As D'Lugo points out in his study of the gaming devices in *Barry Lyndon*:

> The narrative treatment of Redmond Barry's rise to the style and name of Barry Lyndon is set against two distinctive types of ludic structure: the card game and the duel. These two very different patterns of interaction, rather than exemplifying Huizinga's notion of "ultimate perfection" characterize a baser human drive played against greed and passion: the petty striving of individuals to gain and retain their positions in a world apparently devoid of any spiritual essence.[6]

It is this focus on the game of life that moves back and forth in Kubrick's depiction of Barry's rise to position in the aristocracy he so desperately craves.

Like other Kubrick heroes, Barry works his way into and out of situations that tend to control and restrict him while he has no apparent control over many of the incidents that shape his present status or future aspirations. Barry's quest to lead the life of a gentleman seems to be the main unifying element in the film, as Kubrick shows us what this demands of the individual. Both parts of the film seem to advance the idea that from beginning to end Barry risks more than he ultimately gains. Every one of his victories seems tempered by the loss of something he tried to gain, often justifying the sacrifice of the individual's code to that of society. As in earlier Kubrick films, we are looking at a character who attempts to control his fate in a world that continually restricts and impedes the role of the individual. The basic questions of life, death, and survival are still here, but are entwined with eighteenth-century codes of social grace and behavioral standards. It appears as a thin veneer that comes apart for the twentieth-century viewer looking at it from the hindsight of history.

In *Barry Lyndon,* Kubrick has extended his image of being an outstanding visual craftsman by paying close attention to the visual sets and landscapes of Barry's world. He does this as a means of having us constantly see the equation between the individual in the foreground and the background against which he operates. Throughout the film we see private scenes followed by public confrontations, i.e., lovers' meetings and public duels, private conspiracies and public cheating at the gaming tables, private schemings and public charades. The individual is less important in *Barry Lyndon* simply because the worth of an individual is measured by his birth and heritage rather than by his innate qualities or personal behavior. Barry is a loner in a world of organized rules of conduct and decorum which he ultimately violates and is defeated by. The final duel with Lord Bullingdon underscores Barry's faith in the humanity of his fellow man and the tragic consequences of his gullibility.

The critical reception of *Barry Lyndon* was extremely negative in both England and America. Many of the critical studies of the film focused on the breathtaking cinematography and the poor development of character, motivation, and resolution of conflict. Several critics saw Kubrick's film as a definite plunge in his expertise as a film director and pondered why he would take such an uninteresting story about an unusually boring hero to make a film. Another problem that bothered the critics was the length of the film (185 minutes) and the use of a narrator that continually informed the audience about the outcome of events before they happened. Many felt that Stanley Kubrick, the master of telling a good story, had lost his touch and that the enormous production costs of the film appeared only in the spectacular visual qualities of the color and photography amidst poor acting, poor story line, and poor thematic development. Still other critics saw in *Barry Lyndon* the unusual combination of form and content that seemed particularly suitable for showing a twentieth-century film about a nineteenth-century view of eighteenth-century society. The reaction of *Barry Lyndon* was similar in many respects to the critical reception of *2001: A Space Odyssey;* many critics saw spectacular visual effects amidst a film that was essentially a visual rather than narrative experience. This may suggest that future studies of *Barry Lyndon* will explore the very unconventional cinematic methods that Kubrick employs to tell the story of the rise and fall of an unconventional hero.

As a satirist, Stanley Kubrick has focused on the plight of an alienated man in a society that he can only partially understand, control, or ultimately survive in. Much of Kubrick's development as a director has been focused on the extent to which the seeming technical limitations of the film art can be expanded and explored. His four most recent pictures have attempted to exploit the limitations of his audience in examining worlds and ideas that are extremely unconventional.

He has always used the basic form of film technology as the springboard of such daring films as *2001: A Space Odyssey* and *A Clockwork Orange.* In the process, Kubrick has also extended the imagination and understanding of his audiences. With each new film, he seems to demand more audience involvement and commitment to bridging the gap between the real world and the cinematic world by a willed sustaining of belief in the director's vision. One can see the sequential development of Kubrick as a director by paying close attention to the endless rhetorical devices he employs to visually and verbally assault his viewers' imaginations. But, at the same time, Kubrick is constantly aware of the medium of film and what he does with it. What Kubrick has done with film may be best summed up in his own words:

> I think that for a movie or play to say anything really truthful about life, it has to do so very obliquely, so as to avoid all pat conclusions and neatly tied-up ideas. The point of view it is conveying has to be completely entwined with a sense of life as it is, and has to be got across through a subtle injection into the audience's consciousness. Ideas which are valid and truthful are so multi-faceted that they don't yield themselves to frontal assault. The ideas have to be discovered by the audience, and their thrill in making the discovery makes those ideas all the more powerful. You use the audience's thrill of surprise and discovery to reinforce your ideas, rather than reinforce them artificially through plot points or phoney drama or phoney stage dynamics put in to power them across.[7]

NOTES

1. Walker, *Stanley Kubrick Directs,* p. 267.
2. Stanley Kubrick, "Words and Movies," *Sight and Sound,* 30 (Winter, 1961), p.14.
3. Robert Brustein, "Out of This World," *New York Review of Books,* (6 February, 1964), p. 14.
4. Norman Kagan, *The Cinema of Stanley Kubrick,* p. 34.
5. Arthur C. Clarke in Jeremy Bernstein, "Books: Chain Reaction." *The New Yorker,* 44 (21 September, 1968), 180-184.
6. Marvin D'Lugo, "Barry Lyndon: Kubrick on the Rules of the Game," *Film Studies Annual* 1977, (Pleasantville, New York: Redgrave Press, 1978).
7. Quoted in Norman Kagan, *The Cinema of Stanley Kubrick,* p. 6.

III The Films: Synopses, Credits, and Notes

1 DAY OF THE FIGHT (1950)

Synopsis

Presents the last hours before the middleweight prize fighter Walter Cartier enters the ring to fight. Includes footage of his workout and training sessions and scenes of his handlers and manager in the dressing room before the start of the fight. Shows the view of the audience from the fighter's viewpoint in the ring.

Credits and Notes

Producer	Stanley Kubrick
Director	Stanley Kubrick
Writer	Stanley Kubrick
Commentary	Douglas Edwards

Filmed on location in New York City.

Running Time	16 minutes
Distribution	RKO Radio
Released	1950

2 FLYING PADRE (1951)

Synopsis

Examines the life of a 'flying' priest, the Reverend Fred Stadtmueller, who travels around his 400 square mile parish by Piper Cub. Includes footage of the priest ministering to the men, women, and children of Mosquero, New Mexico.

Credits and Notes

Producer	Stanley Kubrick
Director	Stanley Kubrick

Writer	Stanley Kubrick
Photography	Stanley Kubrick
Running Time	9 minutes
Distributor	RKO Radio
Released	1951

3 THE SEAFARERS (1953)

Synopsis

A study of the life of the members of the Seafarers Union as they go about their daily work on ships and docks. The workers are seen reporting for duty and carrying out their assigned tasks.

Credits and Notes

Producer	Lester Cooper
Director	Stanley Kubrick
Writer	Will Chasen
Photographer	Stanley Kubrick
Narrator	Dan Hollenbeck
Technical Advice	Staff of *Seafarers Log*
Running Time	30 minutes
Distributor	Seafarers International Union, Atlantic and Gulf Coast District American Federaton of Labor
Released	1953

*4 FEAR AND DESIRE (1953)

Synopsis

Film opens with these lines spoken by off-screen narrator:

There is a war in this forest
Not a war that has been fought, nor one that
will be
But any war
And the enemies that struggle here do not exist
Unless we call them into being
For all of them, and all that happens now
Is outside history

*Synopsis based on the summary of *Fear and Desire* in Norman Kagan's *The Cinema of Stanley Kubrick*, pp. 9–17.

Only the unchanging shapes of fear and doubt
and death
Are from our world
These soldiers that you see keep our language
and our time
But have no other country but the mind.

A plane flies overhead and four soldiers hit the ground to seek shelter from it. Lieutenant Corby and his three men, Mac, Sidney, and Fletcher, have crashed behind enemy lines and are now building a raft to float down the river to the safety of their own lines. Corby draws a map on the ground indicating their position and the plan of escape. The men begin building the raft near the river, but they soon observe an enemy truck going by and start to doubt their ability to survive.

From his vantage point, Mac spots an enemy airstrip nearby and a command post where one of the generals is giving out his orders to men. Just at this moment, a plane dives overhead and they all seek shelter in the woods. As they move through the woods they spot an enemy shack with two men inside eating a meal. They rush the shack, kill the men, and begin eating the stew that the soldiers were eating before. Another enemy soldier returns and Corby kills him and rushes off to the woods with his men. The men begin to fear that the entire woods are filled with enemy patrols. As they are hiding, they notice a young girl who is wading in the brook nearby. She comes toward one of the soldiers, who jumps out, gags her, and holds her up while the other soldiers surround her and tie her to a tree with two belts. Sidney is left behind to guard her while Corby and the other two return to work on the raft. While Sidney is guarding the girl he begins to talk to her and entertain her by doing an imitation of the general and his actions. He hugs her and asks her to like him even though he knows she must hate him too.

Down at the raft site, the other men find no evidence of the raft or an ambush. Mac observes the command post with his binoculars and wishes that they were really a rifle sight looking at the general. Back in the woods, the girl tries to struggle and twist herself free. Sidney brings her some water in his cupped hand and the girl attempts to play up to him by licking his hands. He then undoes the belt holding her and presses himself against her body. She struggles free but he catches her with the free end of the belts. In the next three shots, the girl runs, Sidney pulls out his gun, fires, and the girl collapses on the ground. At this point the other men return and Sidney invites them to go swimming with him. He then runs off into the woods. Fletcher and the others assume that Sidney has gone out of his mind.

At night, Mac convinces Corby and Fletcher to help him kill the enemy general. Mac will bring the raft downstream to attract the sentries while Corby and Fletcher rush the command post and kill the general and his aide, and escape in the plane. Corby and Fletcher scout the enemy plane and then begin moving in on the command post. When they look through the binoculars they see images of themselves (the actors playing Corby and Fletcher play the general and his aide). Meanwhile, Mac poles the raft downstream thinking all the time of how happy he is that he is not the general about to be killed. He draws the attention of the sentries, who begin to fire at him. Corby and Fletcher rush the command post, Fletcher shoots both occupants at close range, and the general tries to escape. As the general comes out to surrender, Corby fires at point blank range and the general's head turns over, revealing Corby's facial features. A few minutes later the plane takes off.

Mac drifts down the river and sees an apparition of Sidney, who joins him on the raft. At another military airport, Corby and Fletcher have just finished telling the story and are now heading down to the river to watch for Mac. They talk about how war is and how their heads are not ready for accepting it. They see a raft coming into sight with Mac lying down (and maybe dead) with Sidney kneeling on all fours over him. Sidney is singing incoherently. The four soldiers are reunited again.

Credits and Notes

Producer	Stanley Kubrick
Director	Stanley Kubrick
Photography	Stanley Kubrick
Editor	Stanley Kubrick
Associate Producer	Martin Perveler
Screenplay	Howard O. Sackler
Music	Gerald Fried
Unit Manager	Bob Dierks
Assistant Director	Steve Hahn
Makeup	Chet Fabian
Art Director	Herbert Lebowitz
Title Design	Barry Ettengoff
Dialogue Director	Toba Kubrick
Cast	Frank Silvera (Mac), Kenneth Harp (Corby), Paul Mazursky (Sidney), Steve Coit (Fletcher), Virginia Leith (the girl), David Allen (narrator).

The picture was filmed on location in California and was distributed in the United States by Joseph Burstyn Inc. All prints of the film were returned to Stanley Kubrick and the film is no longer available for commercial distribution.

Running Time	68 minutes
Released	April 1, 1953

5 KILLER'S KISS (1955)

Synopsis

Davy Gordon, a boxer, reflects on his life as he waits for a train at New York's Pennsylvania Station. He talks about how you can get yourself in a mess sometimes and reflects back to "taking it easy before my fight with Rodriguez."

Flashback to Davy's room in a rooming house across from an attractive girl's room. Davy gets dressed, shaves, and looks across at Gloria's room. On the way out of the building, the two meet in the lobby. Gloria is picked up by Vince Rapallo, a dance hall owner, and Davy takes the subway down to the arena. As he travels, Davy reads a letter from a relative asking him to come for a visit to Seattle. Gloria goes to work at the Pleasureland Dance Hall where she works as a taxi dancer. In the back office Rapallo watches Gordon on television in his fight. The action moves back and forth from Davy's fight in the arena to the fight between two drunks at the dance hall. During all of this Vince Rapallo is hugging and kissing Gloria in the back room. Later Gloria leaves the dance hall and goes back to her room.

In the darkness, Davy is watching Gloria undress when he is interrupted by a phone call from his uncle, George, who talks to him about the fight on television. After this conversation, Davy goes to sleep and dreams of an alley scene (negative prints on screen) of hollow buildings and loud screaming. Just as he is racing down this alley, he awakens to the sound of Gloria screaming from the room next door. He races over the roof to her room, just after Rapallo has left. He calms Gloria and asks her to explain what has happened. After he settles her in bed, he returns to his own room. The next morning over breakfast, Gloria tells her story to Davy (via flashback) explaining how her sister was a talented ballet dancer who committed suicide after her father's death. Gloria's sister had worked hard to pay for her father's mounting medical bills. After her sister's suicide, Gloria had traveled to New York to help forget her past. Gloria and Davy embrace and later agree to go away together to Seattle.

Back at the dance hall, Rapallo reacts with rage to the idea of Gloria's departure and threatens to kill her. She decides to take her money and leave with Davy, who is waiting downstairs. While Davy is waiting, a group of drunks take his scarf and he runs off in pursuit. When Gloria comes down to meet him, she meets Davy's fight manager, who has come to give Davy his final check. One of Rapallo's thugs sends Gloria up to get her money and, while she is gone, they mistake Davy's manager for Davy, rob him, and leave him in the alley to die.

When Davy returns and finds neither Gloria nor his fight manager, he returns to his room and packs for Seattle. He goes to Gloria's room for one last check and while he is there he observes two detectives searching his own room in connection with the murder of Albert, his fight manager. Davy then spots Rapallo, who is also looking for him, and proceeds to follow him in a cab. Later the next morning, Davy gets in Rapallo's car and threatens him with a gun if he does not take him to Gloria. They proceed to the warehouse area where Gloria is being held as a prisoner.

Davy forces the two men against the wall with Rapallo, but they push Gloria against Davy and he ends up as their prisoner. Davy then jumps through a glass window, falls to the ground, and runs away from the pursuing thugs. The chase proceeds through alleys and over rooftops similar to the earlier "dream sequence" that Davy had. Finally, Rapallo catches up with Davy in an old mannequin warehouse and the chase ends with Davy spearing Rapallo with a crowbar.

Back at Pennsylvania Station, Davy summarizes the last events in his life in New York: Gloria is rescued, the police question and release Davy, Davy sends flowers to Albert's widow, and then leaves for the railroad station. As his train is announced, Davy turns to hear Gloria call for him in the background. The two embrace each other as the music rises.

Credits and Notes

Production Company	Minotaur
Producers	Stanley Kubrick Morris Rousel

Director	Stanley Kubrick
Photography	Stanley Kubrick
Screenplay	Stanley Kubrick
Editor	Stanley Kubrick
Music	Gerald Fried
Choreography	David Vaughan
Cast	Frank Silvera (Vincent Rapallo), Jamie Smith (Davy Gordon), Irene Kane (Gloria Price), Jerry Jarret (Albert, the fight manager), Mike Dana, Felice Orlandi, Ralph Roberts, Phil Stevenson (hoodlums), Julius Adelman (owner of the mannequin factory), David Vaughan, Alec Rubin (conventioneers).

Filmed on location in New York City; New Jersey

Running Time	67 minutes
Distributor	United Artists Release of Minotaur Production
Released	September 28, 1955

6 THE KILLING (1956)

Synopsis

View of the Bay Meadows Racetrack. Marvin Unger comes from the betting area and passes a note to the bartender, Mike O'Reilly. Narrator: "It is 3:45 on a September day." This description of the action is followed by the narrator saying: "Now the addition of the others like fragments in a picture puzzle."

Barroom scene showing Patrolman Randy Kennan meeting a friend of Val Cannon and promising payment of gambling debts. At Johnny Clay's apartment, Johnny is talking to his girl, Fay, about the plans and the role of each of the members of the gang, who are not rich but have "little problems." Fay asks Johnny to quit but he tells her to stay out of his way until it is over. Mike O'Reilly arrives home at his apartment to greet his invalid wife. In yet another apartment scene, George Peatty has a domestic quarrel with his wife over money and tells her that soon she will not complain about how much money he has. She presses him for details but he tells her he cannot tell her anything more. Later that night, Peatty's wife, Sherry, meets with her boyfriend, Val Cannon, and tells him George is involved with something "big" that involves a lot of money.

Back at Johnny Clay's apartment, the robbers are going over the details of the racetrack robbery when they hear someone at the door. They discover Sherry Peatty at the door and send George home while the rest of the gang stay to question her. Sherry offers to compromise her position by resting her head on Johnny's shoulder, but he rejects her and threatens her if she bothers them again. At the apartment, George is upset with the gang's treatment of his wife and asks if Johnny tried anything with Sherry. She replies, "No" and he is left brooding.

Narrator: "Three days later, Johnny began his final preparation." At the Academy of Chess, Johnny meets with Maurice, the owner, and asks him to stage a phoney fight in order to divert attention at the racetrack. Then Johnny meets with Nikki Arane at an abandoned farm where Nikki is taking practice shots with a high-powered rifle. Nikki agrees to shoot "a special horse" for him, and Johnny leaves to return to town and rent a motel room.

Narrator: "Four days later at 7 a.m., Sherry Peatty was wide awake." She teases George at breakfast by saying she knows this is the big day. George asks her what happened the other night and she replies that she tried to resist Johnny but he forced her. George is angry and begins to tell her the whole plan for the robbery. Preparations at the racetrack are shown. Johnny and Marvin Unger meet to go over the plans once more. Johnny thanks him and tells him to stay away from the track until 4:30, when the seventh race begins. Johnny gets his plane reservations, buys flowers in a large box, replaces the flowers with a rifle, and leaves the box in a coin locker at the local bus station. He deposits the key in Mike O'Reilly's mailbox and returns to his apartment.

Mike O'Reilly says goodbye to his wife, takes the key Johnny left, and takes the box to the racetrack with him. O'Reilly goes to his locker room, changes into work clothes, and leaves the box with the rifle inside his locker. The narrator announces that after the first race "Mike was in business" at the bar. Officer Randy Kennan reports that his radio is out of order and races away from a sidewalk brawl to be at the racetrack on time. He parks his car underneath the window at the back of the counting room offices.

At the Academy of Chess, Maurice hears the early races on the radio and then gets up to leave for the track. The announcer at the track announces the start of the seventh race. This scene is repeated three times showing: Maurice in position at the bar, Nikki in position in a vacant parking lot overlooking the track, and Johnny in position near the track office door. We then jump back to Nikki coming to the track and getting himself in position with rifle ready at trackside. As the horses come by Nikki, he shoots the favorite, "Red Lightning." When he tries to escape, Nikki is shot and dies in the parking lot beside his "lucky" horseshoe.

At the racetrack bar, police come out to break up the fight staged by Maurice. After they come out, Johnny enters the door to the office that is left unlocked by George Peatty. Once inside, Johnny puts on a mask and takes the rifle from Mike's locker. He goes across to the office and orders the men to put all the money in a bag. He then sends the men to the locker room, takes off his mask and disguise, and throws the bag with rifle and money out the window into the waiting arms of Patrolman Randy Kennan below. Johnny then goes downstairs and blends into the crowd.

Back at Unger's apartment the robbers are getting nervous waiting for Johnny to return. Suddenly, they are surprised by Val Cannon and his men who order them to give up the money. George comes out of the kitchen and a shootout occurs in which everyone is killed except George, who struggles away wounded. Meanwhile, Johnny has picked up the money at the motel but goes by the apartment when he sees the police arrive. Johnny buys a large suitcase and transfers the money to it and goes off to the airport. Back at Peatty's apartment, George confronts his wife, who is planning to leave with Val Cannon. He shoots her and dies beside her.

At the airport Johnny has an argument with the desk clerk about having to check his large bag. He finally agrees and walks out to the waiting plane. As the bags are being transferred to the plane, a small dog runs in front of the baggage cart upsetting the driver who stops abruptly, throwing the bags all over the runway. Johnny's bag bursts open scattering the money all over. As Johnny turns to leave the airport, two detectives come up from behind him through the glass doors. He turns to his girl, Fay, saying "What's the use?" and awaits his captors.

Credits and Notes

Production Company	Harris-Kubrick Productions
Producer	James B. Harris
Director	Stanley Kubrick
Screenplay	Stanley Kubrick from Lionel White's novel *Clean Break*
Camera	Lucien Ballard
Editor	Betty Steinberg
Music	Gerald Fried
Additional Dialogue	Jim Thompson
Art Director	Ruth Sobotka
Sound	Earl Snyder
Cast	Sterling Hayden (Johnny Clay), Coleen Gray (Fay), Vince Edwards (Val Cannon), Jay C. Flippen (Marvin Unger), Marie Windsor (Sherry Peatty), Ted De Corsica (Randy Kennan), Elisha Cook (George Peatty), Joe Sawyer (Mike O'Reilly), Tim Carey (Nikki), Jay Adler (Leo), Joseph Turkel (Tiny), Kola Kwarian (Maurice), James Edwards (car park attendant).
Running Time	83 minutes
Distributor	United Artists
Released	May 20, 1956

7 **PATHS OF GLORY** (1957)

Synopsis

Exterior view of large chateau headquarters of French Army during World War I. Inside, General Broulard outlines to General Mireau his plans for taking an impregnable position. Mireau says that his men are tired and the Ant Hill objective is almost impossible to take in their present condition. Broulard insists and points out the possible promotion for Mireau in the offing. Mireau agrees and decides to accept the job. Down in the trenches, Mireau visits with the troops on his way to the commander, Colonel Dax. At Dax's room, Mireau insists on Colonel Dax taking the Ant Hill and, after strong objections, Dax agrees to try despite the heavy losses that will result.

During the evening, Lieutenant Roget and two other men leave for a reconnaissance patrol. While they are out on the patrol, Roget leaves one of the men to die and runs like a coward. Corporal Paris tries to save the man, Private LeJeune, but fails. Later, he confronts Roget with his cowardice but the lieutenant tells him that no one will believe an enlisted man against an officer.

During the battle for the Ant Hill, General Mireau observes the attack from behind the lines. Colonel Dax leads the men out of the trenches amidst very heavy artillery shelling by the Germans. As Dax crawls slowly along with his troops, Mireau becomes concerned that the second wave of French troops has not left the trenches. He orders his own artillery to fire on the French troops but the artillery captain refuses the order unless it is in writing signed by the general. Mireau relieves the captain and orders him to report to him at headquarters. After the unsuccessful attack on the Ant Hill, Mireau and Broulard decide to execute three soldiers (selected at random) as an example to the other men of the consequences of cowardice. Dax leaves the generals to bring the bad news to his company commanders. Dax has volunteered to defend the men at the court martial. Colonel Dax then meets with the prisoners and tells them about the court martial and their situation.

At the court martial, all of the prosecution's charges and evidence are accepted. Colonel Dax attempts to introduce evidence, including the war records of the soldiers, but none of it is allowed. Dax appeals to the humanity of the board members. In the next scene, the condemned prisoners await their fate with a visiting priest and their last meal. A fight breaks out and one of the men is injured. Colonel Dax assigns Lieutenant Roget to the firing squad detail and then speaks with the artillery captain who tells him about Mireau's orders. Later, at a ball that evening, Colonel Dax confronts General Broulard with the truth about Mireau's order to fire on his own troops and Broulard tells him he will look into it.

On the morning of the execution the prisoners are led to the firing squad, strapped to the posts, and shot in front of all the assembled troops. At breakfast in the chateau, Broulard confronts General Mireau with the charges made by Colonel Dax the night before. Mireau denies them, but resigns when he is asked to face a board of inquiry. Broulard then offers the job to Colonel Dax, but Dax refuses, saying that he despises everything that General Broulard stands for. As Dax returns to his quarters, he observes his men in a barroom watching a humiliated German girl who is forced to sing for their entertainment. As the girl sings, all of them begin to sympathize with her plight; some cry and they all sing with her. Dax orders his sergeant to allow the men to finish and then prepare to return to battle.

Credits and Notes

Production Company	Harris-Kubrick Productions
Producer	James B. Harris

Director	Stanley Kubrick
Script	Stanley Kubrick, Calder Willingham, Jim Thompson, based on the novel *Paths of Glory* by Humphrey Cobb
Photography	George Krause
Editor	Eva Kroll
Art Director	Ludwig Reiber
Music	Gerald Fried
Sound	Martin Miller
Cast	Kirk Douglas (Colonel Dax), Ralph Meeker (Corporal Paris), Adolphe Menjou (General Broulard), George Macready (General Mireau), Wayne Morris (Lieutenant Roget), Richard Anderson (Major Saint-Auben), Joseph Turkel (Private Arnaud), Timothy Carey (Private Ferol), Peter Capell (Colonel Judge), Susanne Christian (German girl), Bert Freed (Sergeant Boulanger), Emile Meyer (priest), John Stein (Captain Rousseau), Ken Dibbs (Private LeJeune), Jerry Hausner (tavern owner), Harold Benedict (Captain Nichols).
Running Time	86 minutes
Distributor	United Artists, presented by Bryna Productions

Filmed on location in Belgium and Germany.

Released	December 25, 1957

8 **SPARTACUS** (1960)

Synopsis

Panoramic shot of the mines and the slaves working on the rocks. Batiatus arrives to select some new members for his Gladiator School, including Spartacus. The slave travels to the school and undergoes training on how to fight as a gladiator. After the day's work, the slaves are rewarded with slave women who are forced to entertain them. Spartacus meets the beautiful Varinia, but refuses to abuse her as the others do.

In the next scene, Crassus arrives to watch the gladiators put on a fight to the death. Rather than kill Spartacus, whom he has trapped in his net, the Ethiopian slave lunges for Crassus in the stands and is immediately killed by him. Batiatus decides that the Ethiopian slave will hang till he rots. The next day a fight breaks out in the eating quarters and the slaves revolt and take over the whole school, freeing all of the others. In the Senate in Rome, the senators debate the problem of the slave revolt and vow to fight to the death. Later, Spartacus organizes his army of slaves and vows he will never allow two men to fight to the death again as a spectacle for others. As he moves about Italy freeing other slaves, Spartacus meets Varinia again.

In Crassus's home in Rome, Crassus addresses a plea to his slave, the poet Antoninus, but he turns around and finds the slave has fled to Spartacus. In a scene showing Spartacus's camp, we see slaves in training learning how to fight as soldiers. In the evening, the poet Antoninus entertains the slave-soldiers around the camp fire by performing feats of magic. Spartacus and Varinia fall in love with each other and he asks her to teach him how to read and write. Later, Spartacus makes a deal with a trader to buy passage out of Italy for all of his men in exchange for a treasure chest of captured gold coins. In a daring night raid, Spartacus and his men surround a Roman camp, set it afire, and send the leader off to Rome strapped to his horse. In the Senate in Rome, the commander is forced to face the question of the senators, who blame Crassus for the slave revolt.

[Aerial view showing Spartacus and his army making their way across Italy to the sea.] Varinia is taking a bath in a pond and is lifted out by Spartacus. She warns him not to drop her as she is now bearing his child. In Rome the Senate debate continues on whether Spartacus can be stopped. In the baths, Crassus talks to Julius Caesar, asking him why he has decided to join with Gracchus. Caesar only smiles at him. At the slave encampment, celebrations are taking place prior to the impending departure on ships. Soon after this, Spartacus discoveres that the Semitic merchant captain has betrayed the slaves and left them, with all of the money Spartacus had given him. Now the slaves, led by Spartacus, are forced to turn and fight the Roman army in order to save themselves. [Alternating scenes of Spartacus addressing his army and Crassus (in Rome) addressing the Senate.] Spartacus addresses his army of slaves and then turns to embrace Varinia and to touch her stomach, feeling the new child.

[Aerial view of the Roman army advancing against the slave army.] The slaves have prepared large rolls of straw that are now set on fire and rolled at the Roman soldiers. Several scenes depict the hand to hand combat between the two armies, accompanied by loud martial music.

Spartacus is defeated and large piles of dead bodies are taken off the field. Crassus offers a deal to the survivors if they will surrender their leader, Spartacus. One by one all of the slaves jump forward yelling, "I am Spartacus!" Crassus decides to crucify all of the slaves as he makes his way to Rome. As he leaves, he takes Varinia and her newborn son as prisoners with him.

Outside his villa, along the cross-lined road, Crassus pits Antoninus and Spartacus against each other in a fight to the death. The two combatants are surrounded by soldiers and forced to fight. Antoninus vows to kill Spartacus rather than allow the Romans to crucify him. Spartacus kills Antoninus (who forgives him for killing him), and Crassus orders Spartacus to be crucified. As Crassus tries to make Varinia submit to him, she hides from him and eventually escapes to Gracchus and Batiatus. In order to seek revenge against Crassus, Gracchus gives safe conducts and money to Batiatus and Varinia so they can flee Rome. Gracchus then commits suicide. On their way out of Rome, Varinia stops to show the crucified Spartacus his new son. Spartacus looks down at his son, realizing he will grow up a free man. Varinia promises to tell her child about the exploits of his father. Batiatus and Varinia leave Rome.

Credits and Notes

Production Company	Bryna Productions
Executive Producer	Kirk Douglas
Producer	Edward Lewis
Director	Stanley Kubrick
Script	Dalton Trumbo, based on the novel *Spartacus* by Howard Fast
Photography	Russell Metty
Additional Photography	Clifford Stine
Screen Process	Super Technirama 70
Color	Technicolor
Editors	Robert Lawrence, Robert Schultz, Fred Chulack
Production Designer	Alexander Golitzen
Art Director	Eric Orbom
Set Decoration	Russell A. Gausman, Julia Heron
Titles	Saul Bass
Technical Adviser	Vittorio Nino Novarese
Costumes	Peruzzi, Valles, Bill Thomas
Music	Alex North
Music Director	Joseph Gershenson
Sound	Waldon O. Watson, Joe Lapis, Murray Spivack, Ronald Pierce
Assistant Director	Marshall Green
Cast	Kirk Douglas (Spartacus), Laurence Olivier (Marcus Crassus), Jean Simmons (Varinia), Charles Laughton (Gracchus), Peter Ustinov (Batiatus), John Gavin (Julius Caesar), Tony Curtis (Antoninus), Nina Foch (Helena), Herbert Lom (Tigranes), John Ireland (Crixus), John Dall (Glabrus), Charles McGraw (Marcellus), Joanna Barnes (Claudia), Harold J. Stone (David), Woody Strode (Draba), Peter Brocco (Ramon), Paul Lambert (Gannicus), Robert J. Wilke (Captain of the Guard), Nicholas Dennis (Dionysius), John Hoyt (Roman officer), Fred Worlock (Laelius), Dayton Lummis (Symmachus).
Original Running Time	196 minutes
Cut to	184 minutes
Distributor	Universal Pictures
Released	October 6, 1960

Note

The running time of the film shown in Britain was 196 minutes. When Universal released the film in the United States and other countries, the film was cut to 184 minutes. The scenes taken out dealt with an attempt by Marcus Crassus (Laurence Olivier) to seduce his slave Antoninus.

9 LOLITA (1962)

Synopsis

Background music, "Lolita's Theme." A girl's leg is thrust onto the screen and we watch Humbert Humbert painting her toenails with delicate tenderness as the credits for the film are given.

[Scene of a station wagon speeding down a deserted road.] At an old mansion Humbert enters dressed in a raincoat and hat. The room is filled with furniture covered with white sheets. He calls out for Quilty, who soon appears from underneath one of the sheet-covered chairs. He is drunk and parades around the room telling Humbert about the terrible behavior of his guests at his parties. Humbert draws out black leather gloves, puts them on, and aims a gun at Quilty. Quilty begins to move around the room and challenges Humbert to a ping pong game. They play for a few minutes and then Humbert shoots at Quilty, hitting a large boxing glove on his hand. Humbert then pursues Quilty around the cluttered room and shoots at him as he tries to go up a staircase. He wounds Quilty, who seeks shelter behind a large painting. He continues to fire at the painting.

Subtitle: "Four Years Earlier"

[Aerial view of New York City with airplane in foreground.] Professor Humbert Humbert announces he is to spend a restful summer in rural Ramsdale. His station wagon arrives at the home of Mrs. Charlotte Haze, who has advertised a room for rent. Charlotte sees Humbert as a potential future husband and attempts to attract him to her room and cooking. She shows him the room, the urn of her husband's earthly remains, and the backyard scene with her daughter Lolita. As soon as Humbert sees Lolita, he decides to take the room. As he looks at the bikini-clad daughter, Charlotte observes: "I offer you a comfortable home, sunny garden, a congenial atmosphere, my cherry pie!" At a drive-in movie Charlotte and Lolita place their hands on Humbert's knee as they are petrified by the Frankenstein monster on the screen.

In the next few days, Humbert is continually attracted to Lolita and seeks opportunities to observe her as he plays chess and reads in the garden. At a high school dance, he looks at her while Charlotte tries to introduce him to the Farlows and Clare Quilty, a local drama critic who is lionized by all the women. Later that evening Charlotte prepares to seduce Humbert with romantic music, dress, and dancing, but is interrupted by Lolita, who returns early from a party at the Farlows' house. Humbert goes to bed soon after Lolita retires and Charlotte is left weeping (to herself) in the living room.

Later the next day, Charlotte informs Humbert that she is sending Lolita off to camp for the summer and that he will be gone when she returns. When the day arrives for Lolita's departure, Humbert bids the girl goodbye and falls on her bed in anguish over her departure. After Charlotte offers to marry him, Humbert accepts and stays on to become Lolita's stepfather.

After seeking solace with Charlotte, Humbert locks himself in the bathroom and Charlotte begins to read his secret diary in which Humbert confesses his attraction to Lolita and his toleration of the mother, whom he really dislikes. Charlotte threatens Humbert and in her upset condition runs outside in a rainstorm and is killed instantly by an automobile. As Humbert rejoices over getting rid of her, the neighbors come to visit him in the bathroom, where he relaxes by taking a bath. He assures the father of the driver who killed Charlotte that he does not hold the driver responsible and will not press charges. Humbert leaves at once for "Camp Climax for Girls" to pick up Lolita and take her home.

On the way home from camp, Lolita and Humbert spend the night at a large hotel that is also hosting a state police convention. After settling for a single room and a cot for the night, Humbert returns to the lobby and meets another guest (Quilty in disguise), who questions him about his behavior and his beautiful daughter, Lolita. Humbert retires to bed and sleeps in a cot at the bottom of the large double bed that Lolita is in.

In the morning, Lolita wakes Humbert and suggests that they try some of the "games" that Charlie taught Lolita at summer camp. As they drive away from the hotel, Lolita inquires about her mother and suggests they tell her about what they had done together that morning. Later on, Humbert tells Lolita about her mother and she begins a long period of remorse and crying. She asks Humbert to keep her with him and not allow her to be put in a "juvenile delinquent place."

Humbert accepts a position as visiting professor at Beardsley College and he and Lolita move there, set up house, and begin a new life. After Humbert complains of Lolita's after school activities, they quarrel and he refuses to allow her to take the lead in the high school play. On the next day, Humbert receives a visit from the Beardsley High School psychologist, Dr. Zemsh (another disguise of Quilty), who urges Humbert to allow the young girl to be in the play or face a full scale investigation of her home life situation. At the play opening, Lolita smiles to Quilty, who is waiting in the wings as she goes on stage. After the play, Lolita is dragged home by Humbert, who refuses to allow her to attend the cast party. Humbert and Lolita quarrel until a neighbor appears and Lolita escapes. She calls Humbert up and apologizes to him.

Humbert takes a leave of absence from Beardsley, and he and Lolita travel out to Hollywood to work on a film. On their way Humbert notices that they are being followed by a strange car. When they have a blowout, the car makes a U-turn and goes away. After this incident, Lolita becomes very sick, is admitted to a hospital, and is visited by Humbert every day. At his motel room Humbert is threatened with anonymous calls asking about the present state of his "sex life." When he visits Lolita one night, he finds that she has been released from the hospital and taken home by her "uncle." Humbert becomes hysterical and has to be held by a doctor and some orderlies. He is later released and leaves the hospital. After a long period of time, Humbert gets a letter from Lolita telling of her marriage and the impending birth of her child. She asks for money from him and gives him her address.

Humbert finds Lolita living in a poor section of town with a man named Dick, who thinks that Lolita's child is his own. Humbert offers to take her away but she refuses. She tells him that all of the strange men following them were really Clare Quilty in disguise. She went off to live with him (from the hospital) but later left him when Quilty asked her to appear in a "strange" type of film. Humbert breaks down and cries but Lolita refuses to go with him. He leaves her with a check for $13,000. Later we see Humbert heading down the same road as at the beginning of the film. He enters, calling to Quilty. The sound of shots is heard as the screen darkens.

Sub-title: "Humbert Humbert died in prison of coronary thrombosis while awaiting trial for the murder of Clare Quilty."

Credits and Notes

Production Company	Seven Arts/Anya/Transworld
Producer	James B. Harris
Director	Stanley Kubrick
Script	Vladimir Nabokov, based on his novel *Lolita*
Photography	Oswald Morris
Editor	Anthony Harvey
Art Director	William Andrews
Set Design	Andrew Low
Music	Nelson Riddle
Lolita's Theme	Bob Harris
Sound	H. L. Bird, Len Shilton
Assistant Directors	Roy Millichip, John Danischewsky
Cast	James Mason (Humbert Humbert), Sue Lyon (Lolita Haze), Shelley Winters (Charlotte Haze), Peter Sellers (Clare Quilty), Diana Decker (Jean Farlow), Jerry Stovin (John Farlow), Suzanne Gibbs (Mona Farlow), Gary Cockrell (Dick), Marianne Stone (Vivian Darkbloom), Cec Linder (physician), Lois Maxwell (Nurse Mary Lord), William Greene (Swine), C. Denier Warren (Potts), Isobel Lucas (Louise), Maxine Holden (hospital receptionist), James Dyrenforth (Beale), Roberta Shore (Lorna), Eric Lane (Roy), Shirley Douglas (Mrs. Starch), Roland Brand (Bill), Colin Maitland (Charlie), Irvin Allen (hospital attendant), Marion Mathie (Miss Lebone), Craig Sams (Rex), John Harrison (Tom).
Running Time	153 minutes
Distributor	Metro-Goldwyn-Mayer
Released	June 13, 1962 Opened in London, September, 1962. Opened in New York, December 31, 1962.

Filmed on location in Albany, New York and Great Britain.

Note

In the preface to his *Lolita: A Screenplay* [*See* entry 468] Nabokov has acknowledged that Kubrick used only about 20 percent of the original screenplay in the film version of *Lolita.* Most of the final script for the film was written by Kubrick, based in part on the screenplay by Nabokov.

10 DR. STRANGELOVE, OR HOW I LEARNED TO STOP WORRYING AND LOVE THE BOMB. (1964)

Synopsis

The following disclaimer appears at the beginning of the film: "It is the stated position of the U.S. Air Force that their safeguards would prevent the occurrence of such events as are depicted in this film. Furthermore, it should be noted that none of the characters portrayed are meant to represent any real person living or dead."

[Aerial view of arctic waste region.] Narrator: "For more than a year, ominous rumors have been privately circulating among high level leaders that the Soviet Union had been at work on what was darkly hinted to be the ultimate weapon, a doomsday device. Intelligence sources placed the site of the top secret Russian project at the perpetually fog-shrouded wasteland below the Arctic peaks of the Zhukov Mountains. What they were building, or why it should be located in such a remote and desolate place, no one could say."

[Opening scenes with credits superimposed: B-52 bomber being refueled in mid-air with song, "Try a Little Tenderness" on soundtrack. Aerial view of Burpleson Air Force Base.] A phone buzzes in the computer room and General Jack D. Ripper informs his executive officer, Colonel Lionel Mandrake, he is placing the base on condition "red" for airborne alert. Ripper looks out his window as the alarm is sounded for the base. In the cockpit of the B-52, pilot and crew are relaxing when they receive the "go code" on the radio. The pilot asks for confirmation from base and then proceeds with "Wing Attack Plan R." Music: "When Johnny Comes Marching Home Again" begins playing in the background as the pilot takes out plans and describes the attack profile to the crew via radio.

Bedroom of General Buck Turgidson and his girlfriend, Miss Scott, who answers a telephone call from the Pentagon. Buck finally comes to the phone, relays the message to "bump everything up to condition red" and says that he is going over to the war room. Back at Burpleson, General Ripper is giving instructions about confiscating all radios and being alert for the enemy. Mandrake finds a civilian radio and reports to Ripper with radio in hand. He suggests that Mandrake sit down and relax since he (Ripper) does not plan to issue the recall code to the bomb wing. In the B-52, the pilot, Major Kong, continues to follow the directions in the wing attack plan. In Ripper's office, Mandrake realizes his leader is insane and attempts to leave the office. Ripper threatens him with a gun and Mandrake complies.

[Aerial view of the Pentagon in Washington and interior view of the war room with the President and Joint Chiefs assembled.] President Merkin Muffley asks for an explanation of the situation and General Turgidson replies with the provisions of "Wing Attack Plan R," which allows a lower ranking commander to order a nuclear attack on the Soviet Union. Muffley orders the Army Chief of Staff to invade the air base and put Ripper in contact with the President. The President also sends for the Russian Ambassador.

In the B-52, Major Kong goes through a check of the contents of the survival kit issued to all crewmen. At the war room, Turgidson catches the Russian Ambassador taking pictures of "the big board" with a secret camera. They begin to fight but are interrupted by the telephone call to the Russian Premier. Back at Burpleson, Army troops begin the invasion of the base but meet with heavy resistance from base security troops. At the war room the President explains the situation to the Russian Premier on the phone. The ambassador then learns of a doomsday device that will automatically trigger a nuclear disaster. In his office at Burpleson, Ripper begins to tell Mandrake about the threat of water fluoridation as a great big "Commie conspiracy" against the United States. Back at the war room, Dr. Strangelove, a refugee scientist from World War II, begins to explain the threat of the doomsday device. He questions why the Russians had kept it a secret and the Ambassador explains that the Premier had planned to announce it at the next meeting.

At Burpleson, the security troops surrender the base and the fighting stops. Ripper tells Mandrake that he must accept his actions and justify them hereafter. He goes into the bathroom and kills himself. In the B-52 above, the plane has penetrated Russian radar and is now being tracked by a missile that hits the plane and damages it. Back at Ripper's office, a machine gun rips open the door and Colonel Bat Guano arrests Mandrake for suspicion of leading an uprising of "preverts." On board the B-52, damage is assessed and the fires are put out and a new target is set for the plane. On his way out of the office, Mandrake convinces Guano to allow him to call the President of the United States. When he cannot produce enough change to put through the telephone call, Mandrake orders Guano to shoot a Coke machine for the correct change. As the announcement of the recall code is given, scenes of jubilation appear in the war room. But up in the B-52, unable to receive any radio transmission, the pilot and crew continue on to their new designated target even though the plane is severely damaged and flying very low.

Back at the war room a discovery is made that all but one of the planes has returned. Turgidson then describes to the President the chances of the plane getting through to its target. The President advises the Russian Premier to put everything he has into one sector to get that plane. Major Kong has begun his final bomb run and his B-52 comes into position over the target. Since the bomb doors fail to open, Kong goes down into the bomb bay and repairs the damage. When the bomb goes out, Kong rides it down screaming and yelling. The bomb bursts and this is followed by a large mushroom cloud.

Back in the war room, Dr. Strangelove begins planning for a survival colony of key leaders to live through the nuclear fallout in special mine shafts. As he explains this, his right arm keeps trying to strangle his throat and he has to stop to fight off the hand with his other fist. Turgidson is fearful of a possible mineshaft "gap." At this point, Strangelove rises and proclaims to the President, "Mein Fuhrer, I can walk!" A large group of mushroom clouds appears while we hear "We'll Meet Again" in the background.

Credits and Notes

Production Company	Hawk Films
Producer	Stanley Kubrick
Director	Stanley Kubrick
Associate Producer	Victor Lyndon
Script	Stanley Kubrick, Terry Southern, Peter George, based on the novel *Red Alert* by Peter George
Photography	Gilbert Taylor
Editor	Anthony Harvey
Production Designer	Ken Adam
Art Director	Peter Murton
Special Effects	Wally Veevers
Music	Laurie Johnson
Aviation Adviser	Captain John Crewdson
Sound	John Cox
Cast	Peter Sellers (Group Captain Lionel Mandrake, President Muffley, Dr. Strangelove), George C. Scott (General Buck Turgidson), Sterling Hayden (General Jack D. Ripper), Keenan Wynn (Colonel Bat Guano), Slim Pickens (Major T. J. "King" Kong), Peter Bull (Ambassador de Sadesky), Tracy Reed (Miss Scott), James Earl Jones (Lieutenant Lothar Zogg, Bombadier), Jack Creley (Mr. Staines), Frank Berry (Lieutenant H. R. Dietrich, D. S. O.) Glenn Beck (Lieutenant W. D. Kivel, navigator), Shane Rimmer (Captain G. A. "Ace" Owens, co-pilot), Paul Tamarin (Lieutenant B. Goldberg, radio operator), Gordon Tanner (General Faceman) Robert O'Neil (Admiral Randolph), Roy Stephens (Frank), Laurence Herder, John McCarthy, Hal Galili (members of Burpleson Base Defense Corps).

Film on location in England at Shepperton Studios.

Running Time	94 minutes
Distributor	Columbia Pictures
Released	January 30, 1964 New York Opening, December 3, 1963.

Note

The original running time of the film was 102 minutes but it was cut by Kubrick in the released version. The cuts included a pie throwing sequence in the war room at the end of the film. The word "Vegas" was dubbed into the final version to remove the original word "Dallas" because of the reference to the Kennedy assasination in November 1963. This was spoken by Slim Pickens as Major Kong in commenting on the contents of the survival kit.

11 2001: A SPACE ODYSSEY (1968)

Synopsis

Subtitle: "The Dawn of Man"

Opening scenes on earth in prehistoric times showing the gradual evolution of life and the emergence of apes who move about on a desert plateau. The apemen learn how to use tools after finding the remains of an animal carcass and using a bone to hammer with. In the next scene, the apemen observe a large black monolith that appears in the middle of their plateau. One of the apemen uses a bone as a weapon to kill an animal (with the soundtrack music of *Thus Spake Zarathustra*). Finally, the apeman throws the bone up into the air and it continues to rise until we see a jump cut to the image of a spaceship in the year 2001 shaped exactly like the bone. The interior shots of the spacecraft depict the condition of weightlessness encountered in space. One of the passengers in this space shuttle is Dr. Heywood Floyd, who is on his way to a conference dealing with an unusual occurrence that has taken place on Clavius. As he travels, we see scenes of the weightless conditions in space: the stewardess serving meals, the zero-gravity toilet, the electronic guidance systems on the spacecraft, and the exterior shots of planets and comets in outer space. Dr. Floyd arrives on the moon, checks through visual security, and calls his daughter on a picturephone in the lobby of Howard Johnson's Earthlight Room. Floyd then meets some fellow scientists from Russia in the lounge and they begin a brief discussion of the strange rumors circulating about the problems on Clavius. But Floyd responds to the questions by saying: "I am not at liberty to say." The conversation ends and Floyd promises to try and get together with his friends at the next professional meeting. To the music of the "Blue Danube Waltz" we watch the voyage of a larger spacecraft to Clavius, where Floyd briefs a large group of assembled scientists from various countries. He promises to keep them informed of the various developments and then leaves on a smaller space shuttle to visit the large crater created by a huge black monolith. At the site of the black monolith (exactly like the one in the prehistoric plateau) the scientists assemble around the object for a group picture. While this is taking place a loud piercing scream is heard as the space scientists cover their ears.

Subtitle: "Jupiter Mission, 18 Months Later"

On board the *Discovery* spaceship, astronauts Poole and Bowman go about their daily routines as they travel to the planet Jupiter. They are accompanied by five other crew members who have been placed in hibernation until they reach their destination. In addition, another crew member, HAL-9000, a modern computer, monitors all aspects of the mission including the elaborate control systems throughout the spaceship. Poole and Bowman carry on routine tasks including exercises, eating meals, and playing chess with HAL. HAL points out a potential failure of the communications system and Poole goes outside the ship in one of the space pods to fix the problem. He finds that the unit is not defective and HAL is corrected by another computer from Mission Control back in Houston. HAL insists that the error must be a human error and that he is correct about the original prediction. Astronauts Poole and Bowman then retire to one of the space pods and turn off all of the intercom systems. They discuss the problem of HAL's mistaken prediction and both agree that if it happens again they will have no choice but disconnection. While this secret conversation is taking place, HAL is reading their lips and realizes his life is being threatened.

INTERMISSION

Poole goes outside the spaceship to replace the unit that he had taken off. While he is outside the pod, HAL maneuvers the mechanical arms of the pod to cut off Poole's oxygen line and the astronaut begins to hurtle through space. Inside the *Discovery,* Bowman races to rescue his partner and forgets his space helmet in the process. While Bowman is outside the spacecraft, the control board lights up with COMPUTER MALFUNCTION, followed by LIFE SYSTEMS CRITICAL, and LIFE SYSTEMS TERMINATED, indicating the deaths of the five hibernating astronauts. Outside the craft, Bowman has caught Poole in the mechanical arms of the pod and now asks HAL to open the pod door to let him back in. HAL refuses to open the door and says goodbye to Bowman. Bowman then lines himself up against the locked pod door and releases an explosive charge that blasts him into the air chamber where he immediately closes the outside door. Bowman races to the computer brain room to disconnect HAL, who now controls all of the ship's vital systems. HAL pleads for his life and begins to go back in his memory to the time in his "life" when he was first created and demonstrated at the computer factory. He begins to sing "Daisy" and slowly dies. At this point the prerecorded message from Dr. Heywood Floyd is heard: "Good day, gentlemen. This is a prerecorded briefing made prior to your departure, which for security reasons of the highest importance has been known on board during your mission only by your HAL-9000 computer. Now that you are in Jupiter space, and the entire crew is revived, it can be told to you. Eighteen months ago, the first evidence of intelligent life off the Earth was discovered. It was buried forty feet below the lunar surface, near the crater Tycho. Except for a single, very powerful radio emission aimed at Jupiter, the four-million-year-old black monolith has remained completely inert, its origin and purpose a total mystery."

Subtitle: "Jupiter and Beyond the Infinite"

Exterior view of the spaceship *Discovery* in outer space. Astronaut Bowman leaves the *Discovery* and begins to travel through space in one of the pods. The pod moves toward the black monolith as if it were drawn to it by intention, going faster and faster. Bowman plunges through space at ever increasing speeds moving through a tunnel of blazing reds and psychedelic blues, yellows, and greens. Bowman suddenly stops, walks out of his pod, and into a green and white room decorated in Louis XVI style. As he moves across the room, he sees an old man sitting at the table eating. Bowman has aged twenty years and now looks at the old man in front of him. As the old man turns he drops a wine glass. We then see the old man in a large bed looking up at the huge black monolith standing at the foot of the bed. The man has become an ancient figure lying on the bed. Bowman is transformed and becomes an embryo lying in the center of the bed. With the "World Riddle Theme" from *Thus Spake Zarathustra* in the background, we see the image of an embryo "star" child with large eyes looking down on the planet Earth from a position in outer space.

Credits and Notes

Production Company	Metro-Goldwyn-Mayer
Producer	Stanley Kubrick
Director	Stanley Kubrick
Script	Stanley Kubrick, Arthur C. Clarke, based on Clarke's short story *"The Sentinel"*
Photography	Geoffrey Unsworth
Screen Process	Super Panavision, presented in Cinerama
Color	Metrocolor
Additional Photography	John Alcott
Special Photographic Effects	
Designer and Director	Stanley Kubrick
Editor	Ray Lovejoy
Production Designers	Tony Masters, Harry Lange, Ernie Archer
Art Director	John Hoesli
Special Photographic Effects	
Supervisors	Wally Veevers, Douglas Trumbull, Con Pederson, Tom Howard
Music:	Richard Strauss, *Thus Spake Zarathustra;* Johann Strauss, *The Blue Danube,* performed by the Berlin Philharmonic Orchestra; Aram Khatchaturian, *Gayne Ballet Suite,* performed by the Leningrad Philharmonic Orchestra, Conductor Gennadi Rozhdestvensky, Courtesy Deutsche Grammophon; Gyorgy Ligeti, *Atmospheres,* performed by the Southwest German Radio Orchestra, Conductor Ernest Bour; *Lux Aeterna,* performed by the Stuttgart State Orchestra, Conductor Clytus Gottwald; *Requiem,* performed by the Bavarian Radio Orchestra, Conductor Francis Travis
Costumes	Hardy Amies
Sound	Winston Ryder
Cast	Keir Dullea (David Bowman), Gary Lockwood (Frank Poole), William Sylvester (Dr. Heywood Floyd), Daniel Richter (moon-watcher), Douglas Rain (voice of HAL-9000), Leonard Rossiter (Smyslov), Margaret Tyzack (Elena), Robert Beatty (Halvorsen), Sean Sullivan (Michaels) Frank Miller (mission control), Penny Brahms (stewardess), Alan Gifford (Poole's father), and Glenn Beck, Edwina Carroll, Bill Weston, Mike

	Lovell, Edward Bishop, Ann Gillis, Heather Downham, John Ashley, Jimmy Bell, David Charkham, Simon Davis, Jonathan Daw, Peter Delmar, Terry Duggan, David Fleetwood, Danny Grover, Brian Hawley, David Hines, Tony Jackson, John Jordan, Scott Mackee, Laurence Marchant, Darryl Paes, Joe Refalo, Andy Wallace, Bob Wilyman, Richard Wood
Special Photographic Effects Unit	Colin J. Cantwell, Bryan Loftus, Frederick Martin, Bruce Logan, David Osborne, John Jack Malick
Camera Operator	Kelvin Pike
Sound Editor	Winston Ryder
Make-up	Stuart Freeborn
Editorial Assistant	David De Wilde
Sound Supervisor	A. W. Watkins
Sound Mixer	H. L. Bird
Chief Dubbing Mixer	J. B. Smith
Scientific Consultant	Frederick I. Ordway III
Running Time	141 minutes cut from 160 minutes
Distributor	Metro-Goldwyn-Mayer
Released	April 1, 1968 in New York City, New York April 2, 1968 in Washington, D.C. May 1968 in London, England

Filmed at MGM British Studios Ltd., Boreham Wood, England.

Note

Following the New York release of *2001: A Space Odyssey* Kubrick cut out 19 minutes from the original running time of 160 minutes. *See* entry 216.

In the film, Vivian Kubrick (the director's daughter) played the daughter of Dr. Heywood Floyd. She was not listed in the original credits at the end of the film.

12 A CLOCKWORK ORANGE (1971)

Synopsis

Following the credits on a red background, we see the eyes of Alex, the narrator-hero, who introduces himself and his three friends, Pete, Georgie, and Dim. They are all in the Korova Milk Bar trying to make up their minds on what to do with their evening. The bar is filled with white plastic statues of nude women who serve as coffee tables and milk dispensing machines. Alex tells us of how the milk-plus (drugs) will make them ready for a bit of the old ultra-violence. Outside in a culvert, the foursome surround an old man and begin beating him to death with clubs and black boots. Later, at an abandoned theater, Alex and his friends watch a gang of thugs raping a helpless girl and they then join in fighting with knives and canes.

On the road, Alex and his friends speed through the countryside, terrorizing motorists along the way. They come to a house with a neon sign, "HOME," and seek admission by telling the lady of the house that a terrible accident has taken place. Once they gain admission, they terrorize the husband and force him to watch Alex as he rapes the wife to the music of "Singing in The Rain," sung by Alex and his friends. Back at the milk bar, Alex hits one of his friends who dares to poke fun at the famous Ludwig van Beethoven, Alex's favorite composer. Alex then returns to his house, where he lives with MOM and DAD, and goes to his room. He checks on his pet python snake, puts on a recording of Beethoven's "Ode to Joy" and proceeds to masturbate to the sound of the music.

The next morning, Alex meets his mother and father on their way to work and then is greeted by his probation officer. As Alex walks around in his underwear, the probation officer, Mr. Deltroid, looks at Alex's body with envy. Alex picks up two girls sucking phallic popsicles in a shopping center and returns for a sex orgy to the accompaniment of "The Overture to William Tell" (in speeded-up film sequence). Alex then meets his pals in the lobby and they decide to desert him as their leader. In the next scene, at a marina, Alex teaches them a lesson by trying to drown Dim and cutting him with his knife.

At another bar, Georgie proposes that they visit an abandoned health farm run by a strange lady. They use the same story about a terrible accident to gain entrance, but the "Cat Lady" refuses to let them in though she calls the police for them. Alex sneaks in the second floor, confronts the "Cat Lady" in a room full of cats, and beats her to death with a large phallic sculpture that he uses as a weapon. When he runs from the house, his "droogs" are waiting for him and beat him into unconsciousness, leaving him for the police to take. At the police station, Alex exchanges insults with the interrogators, receives facial wounds, and is met by his probation officer. Alex is left with the probation officer's wish that he will be driven to madness in prison for the death of the "Cat Lady."

[Aerial view of the correctional facility that Alex is sent to.] Alex tells us that this begins the "weepy and tragic" part of his story. After being stripped, searched, and examined by one of the prison guards, Alex is issued clothing and begins his sentence. He becomes a model prisoner and serves as a special assistant to the chaplain, who befriends him. Alex inquires about the new Ludovico treatment of rehabilitation, hoping that he can make the rest of his life "one act of goodness." The chaplain expresses concern over the treatment, since when a man ceases to choose, he ceases to exist.

During exercise period (to the music of "Pomp and Circumstance"), Alex attracts the attention of a high government official interested in getting volunteers for the Ludovico treatment. Following his release from prison, Alex reports to the Ludovico Treatment Center and begins the series of brainwashing sessions designed to rid him of his violent ways. Alex is drugged, strapped in a chair with a strait-jacket, and forced to watch films showing violent physical crimes. In order to keep his eyes open, he is fitted with a special helmet and clamps to keep his eyes focused on the screen. After watching numerous films of rapes, assaults, and beatings, Alex becomes physically sick. The doctor in charge, Brodsky, continues the treatment despite the violent screams of anguish from Alex. One of his film sessions includes views of Adolf Hitler marching to the music of Beethoven's *Ninth Symphony*. Alex pleads with the staff to stop the session, but the treatment continues.

After his treatment is finished, Alex is exhibited to an audience of government officials who watch him being tested by a bully and beautiful young girl dressed only in panties. In both cases, Alex refuses to be tempted by thoughts of violence or rape and becomes physically ill at the thought of such acts. The minister proclaims Alex cured and ready to return to society. The chaplain protests that Alex is nothing more than a being incapable of moral choice but the minister maintains that they are only concerned with cutting down society's crime rate.

Alex returns to his home, where he is rejected by his parents and replaced by a lodger named Joe, who has taken over his room. Alex runs off to the Thames bankside where he meets the old man he had beaten up earlier. Alex is set upon by the old man along with some friends. He is rescued by two policemen (who turn out to be Georgie and Dim). Georgie and Dim take him out into the country and hold him in a trough of water while they beat him with their clubs.

Amidst thunder and lightning, Alex makes his way out of the woods he has been left in to die. He struggles to the same house ("HOME") that he had been to earlier. The owner and his companion, a large, strong man, take him in, clean him up, and allow him to take a bath. While he is washing, Alex begins to sing "Singing in the Rain" and the owner, a writer, realizes that this is the same person who raped his wife and tortured him. Alex is given a meal of meatballs and spaghetti. While he eats, the writer and his friends tell Alex of the terrible rape of the writer's wife and her ultimate death as a result of her suffering. Alex collapses after drinking some wine and his face hits the plate of spaghetti. When he wakes up, he is in a large upstairs room without any means of escape. The writer has two large speakers downstairs and plays the *Ninth Symphony* of Beethoven until Alex is driven to the point of distraction. Alex breaks the window and plunges to his "death" outside.

Later on, Alex wakes up in a hospital room with both legs in large plaster casts. He is greeted by his mother and father and a host of well-wishers from the government ministry. Since he has now become a hero and the victim of the terrible state treatment, Alex is catered to by everyone. The minister visits him and promises him a well paid job and complete recovery. A large set of speakers is wheeled in and Alex is photographed with the minister at his bedside and the "Ode to Joy" blaring in the background. There is a cut to Alex copulating in the snow with a blonde dressed only in stockings, surrounded by Victorian dressed ladies and gentlemen applauding Alex. Alex comments, "I was cured all right!" End titles to the music of Gene Kelley singing, "Singing in the Rain."

Credits and Notes

Production Company	Hawk Films
Producer-Director	Stanley Kubrick
Executive Producers	Max L. Raab, Si Litvinoff
Associate Producer	Bernard Williams

Script	Stanley Kubrick, based on the novel by Anthony Burgess
Photography	John Alcott
Color	Warnercolor
Editor	Bill Butler
Production Designer	John Barry
Art Directors	Russell Hagg, Peter Shields
Music	Ludwig van Beethoven, Edward Elgar, Gioacchino Rossini, Terry Tucker, Erika Eigen
Original Electronic Music	Walter Carlos
Sound	John Jordan
Assistant Directors	Derek Cracknell, Dusty Symonds
Costumes	Milena Canonero
Cast	Malcolm McDowell (Alex), Patrick Magee (Mr. Alexander), Michael Bates (chief guard), Warren Clarke (Dim), John Clive (stage actor), Adrienne Corri (Mrs. Alexander), Carl Duering (Dr. Brodsky), Paul Farrell (tramp), Clive Francis (lodger), Michael Gover (prison governor), Miriam Karlin ("Cat Lady"), James Marcus (Georgie), Aubrey Morris (Deltroid), Godfrey Quigley (prison chaplain), Sheila Raynor (Mum), Madge Ryan (Dr. Barnom), John Savident (conspirator), Anthony Sharp (Minister of the Interior), Philip Stone (Dad), Pauline Taylor (psychiatrist), Margaret Tyzack (conspirator), and Steven Berkoff, Lindsay Campbell, Michael Tarn, David Prowse, Barrie Cookson, Jan Adair, Gaye Brown, Peter Burton, John J. Carney, Vivienne Chandler, Richard Connaught, Prudence Drage, Carol Drinkwater, Lee Fox, Cheryl Grunwald, Gillian Hills, Craig Hunter, Shirley Jaffe, Virginia Wetherell, Neil Wilson, Katya Wyeth

Filmed at MGM British Studios, Boreham Wood, England.

Running Time	135 minutes
Distributor	Warner Brothers
Released	December 20, 1971, New York City, New York.
MPAA Code Rating	"R"

Note:

"Singing in the Rain," sung by Gene Kelley, appeared on the soundtrack of the film at the end of *A Clockwork Orange*.

13 BARRY LYNDON (1975)

Synopsis

PART ONE

Opening shot showing Redmond Barry's father being killed in a duel in eighteenth-century Ireland. In a garden house Redmond Barry is engaged in a lover's game with his cousin Nora, who hides a scarf in her bosom and asks Barry to find it. After the British regiment visits the town, Nora falls in love with Captain Quin and spends a great deal of time with him, ignoring Barry altogether. At a banquet scene, Barry refuses to toast Quin and the insult leads to a duel in which Barry kills Quin and is urged to leave Ireland before the authorities catch up with him. Barry leaves his mother at her cottage and travels away with part of his father's inheritance. Along the way Barry is robbed of his money and horse, and decides to join the army as a means of surviving. Barry soon proves himself to his fellow soldiers by taking on one of the tough recruits in a hand to hand battle. Later, Barry meets Captain Grogan, who tells him of Nora's marriage to Captain Quin and the staged duel in which Barry wounded Quin with a paper wad in order to keep Quin's fortune in the family.

Barry and Captain Grogan travel to the continent to fight in the Seven Years War. Grogan is killed in the first skirmish; Barry is disillusioned with war and deserts the British forces in a stolen officer's uniform. As a disguised courier, Barry travels behind the lines and is eventually discovered by the Prussian Captain Potzdorf, who offers Barry the choice of returning to the British or joining the ranks of the Prussian Army. Barry accepts the offer to stay and soon distinguishes himself in battle by saving a fellow soldier's life.

After the war is over, Barry finds employment with the state police in Berlin, spying on one of his countrymen, the Chevalier. Before Barry begins his service as a disguised footman to the Chevalier, he breaks down and confesses the plot to the Chevalier. The two of them decide to continue the ruse and Barry reports back to Potzdorf with information supplied from the Chevalier. When one of the Chevalier's gaming partners threatens him, the police decide to deport the Chevalier and confiscate all of his money and possessions. Under a police escort Barry leaves the country disguised as the Chevalier. The real Chevalier left the night before with all the money.

Barry and the Chevalier travel through all the courts of Europe where they are welcomed with royal treatment. As a professional gambler, the Chevalier earns all of the expenses necessary for the pair to live. Barry takes care of all of the duels that develop from any of the Chevalier's victims unwilling to pay their debts.

Amidst the candlelight splendor of the home of Sir Charles Lyndon, Barry meets and woos the beautiful Lady Lyndon, who accepts the clandestine meetings with Barry behind the back of her aging, infirm husband. Sir Charles sends for Barry and accuses him in public of seducing his wife. Barry responds by challenging Sir Charles to prove his accusations and Sir Charles ends up in a coughing fit and chokes to death. Part One ends with the details of Sir Charles Lyndon's obituary spoken by the narrator.

INTERMISSION

PART TWO

Barry and Lady Lyndon are married by the Reverend Runt on June 15, 1773, and as a consequence Barry takes on the name of Barry Lyndon, Esquire. From the beginning of the marriage, Barry dominates his wife and alienates his stepson, Lord Bullingdon. When Barry's first son is born, he celebrates the event in the arms of naked women at a local gentlemen's club. As the relationship between Barry and Lady Lyndon begins to dissolve, she observes him making passes at one of her ladies in waiting. Later on, Barry seeks Lady Lyndon's forgiveness as she is bathing.

When Lord Bullingdon refuses to acknowledge Barry as his real father, Barry takes him aside and beats him into submission. Bullingdon becomes even more embittered toward Barry and begins to plan his ultimate revenge.

Following a birthday party for Bryan, Barry's own son, Barry's mother advises him to seek a peerage since that is the only way he will ever be independent of the financial control of Lady Lyndon and his stepson. Barry undertakes a concentrated campaign to wine and dine the peers of the realm in order to curry favor for his eventual acceptance by them. Elaborate dinner parties, expensive furnishings, and custom tailored clothes consume Barry's financial resources as he works his way upward in society. The end result is Barry's introduction to Lord Wendover, who greets him at the court.

Bullingdon undergoes further punishment from Barry after he has beaten up the younger, favored child, Bryan. At a formal concert with invited guests, Bullingdon again angers Barry and Barry chooses to beat the young man up in the midst of the elegant room in front of horrified spectators. After this incident, Bullingdon is banished, Barry is rejected by the aristocracy, and he and Lady Lyndon grow further apart. Barry spends most of his time with young Bryan showing him how to duel, fish, and ride horses. Barry gives young Bryan a pony on condition that the child not ride it until his birthday. Bryan sneaks out to ride the horse and is thrown off it. After a lingering illness, young Bryan dies and Barry lapses into a period of remorse and heavy drinking. Lady Lyndon is also despondent and eventually tries to kill herself. After the Reverend Runt is discharged, Bullingdon learns of his mother's condition and returns home to seek satisfaction from Barry.

Bullingdon returns to the financially ruined estate and challenges Barry to a duel to avenge his honor. After Bullingdon's first shot misfires, Barry decides to fire off to the side rather than to shoot his stepson. Bullingdon refuses to accept the gesture of kindness and forces Barry to stand and face another shot. Barry is wounded in the leg and is taken to a nearby inn where a doctor must amputate his leg below the knee. Barry's mother returns to take him back to Ireland and he is given an annual allowance from Bullingdon and Lady Lyndon on condition that he never leave his native country for the rest of his life. As Lady Lyndon writes the draft of the payment to "Redmond Barry, Esquire" she pauses and stares off into space under the watchful eye of Lord Bullingdon.

EPILOGUE

"They lived and quarreled, the good and the bad, the handsome and the ugly, the rich and the poor. They are all equal now."

Credits and Notes

Production Company	Warner Brothers
Producer/Director	Stanley Kubrick
Writer	Stanley Kubrick, based on the novel by William Makepeace Thackeray, *The Luck of Barry Lyndon*
Director of Photography	John Alcott
Production Designer	Ken Adam
Editor	Tony Lawson
Art Director	Roy Walker
Music Adapted and Conducted by	Leonard Rosenman
From Works by	Johann Sebastian Bach, Frederick the Great, Handel, Mozart, Giovanni Paisiello, Franz Schubert, Antonio Vivaldi, with Irish traditional music by the Chieftains
Historical Advisor	John Mollo
Cast	Ryan O'Neal (Barry Lyndon), Marisa Berenson (Lady Lyndon), Patrick Magee (the Chevalier), Hardy Kruger (Captain Potzdorf), Steven Berhoff (Lord Ludd), Gay Hamilton (Nora), Marie Kean (Barry's mother), Diana Koerner (German girl), Murray Melvin (Reverend Runt), Frank Middlemars (Sir Charles Lyndon), Andre Morell (Lord Wendover), Arthur O'Sullivan (highwayman), Godfrey Quigley (Captain Grogan), Leonard Rossiter (Captain Quin), Philip Stone (Graham), Lion Vitale Lord Bullingdon), Michael Hordern (narrator).
Color	Warner Color
Running Time	185 minutes
Distributor	Warner Brothers
Released	December 1975

Filmed on location in Ireland and at the MGM British Studios Ltd., Boreham Wood, England.

14 THE SHINING (1980)

Synopsis

Aerial shot of a car traveling along the highway to the Overlook Hotel in Colorado. Front view of a large tourist hotel and parking lot.

Subtitle: "The Interview"

Jack Torrance, a former teacher from Vermont, reports to Stuart Ullman, the manager of the Overlook Hotel. Mr. Ullman tells Torrance of the need for a winter caretaker to live in the hotel between October and May to keep the building in shape against the ravages of the seasons. Torrance looks forward to the job and listens eagerly to Ullman's description of the duties. Cut to Wendy Torrance in their apartment where she listens to her young son Danny talking to his imaginary friend "Tony," through whom Danny can see into the future. Danny creates the character of Tony by changing his own voice and talking to his finger as the imaginary character. Back at Ullman's office, Ullman warns Torrance about the solitude at the resort and the strange events of 1970. Delbert Grady, a former caretaker, became depressed by the isolation of the mountain retreat and killed his twin daughters and chopped up his wife before blowing his own brains out with a shotgun. Torrance replies that there is no danger of anything like that happening and that he looks forward to the isolation in order to work on his writing.

Torrance calls his wife to report that he has the job. In the next scene, Danny is in the bathroom brushing his teeth. Tony tells Danny that his father got the job. He also shows Danny a vision of two young girls (Grady's children), and a second vision of a hotel corridor with huge amounts of blood coming from the sides of the elevator doors. Danny is visited by a doctor, who hears of Danny's strange behavior, and is told of a time when Danny's father came home drunk and dislocated the child's shoulder. Wendy Torrance assures the doctor that it had been an accident and that her husband has not touched liquor since.

Subtitle: "Closing Day"

The Torrances drive to the Overlook Hotel, are met by Ullman, and are conducted on a tour of the different parts of the hotel, starting with the Colorado Lounge, the main guest lounging area near the check-in desk. Meanwhile Danny stays in a gameroom playing darts. There he sees a vision of the two girls again. In the meantime Jack and Wendy have been shown the grounds of the hotel, the "maze" (a thirteen foot hedge set up in the formal garden), their apartment where they will live, and "The Gold Room" ballroom. Here Danny meets up with them. They are all introduced to Dick Hallorann, a black cook. After a brief tour of the kitchen Wendy and Jack leave Danny alone with Hallorann. He tells Danny about the gift that the two of them share: both Danny and Hallorann are able to see into the future and the past and to understand things before they happen. Hallorann tells Danny that his grandmother called the gift "shining" and that they could hold conversations without moving their mouths. Danny asks about room 237; Hallorann says that he should forget about it and not go into the room. Danny tells Dick about his friend Tony, and how he sees things from the hotel's past.

Subtitle: "A Month Later"

Danny amuses himself by riding around the hotel corridors on his tricycle and passes room 237. Wendy takes Jack some breakfast and they talk about the hotel. Jack talks about a sense of deja vu, as if he'd been there before. Jack sets up his typewriter and writing materials on a table in the Colorado Lounge, so that he can start writing. Wendy and Danny explore the hotel together and walk in the "maze" outside. Jack diverts himself from writing by throwing a ball against the walls in the lounge.

Subtitle: "Tuesday"

Wendy is preparing a meal in the kitchen and hears about a severe snowstorm that is approaching. Danny is again seen riding his tricycle. He comes to room 237. He tries to open the door, but it is locked. He sees the two girls again. Wendy goes to tell Jack about the snowstorm. He becomes very upset with her and forbids her to enter the room when he is typing, saying it breaks his concentration.

Subtitle: "Thursday"

The snowstorm intensifies and Torrance becomes more and more upset with his isolation and loneliness. He continues to write but seems frustrated with his efforts.

Subtitle: "Saturday"

While Jack writes, Wendy tries to call out on the hotel switchboard. All the lines are down. She calls the rangers on the CB radio and is assured that if she needs anything, they will be there to help. Danny rides down the hotel corridor and sees the two Grady girls, who invite him to play with them "forever and ever and ever." In the next scene he sees their two dead bodies surrounded by blood. He turns, covers his eyes, and begins talking in Tony's voice saying he is scared.

Subtitle: "Monday"

Wendy and Danny are watching the film *Summer of '42* on television and Danny asks to go to his room to get a toy fire engine. He promises his mother he will not wake his father. When he gets to the room, his father is sitting on the edge of the bed. Jack asks if Danny is having a good time; Danny inquires whether his father likes the hotel. Jack says he wants to stay at the hotel forever and ever and ever. Danny then asks if he would ever hurt him or his mother. Jack asks if his mother had said anything to Danny, he assures him that he would never do anything to harm either one of them.

Subtitle: "Wednesday"

While Danny is playing with his toy trucks in the corridor a ball rolls by and Danny goes to investigate the opened door of room 237. Wendy hears noises upstairs and runs from the boiler room to her husband's study. Jack has collapsed at his typewriter; he recounts a horrid nightmare that he had in which he killed Danny and Wendy and chopped them to pieces. Just at that moment, Danny appears, sucking his thumb. He has been bruised around his neck and cannot speak. Wendy screams, accuses Jack of doing this to Danny, and leaves the room.

Jack wanders through the corridors, ending up in "The Gold Room." He sits at the empty bar and begins "talking" to a bartender, Lloyd, who listens to Jack's problems about his wife and son. Jack explains how Danny's shoulder was dislocated and how he went "on the wagon" for five months afterward. Lloyd observes that "Women, can't live with 'em, can't live without 'em." Wendy appears in the ballroom and tells Jack that Danny told her a woman tried to strangle him in room 237. Abrupt cut to the Miami bedroom of Dick Hallorann who is listening to the television news and hears about the terrible storm in Colorado. With the sound of an intense heartbeat on the soundtrack, there is a closeup of Hallorann's terrified face. Cut to a vision of Danny trembling terrified in room 237. Jack enters room 237 and walks about the empty room and into the bathroom. A beautiful naked woman gets out of the bathtub and walks over to embrace him. As Jack is hugging her, he looks in the full length mirror and realizes that he is hugging the decaying body of an old woman. Cut to vision of the old woman getting out of the bathtub and walking towards Danny to strangle him. Cut back to the old woman walking towards Jack laughing. He races from the room.

Dick Hallorann tries to call from Miami but is unable to get through because of the downed phone lines. Jack reports to Wendy that he saw nothing in room 237 and says that Danny inflicted the bruises on himself. In the bedroom, Danny begins to see visions of a room door marked "redrum" (*murder* in reverse) and hears warnings from Tony to get out of the hotel. This is followed by the same scene of torrents of blood coming out of the elevator.

Wendy says they have to take Danny and get out of the hotel. Jack leaves the apartment very upset. He wanders through the hotel. Cut to Hallorann calling the rangers to ask them to try and contact the hotel via CB. Jack enters The Gold Room where he finds a 1920s style party in full swing. He meets Lloyd, the bartender, who gives him a drink but says he does not have to pay. While Jack is walking around the crowded ballroom, he bumps into a waiter, who spills drinks on him and then escorts him to the men's room to clean off the spills. While he is there, the waiter identifies himself as Grady and tells Jack that he must take care of his family in the same way that he (Grady) took care of his wife and two daughters. Jack responds by saying "You were the caretaker" and Grady replies to Jack: "You are the caretaker. You've always been the caretaker." Grady tells Jack to give his wife a good talking to and perhaps a bit more. He cautions Jack that his son is trying to bring in an outside party, the black cook.

Back in the apartment, Wendy asks herself what to do. Danny's voice has been taken over by "Tony," and she is told that Danny is no longer here. Jack hears the rangers trying to contact them on the CB. He removes the crystals from the set.

Subtitle: "8 A.M."

Dick Hallorann flies from Miami to Denver. Hallorann arranges with a friend to borrow a snow cat so that he can get up the mountain to the hotel. At the hotel, Danny is watching a "Road Runner" cartoon on television. Wendy takes a baseball bat and leaves the room, locking the door behind her. She goes to Jack's study. Jack is not there; she looks at his manuscript, which contains page after page of the same sentence repeated over and over: "ALL WORK AND NO PLAY MAKES JACK A DULL BOY." Jack comes up behind her and asks how she likes the manuscript. She retreats from the room wielding the baseball bat. Jack asks her what should be done about Danny. Cut to Danny seeing corridor of blood again. They talk about Danny as she backs up the stairs swinging the bat at him. He tells her that he is going to bash her brains in. He grabs at the bat, but Wendy hits him on the head with it. He reels backwards, falls down the stairs hurting his ankle in the process and is knocked out. She drags him to a storeroom in the kitchen and locks him in it just as he regains consciousness. Jack pleads with Wendy to let him out. Wendy says that she is going to get a doctor for him. Jack tells her to check the radio and the snow cat. She races to the garage to find that he has taken the distributor cap apart. She returns to the apartment armed with a butcher knife with which to defend herself.

Subtitle: "4 P.M."

Jack wakes up. He is chastised by Grady for not carrying out his purpose; Jack promises to keep his word and follow Grady's example. Grady releases the lock on the door to free Torrance. Outside, Hallorann is working his way up the snow covered mountain in a snow cat. In the apartment, while his mother lies on the bed sleeping, Danny picks up the knife. He takes some lipstick and writes "redrum" on the bedroom door. Wendy wakes up and takes the knife from Danny. She looks in the mirror and sees "redrum" reversed in the mirror to spell "murder." She races into the bathroom, opens a small window, and pushes Danny to safety telling him to run. She will not fit through the window. Jack smashes the outer door with an axe and announces, "Wendy, I'm home." Jack bashes a large hole through the bathroom door and yells: "Here's Johnny!" As he reaches in to unlatch the door, Wendy slashes his hand with the knife. The two of them then hear the sound of Hallorann's snow cat approaching the hotel. Jack leaves Wendy to investigate the sound. Danny has since come back into the hotel and hidden in a large cabinet in the kitchen. As Hallorann walks about the deserted hotel calling out for someone, Jack jumps out from behind a piller and kills him with an axe blow to the chest. Danny sensing Hallorann's death screams. Hearing the scream Jack limps towards the kitchen looking for Danny. Wendy is also looking for Danny. As she walks through the hallways looking for him she encounters the horrid sights her son has seen, including torrents of blood coming out of the elevator. Danny runs from his hiding place out of the hotel into the maze. Jack throws on the outdoor floodlights and pursues Danny, still armed with his axe. Danny runs along the maze and manages to trick Jack by backtracking in his footsteps in the snow. As Wendy races to the front door, she is surrounded by nightmare visions of death and skeletons. She meets Danny at the entrance to the maze and races off with him in the snow cat that Hallorann left in front of the hotel.

Inside the maze, Torrance collapses from exhaustion. In the next daylight scene he is shown frozen to death. As the film ends, the audience is presented a closeup of a group photograph taken at the Overlook Hotel Ball on July 4, 1921. In the center of the photgraph is the face of Jack Torrance.

Credits and Notes

Production Company	The Producer Circle Company
Executive Producer	Jan Harlan
Producer/Director	Stanley Kubrick
Writer	Stanley Kubrick and Diane Johnson, based on the novel by Stephen King
Director of Photography	John Alcott
Production Designer	Roy Walker
Editor	Ray Lovejoy
Art Director	Les Tomkins
Music from Works by	Bela Bartok, conducted by Herbert von Karajan; Wendy Carlos and Rachel Elkind; Gyorgy Ligeti; Krzysztof Penderecki
Cast	Jack Nicholson (Jack Torrance), Shelley Duvall (Wendy Torrance), Danny Lloyd (Danny Torrance), Scatman Crothers (Dick Hallorann), Barry Nelson (Stuart Ullman), Philip Stone (Grady), Joe Turkel (Lloyd), Anne Jackson (Doctor), Tony Burton (Durkin), Lia Beldam (young woman in bath), Barry Dennen (Watson), David Baxt (ranger 1), Manning Redwood (ranger 2), Lisa Burns, Louise Burns (Grady twins), Robin Pappas (nurse), Alison Coleridge (secretary), Burnell Tucker (policeman), Jana Sheldon (stewardess), Kate Phelps (receptionist), Norman Gay (injured guest).
Running Time	145 minutes
Released	May 23, 1980

IV Writings About Stanley Kubrick

1953

15 Anon. Review of *Fear and Desire. Commonweal,* 58 (24 April), 73.
Examines Kubrick's attitude toward war in the film.

16 Anon. Review of *Fear and Desire. Newsweek,* 41 (13 April), 106–108.
Discusses the mixture of promise and frustration in *Fear and Desire.* The camera work is impressive and the film should be seen by anyone interested in making movies.

17 Anon. Review of *Fear and Desire. Theatre Arts,* 37, no. 5 (May), 82-83.
Calls attention to the importance of Kubrick's first film: "a most impressive might-have-been comprises an abstract of what serious inspiration and thought could accomplish in film medium but actually accomplishes so seldom."

18 Anon. Review of *Fear and Desire. Variety* (1 April) p. 6.
The overall effect of the film is not fully realized, although individual scenes stand out. Outstanding for its "fresh camera treatment and poetic dialog." Preview screening of Kubrick's first film, 26 March, 1953.

19 Gurnsley, Otis L., Jr. Review of *Fear and Desire.* New York *Herald Tribune* (1 April), p. 34.
Discusses attempts of young film makers who are "carried away on the wings of their own zeal" in *Fear and Desire.*

20 McCarten, John. "The Current Cinema: Amateur" *New Yorker,* 29 (11 April), 128.
Negative review of the film. Dislikes the acting and the overplaying of the theme of anti-war drama.

21 Weiler, A. "The Screen in Review" *New York Times* (1 April), p. 35.
Sees Kubrick as turning out a "moody and often visually powerful study of subdued excitements." Praises Kubrick's professionalism as a photographer.

1955

22 Anon. Review of *Killer's Kiss. National Parent Teacher,* 50 (December), 39.
Describes the world of film and the treatment of crime.

23 Anon. Review of *Killer's Kiss. Film Daily* (29 September), p. 15.
Discusses the story of the film and its visual effect. The delivery of the lines makes some of them "unconsciously" comic.

24 Gilbert. Review of *Killer's Kiss. Variety* (21 September), p. 6.
Discusses Kubrick's low key lensing and praises his depiction of "the seamy side of Gotham life." Kubrick's "direction is no better while his editing is fair."

1956

25 Anon. Review of *The Killing. Catholic World,* 183 (July), 304.
Analyzes the treatment of suspense in the film.

26 Anon. "Personality of the Month: Stanley Kubrick." *Films and Filming,* 2, no. 12 (September), 5.
Discussion of Kubrick's film career.

27 Anon. Review of *The Killing. National Parent Teacher,* 51 (September), 39.
Analysis of the development of plot in the film.

28 Anon. Review of *The Killing. Newsweek,* 47 (18 June), 58.
Compares the film to *Rififi.* Kubrick's film derives its effectiveness from its avoidance of almost every "cliché in the Hollywood book on crime."

29 Anon. Review of *The Killing. Monthly Film Bulletin,* 23 (July), no. 270, p.1.
Praises Kubrick's development as a director from *Killer's Kiss.* Singles out: his handling of a large cast, harsh unflattering use of light, and percussive score; all reflect Kubrick's personality. Calls earlier film, *Killer's Kiss,* "a small scale film of distinct quality."

30 Anon. "The New Pictures." *Time,* 67 (4 June), 106.
Review of *The Killing.* Contains a biography of Kubrick and praises his ability as a director. Compares the dialogue and camera work of Kubrick with that of Orson Welles. Photograph of Kubrick and James Harris.

31 Anon. Review of *Fear and Desire. Saturday Review,* 39 (19 May), 51.
Analysis of the film's treatment of the war theme.

32 Anon. Review of *The Killing. Saturday Review,* 39 (4 August), 32.
Examines the use of time in the story in the film.

33 Baker, Peter G. Review of *The Killing. Films and Filming,* 2, no. 12 (September), 26-27.
Describes the use of multiple points of view in the film.

34 Beckley, Paul V. Review of *The Killing.* New York *Herald Tribune* (21 May), p. 21.
Describes the film "as an excellent portrait of a crime, unusually taut, keenly directed and acted, and with a sharp, leanly written script."

35 Croce, Arlene. Review of *The Killing. Film Culture,* 2, no. 3 (Spring), 30-31.
Favorable review of the film. This new film of Kubrick's bears evidence of a

fresh and maturing talent. Points to the visual authority of *The Killing* as dominating a flawed script.

36 Lambert, Gavin. Review of *Killer's Kiss. Sight and Sound*, 25, no. 4 (Spring), 198.
The real originality of Kubrick's film lies in its approach to characterization and atmosphere. The director's most remarkable talent is a "kind of neo-realist approach to human behavior, a feeling for the place and the moment." Cites the lighting and composition as examples of Kubrick's skills as a photographer.

37 ______. Review of *The Killing. Sight and Sound*, 26, no. 2 (Autumn), 95-96.
Positive review of the film. Finds Kubrick making a film he thought Hollywood was no longer capable of making. Focuses on Kubrick's use of the camera and long takes that draw attention to characters and gestures.

38 Weiler, A. H. Review of *The Killing. New York Times* (21 May), p. 20.
Compares the film to *The Asphalt Jungle;* it "evolves as a fairly diverting melodrama."

1957

39 Alpert, Hollis. "War and Justice." *Saturday Review*, 40 (21 December), 31-32.
Paths of Glory is unquestionably the finest film of the year. The film is so searing in its intensity that it "will probably take its place, in years to come as one of the screen's most extraordinary achievements."

40 Anon. "Twenty-Nine and Running: The Director With Hollywood by the Horns." *Newsweek*, 50 (2 December), 96-97.
Article about Kubrick as a director and the making of the film *Paths of Glory*. Kubrick quoted on the subject of criminals in film. Adolphe Menjou compares Kubrick to Charlie Chaplin as a director.

41 Anon. "To A Shocking Climax." *Newsweek*, 50 (9 December), 96-99.
Review of *Paths of Glory*. Discusses the film as giving new meaning to the horror film category. Sees the film as "as hard as iron and just as hard to take."

42 Anon. Review of *Paths of Glory. New York Times Magazine* (15 December), p. 16.
Analyzes the film's treatment of war and injustice.

43 Anon. Review of *Paths of Glory. Time*, 70, no. 24 (9 December), 108-112.
Paths of Glory's only real mistake is that "it attacks an unfashionable devil." The film is powerful but somewhat out of time in the effect of the pacificism theme. It leaves the spectator "often confused and numb, like a moving speech in a dead language."

44 Crowther, Bosley. Review of *Paths of Glory. New York Times* (26 December), p. 23.
Finds two central problems with the film: actors playing Frenchmen in colloquial English and the horribly freakish incident at the center of the plot. Feels the film comes to an inconclusive point.

45 Haine, Raymond. "Bonjour, Monsieur Kubrick." *Cahiers du Cinéma* 13, no. 73 (July), 10-18.

Extended interview with Kubrick on location in Munich for the filming of *Paths of Glory*. Discusses Kubrick's career, early vocation, favorite directors—Max Ophuls and Elia Kazan. Interview with James Harris and Kubrick on their work on *Paths of Glory*. In French.

46 Sternberg, Jacques. Review of *The Killing*. *Positif*, no. 21 (February), pp. 36-38.

Introduces Kubrick to the French audience. Since Kubrick's first two films were not released in France, Sternberg presents a discussion of his subtle development of character in his films. Predicts he will go on to be a name to remember. In French.

47 Zinsser, William K. Review of *Paths of Glory*. New York *Herald Tribune* (26 December), p. 25.

Analysis of the film and the treatment of war. Calls *Paths of Glory* "a good hard film . . . powerful in design and execution." Addresses the question of realistic villains in film.

1958

48 Anon. "Après Vision." *Cahiers du Cinéma*, 14, no. 82 (April), 49.

Praises Kubrick's film *Paths of Glory* and compares him with Robert Aldrich, Robert Mulligan, and Sidney Lumet. Discusses the presentation of the French Army in film. In French.

49 Anon. Review of *Paths of Glory*. *Catholic World*, 186 (January), 302-303.

Discusses the treatment of the war theme in *Paths of Glory*.

50 Anon. Review of *Paths of Glory*. *Coronet Magazine*, 43 (January), 14.

Analyzes the acting and realism of the film.

51 Anon. Review of *Paths of Glory*. *Library Journal*, 83 (15 January), 174.

Details the development of the theme in *Paths of Glory*.

52 Anon. Review of *Paths of Glory*. *National Parent Teacher*, 52 (January), 39.

Examines the inhumanity of man theme in *Paths of Glory*.

53 Anon. Review of *Paths of Glory*. *New York Times* (12 January), Section 2, p. 1.

Film is a powerful statement of war's tragedy.

54 Anon. "Infortunes de la Liberté." *Positif*, no. 29 (Fall), pp. 55-57.

Presents various hostile reactions of the French press to the release of *Paths of Glory* which opened in Brussels. Film was banned in France because of its treatment of the French Army. In French.

55 Baker, Peter. Review of *Paths of Glory*. *Films and Filming*, 4, no. 5 (February), 26.

Analyzes the theme of war and suffering in the film.

56 Baumbach, Jonathan. Review of *Paths of Glory. Film Culture,* 4, no. 2 (February), 15.
Discusses the realism of *Paths of Glory.*

57 Bitsch, Charles. "Kubrick Contre L'Armée." *Cahiers du Cinéma,* no. 81 (March), p. 48.
Because of the content of *Paths of Glory,* the film will probably never be seen in France but readers are encouraged to see it in Brussels or at private showings. In French.

58 Brief, Adela. Review of *Paths of Glory. Village Voice,* 3, no. 16 (12 February), 10.
Presents a plot summary of the film *Paths of Glory.* Calls it a good picture but says it lacks honesty. Praises Kirk Douglas and comments on the ending of the film.

59 Bruce, Louise. Review of *Paths of Glory. Films in Review,* 9, no. 1 (January), 30-31.
Negative review of the film. Kubrick is more concerned with camera angles than political angles. Feels that those who have admired Kubrick's earlier films will be unhappy with *Paths of Glory.*

60 Godard, Jean-Luc. Review of *The Killing. Cahiers du Cinéma,* no. 80 (February), pp. 61-62.
Compares the film to *The Asphalt Jungle* and *Treasure of Sierra Madre.* Kubrick is a good director and one to watch for in the future. In French.

61 Hartung, Philip T. "The Screen: The Face of War." *Commonweal,* 67 (17 January), 408-409.
Paths of Glory is not entirely successful. The film is so relentlessly determined to condemn war that it becomes unfeeling to war.

62 Lambert, Gavin. Review of *Paths of Glory. Sight and Sound,* 27, no. 3 (Winter), 144-45.
Difficult to imagine a film about war that could have a more stunning impact today. *Paths of Glory* shows war as an extended struggle for power, both internal and external. Not only a film of unusual substance but a powerfully realized and gripping work of art. Discusses the use of cutting and the execution scenes with grim details of war.

63 McCarten, John. "The Old Army Game." *New Yorker,* 33 (4 January), 70.
Kubrick has succeeded quite well in getting first class performances from his actors. The film packs quite a "dramatic wallop anyhow."

64 Stang, Joanne. "Film Fan to Film Maker." *New York Times Magazine* (12 October), pp. 34, 36, 38.
Presents a biography of Kubrick and a study of his films up to Paths of Glory. Kubrick's early life in Brooklyn. Kubrick talks about films and the purchase of film rights to *Lolita.* Kubrick's films are noted for natural lighting and attention to details. Photos from *Fear and Desire* and *Paths of Glory.*

65 Tailleur, Roger. Review of *The Killing. Positif,* no. 29 (Fall), pp. 32-34.
Discusses the similarities between *The Killing* and *The Asphalt Jungle.* In French.

66 Walsh, Moira. Review of *Paths of Glory. America,* 98 (4 January), 404.
Stanley Kubrick brings a controlled power to his direction of *Paths of Glory.*

1959

67 Anon. Review of *Spartacus. Films and Filming,* 5, no. 12 (September), 20.
Analysis of the epic film and the special effects in making the film.

68 Anon. "Dream Coming True." *Newsweek,* 53 (9 March), 110-111.
On location with the set of *Spartacus* in Hollywood. Interviews with Kirk Douglas and other stars of the film, including director Stanley Kubrick. Discussion of camera techniques and elaborate sets for filming the epic drama.

69 MacDonald, Dwight. "No Art and No Boxoffice." *Encounter,* 13, no. 1 (July), 51.
In a review of *Miss Lonely Hearts,* MacDonald talks about his conversation with a new film director he met in Hollywood, Stanley Kubrick. Discusses the state of the movie industry and a number of other topics, including Whitehead, Kafka, and the decline of Western culture. Kubrick observes that the trouble with film makers is that they make films with heads and not hearts.

70 Young, Colin. "The Hollywood War of Independence." *Film Quarterly,* 12, no. 3 (Spring), 4-15.
Discusses Kubrick's career and the cost of making *Paths of Glory* ($900,000), including $350,000 for star Kirk Douglas. Presents a brief biography of Kubrick and commentary on his films, *The Killing* and *Paths.* Kubrick explains his feelings about completing the script and signing the star and cast before seeking money from major studios. Discusses war and crime as focal points of Kubrick's films. Next film by Kubrick will probably be *The German Lieutenant* by Richard Adams. Discussion of Kubrick as an independent film maker.

1960

71 Alpert, Hollis. "The Day of the Gladiator." *Saturday Review,* 43, no. 40 (1 October), 32.
Praises acting of Kirk Douglas and the sharp direction of Stanley Kubrick. *Spartacus* breathes "new life into ancient Rome."

72 Anon. Review of *Spartacus. Films in Review,* 11, no. 9 (November), 553-554.
Finds the film unsuccessful. It is least satisfying emotionally. The acting of Peter Ustinov and the technical effects are exceptions to the overall failure of the film. Kubrick as a young director took on quite a task for one of his years but he was aided by a cast of talented and experienced players.

73 Anon. "Spartacus." *Filmfacts,* 3:241.
Presents the cast and credits for *Spartacus* along with a plot summary.

74 Anon. Review of *Spartacus. Film Quarterly,* 14, no. 1 (Fall), 61-62.
The film is distinguished by flawless photography, beautiful landscapes, and inordinate length. Finds the film wanting in everything except battle scenes.

75 Anon. "A Mighty Tale Told Large." *Life,* 49 (24 October), 74-79.
Photo essay about how Kubrick filmed *Spartacus,* with explanations of the special effect sequences and battle scenes.

76 Anon. "Stanley Kubrick: Thirty-Two Year Old Director of a $12,000,000 Movie." *Look,* 24 (22 November), 88.
Photographic article on the filming of *Spartacus* and on Kubrick as a director.

77 Anon. Review of *Spartacus. Look,* 24 (22 November), 74-79.
Discusses the epic film and the special effects in the battle sequences.

78 Anon. "Spotty Spectacular." *Newsweek,* 56 (17 October), 117.
Negative review of *Spartacus.* Calls the film a "ragged toga saga" with only Olivier giving the motion picture any real character.

79 Anon. "Nymphet Found." *Time,* 76, no. 15 (10 October), 92.
Discussion of casting the lead role for Kubrick's film of Nabokov novel, *Lolita.* After a national talent search, Kubrick selects Sue Lyon, a 14-year-old from Davenport, Iowa, to play the lead in the film version.

80 Anon. Review of *Spartacus. Time,* 76, no. 17 (24 October), 102.
Director Stanley Kubrick shows mastery in all departments: cast, camera, and cutting. In this type of film "quality is not permitted to inhibit quantity."

81 Crowther, Bosley. Review of *Spartacus. New York Times* (7 October), p. 28.
Spartacus is a "spotty uneven drama" that offers a vast panoramic display of "synthetic Romans." Compares the film version of *Spartacus* to the original novel by Howard Fast.

82 Gill, Brendan. "Love and Slavery." *New Yorker,* 36 (15 October), 133.
To his surprise, Gill finds *Spartacus* a fine film. No one could be more beautiful than Jean Simmons on the screen. Kubrick handles the crowd scenes with extraordinary grace.

83 Hacker, Seymour. "If Spartacus Had Money." *Village Voice,* 5, no. 51 (13 October), 11-12.
Negative review of the film. Both acting and directing show how far Kubrick has fallen from his previous film *Paths of Glory.* Urges readers to stay away from the film.

84 Hartung, Philip T. "The Screen: The Twenty-Fourth Million." *Commonweal,* 73 (28 October), 124.
Positive review of *Spartacus.* Kubrick has succeeded in directing the film as a spectacular epic that makes his audiences think.

85 Kauffman, Stanley. "It Needn't be Bad If It's Big." *New Republic,* 143 (14 November), 19-20.

"Because of the nature of this film, Stanley Kubrick's direction will probably be underrated but by and large he has done a penetrating and imaginative piece of work." The type of film that *Spartacus* is will cause a lot of people to dislike it. The film is a trap for snobs.

86 Kubrick, Stanley. "Interview." *Observer* [London], (4 December), p. 20.
Kubrick discusses film and the making of films by directors. He does not think film directors are motivated by a didactic purpose.

87 Noble, Robin. "Killers, Kisses, and *Lolita.*" *Films and Filming,* 7, no. 3 (December), 11-12, 42.
Discussion of Stanley Kubrick's film career and his present project of *Lolita.*

88 Reynolds, Charles. "Interview with Kubrick." *Popular Photography,* 47 (December), 144-145.
Discussion with Kubrick about his film career and the process of selection of film ideas. Kubrick says: "A good film is, in the end, a film for which you have great affection."

89 Walsh, Moira. Review of *Spartacus. America,* 104 (12 November), 230.
Negative review of the film. Compares *Spartacus* with the film *The Alamo* because it has an "intolerable amount of graphic brutality."

1961

90 Anon. Review of *Spartacus. Monthly Film Bulletin,* 28, no. 324 (Janaury), 6.
Negative review. Despite enormous amounts of money, time, and talent, so much of the film falls into the category of cliché treatments. Praises Kubrick's use of widescreen techniques, but finds the characterization and motives superficial. Excellent use of panoramic shots in the big action scenes.

91 Anon. Review of *Spartacus. McCalls,* 88 (January), 8.
Discusses the scope of the epic spectacular.

92 Anon. Review of *Spartacus. Redbook,* 116 (January), 11.
Analyzes the color, acting, and scope of *Spartacus.*

93 Cutts, John. Review of *Spartacus. Films and Filming,* 7, no. 4 (January), 32-33.
Examines the use of special photographic effects and the overall quality of the film.

94 Dyer, Peter John. Review of *Spartacus. Sight and Sound,* 30, no. 1 (Winter), 38.
Negative review. Stanley Kubrick has been notable for his insight into stark Freudian tensions. There is nothing in the film *Spartacus* to advance any claims that it is a "film which stands up for life."

95 Kubrick, Stanley. "Words and Movies." *Sight and Sound,* 30, no. 1 (Winter), 14.
Kubrick comments on the adaptation of novels to the screen and on the writer-director relationship. The relationship is critical to the adaptation of the literary work. "Directing should be nothing more or less than a continuation of the writing."

96 Lightman, Herbert A. "Filming *Spartacus* in Super Technirama." *American Cinematographer,* 42, no. 1 (January), 42-46.
Discusses the uses of film and special film techniques with Russell Metty, A.S.C. as director of photography at Universal-International Studios. Explains the different types of crane and dolly shots used in *Spartacus.*

97 MacDonald, Dwight. "Films: Mostly on Roman Corruption." *Esquire,* 55, no. 3 (March), 24, 28, 30.
Describes Kubrick as a major director who goes down under the weight of the script in *Spartacus.*

98 Tavernier, Bertrand. Review of *Spartacus. Positif,* no. 41 (September), pp. 60-61.
Kubrick makes good use of the wide screen not only in the battle scenes but also in the intimate scenes. Praises the acting of Kirk Douglas and the superb direction of Stanley Kubrick. In French.

1962

99 Alpert, Hollis. *The Dreams and the Dreamers.* New York: Macmillan, p. 132.
Article on Kubrick.

100 ______. Review of *Lolita. Saturday Review,* 45 (23 June), 40.
Examines the use of comedy in the film and the acting of James Mason and Sue Lyon.

101 [Anby.] Review of *Lolita. Variety* (22 June), p. 6.
Discusses the effect of the film and the treatment of erotic love.

102 Anon. "Lolita." *Show,* 2 (August), 63-69.
Photographic essay on Sue Lyon, star of Kubrick's new film *Lolita.* Photographic impressions are by Bert Stern with comments on Stanley Kubrick's adaptation of Nabokov's novel.

103 Anon. Review of *Lolita. Monthly Film Bulletin* (September), p. 137.
Sees the film's major achievement as charting the obsession in terms of sadness, irony, rage, and genuine compassion. Kubrick is an intellectual director with little feeling for erotic tension. The first scenes in the film remind one of Orson Welles. It is difficult to see how an erotic film about a 12-year-old girl could have passed the censor. Kubrick does some interesting sexy tableaus but does not begin to do justice to the original novel.

104 Anon. Review of *Lolita. Films and Filming,* 8, no. 12 (September), 25.
Discusses the relationship between the book and the film version.

105 Anon. Review of *Lolita. Films in Review,* 13, no. 7 (August-September), 426-427.
Stanley Kubrick's direction of this film is the only "teenage thing" about it. Refers to the film as a "money grabber" and takes issue with Arthur Schlesinger in *Show Magazine,* saying: "It is therefore something of a minor national disgrace to see him [Schlesinger] quoted in advertisements for this worthless picture, as having said in *Show* that *Lolita* is a 'brilliant and sinister film . . . wildly funny and wildly poignant.'"

106 Anon. *Lolita. Filmfacts,* 5. 131.
Presents the credits and cast of *Lolita* along with a plot summary.

107 Anon. Review of *Lolita. Movie,* no. 3 (October), p. 36.
Discusses the treatment of the love story in *Lolita* and the acting of Mason and others.

108 Anon. Review of *Lolita. New York Times,* (24 June), Section 2, p. 1.
Analyzes the tenuous love story of Humbert and the depiction of Lolita in the film.

109 Anon. "Nymphet's Return." *Newsweek,* 59, no. 25 (18 June), 86.
Finds the problems with the film in its distinct differences from original book. But despite these faults *Lolita* is continually interesting as a story. Kubrick's camera work is enjoyable.

110 Anon. Review of *Lolita. Time,* 79 (22 June), 94.
Compares the film version with the original book.

111 Barr, Charles. "Wider Still and Wider." *Motion,* 2 (Winter), 30-33.
Presents argument for increased use of the wide screen or cinemascope based on several films by Nicholas Ray, Stanley Kubrick and others.

112 Beckley, Paul V. "*Lolita*: The New Movies." New York *Herald Tribune* (14 June), p. 28.
Examines the differences between the novel and the film versions of *Lolita.*

113 Benayoun, Robert. Review of *Lolita. Positif,* no. 48 (November), pp. 35-36.
Brief notice about *Lolita* praising various scenes with James Mason. Discusses the central problem of the differences between Nabokov's book and Kubrick's film. In French.

114 Bunzel, Peter. "Yes, They Did It: *Lolita* is a Movie." *Life,* 52 (25 May), 93-97.
Picture story of the filming of *Lolita* and how Kubrick adapted Nabokov's novel to the screen. Photographs.

115 Croce, Arlene. Review of *Lolita. Sight and Sound,* 31, no. 4 (Autumn), 191-192.
Negative review of the film. Praises the acting of James Mason but finds fault with Shelley Winters, Sue Lyon, and Peter Sellers. "The film had everything it needed to be as brilliant and beautiful as the novel, except great direction." Singles out two passages of "great atmospheric proficiency"–the death of Charlotte and the hospital sequence. Film does not capture the flavor of the book in the roles of Charlotte, Quilty, or Lolita. The role of Humbert is much more frustrating in the novel.

116 Crowther, Bosley. Review of *Lolita. New York Times* (14 June), p. 23.
The structure and climate of the novel are not the same in Mr. Kubrick's film although he does have "a lot of fun and frolic in his film." Discusses the differences between the novel and the film and the pathos and irony in the film's ending. Describes it as a "provocative sort of film." Novel and film are two conspicuously different things.

117 Douchet, Jean. Review of *Lolita. Cahiers du Cinéma,* no. 136 (October), p. 46.
Returning to film in England, Kubrick has adopted the style of his country's cinematographers: tedious, boring, and without any spice of life. Describes *Lolita* as a catastrophe for Kubrick which in no way resembles the original novel. In French.

118 Durgnat, Raymond. Review of *Lolita. Films and Filming,* 9, no. 2 (November), 35.
Examines the film version of *Lolita* in comparison with the novel.

119 Gill, Brendan. "Little Girl, Big Girl." *New Yorker,* 38, no. 18 (23 June), 90.
As a movie *Lolita* lacks the beguilement of Nabokov's style. The film does have an inspired cast that helps to save the story.

120 Hartung, Philip T. "The Screen: Of Human Bondage." *Commonweal,* 76 (13 July), 401-402.
Although he lost some of Nabokov's book in the transition to the screen, Kubrick has done a fine job in directing Sue Lyon as Lolita.

121 Hatch, Robert. Review of *Lolita. Nation,* 194 (23 June), 563-564.
Negative review of the film. Kubrick's film is too long and should be cut. The acting of James Mason and Sue Lyon is poor and adds to the failure of the film.

122 Kauffman, Stanley. "Movies: Humbug, Humbug." *New Republic,* 147 (2 July), 29-30.
While some elements of the film "are far above ordinary," he finds the film a failure in converting novel into film. James Mason lacks depth of development.

123 Knight, Arthur. "Cinema on a Shoestring." *Playboy,* 4 (April), 64-66.
Discussion of the progression of directors who started with low budget films like Stanley Kubrick's *Killer's Kiss.* Cites examples among the new film makers.

124 Legrand, Gerard. "La Gloire et ses Chemins." *Positif,* no. 45 (May), pp. 15-21.
Review essay on *Spartacus.* Discussion of the various visual qualities that Kubrick brings to the screen. Compares the film to *Alexander Nevsky.* In French.

125 MacDonald, Dwight. "Of Nymphets and Monsterettes." *Esquire,* 58 (September), 45-46.
Lolita is a disappointment because we have a right to expect more from Kubrick. There is no need for the bowdlerization of the book that Kubrick was responsible for in adapting it to the screen.

126 Russell, Francis. "Petronius Redivivus." *National Review,* 13 (11 September), 198, 200.
Lolita is a convincing picture due to the acting of Shelley Winters, Sue Lyon and Peter Sellers. The acting is varied but fairly strong. Compares *Lolita* to *The Satyricon.*

127 Sarris, Andrew. "Movie Journal." *Village Voice,* 7 (5 July), 11.
Negative review. Kubrick has a weakness for long scenes where everything is explained, and then explained again. Several problems with the film. The acting never meshes. What *Lolita* needed more than anything else was a director in tune with Nabokov's delirious approach to his subject. We face "problem without passion, badness without the beauty, the agony without the ecstasy."

128 Walsh, Moira. Review of *Lolita. America,* 107 (30 June), 448.
Positive review of the film. Discusses the satiric aspects of *Lolita.*

1963

129 Anon. "erratum." *Cahiers du Cinéma,* no. 140 (February), p. 44.
Correction of information in a discussion of *Killer's Kiss* (*See* entry 45) confusing Frank Silvera with Jamie Smith.

130 Anon. "The Directors Choose the Best Films." *Cinema* [Beverly Hills], 1 (August-September), 14.
Selection of films by directors, including Stanley Kubrick. Directors selected the best films.

131 Anon. "Stanley Kubrick." *Current Biography,* 24 (February), 224-227.
Presents a complete biography of Kubrick up through his work on *Dr. Strangelove.* Discusses early still photography work on the staff of *Look* magazine and the early reviews of Kubrick's films *Fear and Desire* and *Killer's Kiss.* Kubrick's work in Hollywood and the attention he received from the films *The Killing* and *Paths of Glory* established him as one of the leading independent film makers in America. Kubrick's films are noted for the use of natural lighting and accuracy of details that create an almost documentary realism "rare in Hollywood films." Offers excerpts from critical reviews of Kubrick's films, including *Fear and Desire, Killer's Kiss, Lolita, Paths of Glory, Spartacus,* and *The Killing.*

132 Barr, Charles. "Cinemascope: Before and After." *Film Quarterly,* 16, no. 4 (Summer), 4-25.
Discusses the use of wide screen techniques in a number of major films, including *Spartacus* by Stanley Kubrick. Analyzes the film techniques used by Kubrick in scenes at the gladiator camp and the distinct differences in cinemascope and regular film versions. (*See* entry 195).

133 Fenin, G. "The Fall of '63–United States." *Films and Filming,* 9, no. 6 (March), 55.
Discusses Kubrick's next film *Dr. Strangelove* and the production of the film.

134 Hrusa, Bernard. Review of *Lolita. Film Journal,* no. 21 (April), pp. 105-106, 118.
Analyzes the similarities between the film and the novel.

135 Kubrick, Stanley. "How I Learned to Stop Worrying and Love the Cinema." *Films and Filming,* 9, no. 9 (June), 12-13.
Kubrick discusses his own films and his career in the cinema along with information about his newest film *Dr. Strangelove.*

136 Marcorelles, Louis. Review of *Lolita. Cahiers du Cinéma,* no. 141 (March), pp. 43-45.

Negative review of *Lolita*. The script, locale, acting, and direction of the film are all poor. Finds many things in the film faulty in comparison with the book. In French.

137 Prideaux, T. "Take Aim: Fire at the Agonies of War." *Life,* 55 (20 December), 115-118.

Discussion of two new anti-war films: *The Victors* and *Dr. Strangelove*. Contains still photos from the films. Includes partial credits.

138 Sarris, Andrew. "The American Cinema." *Film Culture,* no. 28 (Spring), p. 42.

Discusses Kubrick as a major disappointment as a film director. "His metier is projects rather than films, publecite [sic] rather than cinéma." Explains that *Lolita* is his most irritating failure to date, especially considering the material he had to work with. He may end up as the best director but time is running out on "his projected evolution" into a major artist.

139 Schiff, William, Jesse Smith and Lorie Ryback. "Letters." *Sight and Sound,* 32 (Spring), 101.

In response to Arlene Croce's review (*See* entry 115) this letter to the editor suggests that the struggle of Humbert and Quilty over Lolita suggests the same struggle between Kubrick and Nabokov over the film *Lolita* as it was adapted from the novel.

140 Tornabene, Lyn. "Contradicting the Hollywood Image." *Saturday Review,* 46 (28 December), 19.

Discusses the anti-formula films of Kubrick and his two areas of expertise: his visual power and his persuasive power. The roots of his success are in his skill as a still photographer. Kubrick wants his films to have the widest possible audience. Discusses Kubrick's ideas and techniques while filming *Dr. Strangelove*. He emphasizes attention to details and the study of scenes before shooting of them.

1964

141 Albert, Hollis. Review of *Dr. Strangelove. Saturday Review,* 47 (25 January), 24.

Discusses the use of satire and comedy in the film of *Dr. Strangelove*.

142 Anon. Review of *Dr. Strangelove. Reporter,* 30 (27 February), 48.

Discusses the treatment of nuclear warfare in the film.

143 Anon. Review of *Dr. Strangelove. Senior Scholastic,* 84 (21 February), 10.

Discussion of Kubrick's new film with credits.

144 Anon. Review of *Dr. Strangelove. Time,* 83 (31 January), 69.

Film is bitter attack on the futility of war and the threat of the bomb.

145 Anon. "Petit Journal." *Cahiers du Cinéma,* no. 151 (January), p. 46.

Brief comparison of the two films *Fail-Safe* and *Dr. Strangelove*. Both films deal with the subject of questioning the safety of the bomb in today's world. Contains a photograph of George C. Scott in *Dr. Strangelove.* In French.

146 Anon. "Les sentiers de la gloire." *Cahiers du Cinéma,* no. 150-151 (December-January), p. 245.

Brief comment by Kubrick on *Paths of Glory* and the reaction to the film in France. In French.

147 Anon. "Ten Questions to Nine Directors." *Sight and Sound,* 33 (Spring), 62-67.

Questions directed to Kubrick and other directors like Jean-Luc Godard and Clive Donner about their latest films. Kubrick discusses *Dr. Strangelove* and the ideas for the film, financing, distribution, and production costs and problems.

148 Anon. "Stanley Kubrick." *Cahiers du Cinéma,* nos. 150-151 (December-January), 138.

Biography of Kubrick and a discussion of his films up to and including *Dr. Strangelove.* Presents an insight into the production of *Lolita* and the reaction to his other films. In French.

149 Anon. "Direct Hit." *Newsweek,* 63 (3 February), 79-80.

"Kubrick and his biting, bitter satire stands as eloquent testimony not only to the possibilities of intelligent comment in film, but to the great freedom which movie-makers have." Includes photos from *Strangelove* and plot analysis of the film. Talks about Kubrick's next project, a film about outer space.

150 Anon. "Sue Lyon: Modern American Gothic." *Cinema,* 42 (July), 24-28.

Photographic essay on Sue Lyon, star of Stanley Kubrick's film *Lolita.*

151 Batz, Jean-Claude. "La Mutation." *Cahiers du Cinéma,* nos. 150-151 (December-January), p. 233.

Article on the high costs of film productions presents a photograph of Kubrick and Charles Laughton on the set of *Spartacus.* In French.

152 Brustein, Robert. "Out of this World." *New York Review of Books* (6 February), pp. 12-14.

Critical analysis of *Dr. Strangelove* citing Kubrick for "courage" in his treatment of the nuclear arms race question. Relates Kubrick to the satiric mode in drama and discusses the different types of visual and verbal satire in the film. Kubrick has taken on many of the myths and sacred cows of Hollywood in directing a film that dares to attack and address the question of nuclear war. Calls the film Juvenalian satire, saying: "Kubrick has flushed a monster from its psychic lair—the universal fear of nuclear accident—and then proceeded to feed and nourish it, letting it perform its worst before your eyes. The consequence of the spectacle is . . . a temporary purgation; to witness the end of the world as a comic event is, indeed, to stop worrying and to love the bomb." Concludes his discussion of *Strangelove* by saying, "it releases, through comic poetry, those feelings of impotence and frustration that are consuming us all and I can't think of anything more important for an imaginative work to do." *See* entries 286, 591.

153 Burgess, Jackson. "Dr. Strangelove." *Film Quarterly,* 17, no. 3 (Spring), 41-42.

Review of *Strangelove* citing the satiric attack on war training films and the heroic Hollywood image as definite pluses in Kubrick's film. Villains in the film are "courage, resourcefulness, ingenuity, and optimism." Praises the acting of Sterling Hayden, George C. Scott, and Keenan Wynn but finds Peter Sellers in his triple role disappointing. The final irony of the film is that one goes away from the ending admiring it.

154 ______. "The Antimilitarism of Stanley Kubrick." *Film Quarterly*, 18, no. 1 (Fall), 4-11.

Discussion of the three of Kubrick's seven films that deal with war and anti-war feelings: *Fear and Desire, Paths of Glory,* and *Dr. Strangelove.* Kubrick's films are bloody and cruel and all of them except *Killer's Kiss* have an "optimistic gloomy ending." Kubrick's films are "the obsession with the disturbing imperfections of man, with the harrowing doubts which shadow every act of the will . . . an obsession with the central question of political theory: who should decide?" Finally, Kubrick's films are concerned with public morality and often employ a narrator to impart "a ritualistic and documentary distance to the story."

155 Chateau, René. "Entretiens avec Michel Wilson et Dalton Trumbo." *Positif,* nos. 64-65 (Fall), pp. 91-102.

Brief discussion of Trumbo's feelings about the way Kubrick changed the ending of *Spartacus* and his dissatisfaction with him for doing it. (pp. 100–102). Contains filmography of Trumbo. In French.

156 Cohn, Bernard. Review of *Dr. Strangelove. Positif,* nos. 64-65 (Fall), pp. 130–133.

Dr. Strangelove is both the most comic and the most tragic film of the year. Praises Kubrick for his work in attacking and satirizing many of the basic beliefs in American folklore about war and heroes. Talks about truths about life present in Kubrick's films. In French.

157 Crist, Judith. "*Dr. Strangelove*: Committed, Bitter, One of the Best." New York *Herald Tribune* (30 January), p. 21.

Review of *Strangelove* talking about the use of satire in the film and the bitter reaction of Kubrick as a critic of nuclear warfare.

158 Crowther, Bosley. Review of *Dr. Strangelove. New York Times* (30 January), p. 24.

Dr. Strangelove is "beyond question the most shattering sick joke I have ever come across." But the film is also "one of the cleverest and most incisive satiric thrusts at the awkwardness and folly of the military that have ever been put on screen." Discusses the acting and the depiction of exaggerated characters in the film.

159 Decter, Midge. Review of *Dr. Strangelove. Commentary,* 37 (May), 75-77.

Positive review of the film praising the satiric aspects of *Dr. Strangelove.*

160 Forbes, Bryan. Review of *Dr. Strangelove. Films and Filming,* 10, no. 5 (February), 26.

"I consider *Dr. Strangelove* to be a tragic-comic masterpiece the first truly moral film of our time: courageous, outrageous, borrowing nothing, admitting of no compromise."

161 George, Peter Bryan. *Dr. Strangelove.* New York: Bantam Books. 161 pp.
The film script of *Dr. Strangelove,* made from the book *Red Alert.*

162 Gill, Brendan. Review of *Dr. Strangelove. New Yorker,* 39 (1 February), 75-76.
Discusses the use of satire and the comic scenes in the film.

163 Goldberg, Joe. "Dr. Kubrick." *Seventh Art,* 2, no. 2 (Spring), 2-3.
Analysis of the satiric attacks in *Dr. Strangelove.*

164 Hart, Henry. Review of *Dr. Strangelove. Films in Review,* 15, no. 2 (February), 113-114.
Negative review of *Strangelove.* Considers the film a farce. "*Dr. Strangelove* is not really farce for farce's sake, but farce for the expression of the private world of Mr. Kubrick and if you have been under any illusion about Kubrick's competence as a director look at the absurd performance he allowed George C. Scott to give as a U.S. general, whose mind, what there is of it, is on his secretary in bed."

165 Hartung, Philip T. Review of *Dr. Strangelove. Commonweal,* 79 (21 February), 632-633.
Discusses the effective use of comedy in *Strangelove* but feels Kubrick overdoes it: "in going to such extremes in his comedy, he detracts from the important theme."

166 Hatch, Robert. "Films." *Nation,* 198 (3 February), 127-128.
Review of *Strangelove.* Discusses the role of Kubrick and Terry Southern in adapting *Red Alert* as a film. "In any case they have made from Peter George's novel a picture that is hideously funny in the full meaning of the adverb." Describes *Strangelove* as "more effective as sadistic humor than adult education."

167 Kauffmann, Stanley. "Dean Swift in the 20th Century." *New Republic,* 150 (1 February), 26-28.
Praises Kubrick's film *Dr. Strangelove* and the director's abilities as a modern day satirist. "In its mode it stands alone, too much so, among recent American films."

168 ______. "Dr. Strangelove." *New Republic,* 150 (21 March), 28.
Pesents a quotation from a letter to *New York Times* by Lewis Mumford in praise of *Strangelove.* (*See* entry 173). Discusses the effectiveness of the film as satire.

169 Lyon, Peter. "The Astonishing Stanley Kubrick." *Holiday,* 35, no. 2 (February), 101-105, 146-150.
Picture story on the filming of *Dr. Strangelove* with biography and comment on Kubrick's career as a film director. "He [Kubrick] has caught hold of one simple truth: audiences are not necessarily interested by, and may even be bored by, sex appeal or spectacle. To put the thing more positively: an idea presented in entertaining fashion, will enthrall an audience." Discusses Peter Sellers' reaction to Kubrick, calling him the "*complete* director."

170 MacDonald, Dwight. Review of *Dr. Strangelove. Esquire,* 61, no. 2 (February), 26-28.

Analysis of the successful film *Dr. Strangelove.* "*Dr. Strangelove* is the funniest and most serious American movie in a long time. With this *comédie noue,* Stanley Kubrick clinches his title—one I conceded him years ago—to Best of Show among our youngest directors and why stop there, also, boldest." Shows how Kubrick takes every idea about the cold war and methodically rakes them over with a "barrage of satire."

171 Milne, Tom. Review of *Dr. Strangelove. Sight and Sound,* 33, no. 1 (Winter), 37-38.

Each of Kubrick's films shows characters entrapped in situations. Compares *Strangelove* and Kubrick's other films to classical tragedy.

172 ______. "How I Learned to Stop Worrying and Love Stanley Kubrick." *Sight and Sound,* 33, no. 2 (Spring), 68-72.

Discussion of all of Kubrick's films through *Dr. Strangelove* with an analysis of each theme. All of his films chart an obsession with something that brings about disaster.

173 Mumford, Lewis. "Letter." *New York Times* (1 March), p. 25.

Commentary on *Dr. Strangelove*: "What the wacky characters in *Dr. Strangelove* are saying is precisely what needs to be said; this nightmare eventuality that we have concocted for our children is nothing but a crazy fantasy, by nature as horribly crippled and dehumanized as Dr. Strangelove himself. It is not this film that is sick; what is sick is our supposedly moral, democratic country, which allowed this policy to be formulated and implemented without even the pretense of open public debate. . . . The film is the first break in the catatonic cold war trance that has so long held our country in its rigid grip."

174 Narboni, Jean. "Homo Ludens." *Cahiers du Cinema,* no. 155 (May), pp. 45-47.

Review of *Dr. Strangelove.* Praises Kubrick as a director and says that many elements in the film are like the tradition of the Marx brothers. In French.

175 Noames, Jean Louis. "Letters." *Cahiers du Cinema,* no. 160 (November), p. 77.

Brief note about Kubrick hoping that the next film he makes dealing with extra-terrestrial life will not be a failure like *Lolita.* In French.

176 Price, James. "Stanley Kubrick's Divided World." *London Magazine,* new series 4, no. 2 (May), 67-70.

Kubrick's new film *Dr. Strangelove* provides a focus for a review of Kubrick's career. Kubrick's main strength lies in his development of conflict. Humbert Humbert (*Lolita*) is the only sympathetic character in all of his films. Kubrick's other characters are "there not as people but as demonstrators of ideas, or alternately, as mouthpieces for their author's wit. In all cases Kubrick uses the physical world as, when, and in whatever way it suits him . . . it is on a level with wardrobe, makeup, special effects and the other items listed in the credits." Kubrick's world is a violent world and a divided world "in which violent antipathies work themselves up to a violent climax; and the climax involves death." Instead of referring to some other standard or normal order, Kubrick "refers us to a standard of madness personified." The result is that Kubrick sends *Strangelove* "with a double purpose: to destroy our apathy as citizens and as movie goers."

177 Ross, T. J. "Strange Loves and Stranger Deaths." *New Politics,* 3, no. 2 (Spring), 94-99.

In-depth analysis of *Strangelove* as a "streamlined variation for a broad public on the theme of civilization and its discontents." Ross identifies the film as "a sustained identification of violence with loveless sexual malaise" and relates its form to both science fiction and science horror film minus the "last minute save." Finally, *Dr. Strangelove* is Kubrick's "bleakest rendering of an anti-Arcadia. . . . Its world of schizophrenics 'sealed off' from one another is without emotional hitches." While Kubrick's compact films lack "the posed grandeur of those by such masters as Sternberg or Stroheim. . . . *Dr. Strangelove* marks a high flight in a career which has, after all, a way to go."

178 Russell, Lee. "Stanley Kubrick." *New Left Review,* no. 26 (Summer), pp. 71-74.

Study of Kubrick's films including *Dr. Strangelove.*

179 Sarris, Andrew. "Come Now, Dr. Strangelove." *Village Voice,* 9 (13 February), 13-14.

Positive review of *Dr. Strangelove.* Sees problems in Kubrick's structuring the film with a consistent camera viewpoint. Kubrick's direction is "efficient without being inspired." Critical of the acting of both George C. Scott and Sterling Hayden but feels ultimately that *Dr. Strangelove* is not a bad movie.

180 ______. "Films." *Village Voice,* 9 (11 June), 13.

Brief commentary on the revival of popularity of *Dr. Strangelove* during a Peter Sellers festival. Sees *Strangelove* as particularly "victimized by retrospection" and notes the backlash against the film in the pages of *Commentary* and *The New Leader.*

181 Schickel, Richard. *Movies.* New York: Basic Books, pp. 89-90.

Brief discussion of Kubrick's films and *Dr. Stranglove.* Comments: "but it does seem that this [*Strangelove*] may be the best comedy since sound came to Hollywood, or if not that, the best of the post war years."

182 Taylor, Stephen. Review of *Dr. Strangelove. Film Comment,* 2, no. 1 (Winter), 40-43.

Finds *Strangelove* inept as cinema. "While it succeeds beautifully as both anticipation and afterthought, it nonetheless falls short in execution. Mingled with our satisfaction, or lack of it, is a sense of puzzlement." *Dr. Strangelove's* attempts to be funny with nightmarish humor "fall dead on encounter with the viewer's prescience." Film overshoots its mark in that Kubrick "failed in not allowing us to look long enough and deep enough at Strangelove."

183 Von Dreele, W. H. "Satirist with Astigmatism." *National Review,* 16 (10 March), 203-204.

Discussion of the purpose and scope of *Strangelove.* Basic purpose of the film is ridicule. Explains how Kubrick made the film, including the cockpit sequences in the B-52.

184 Wainwright, Loudon. "The Strange Case of Strangelove." *Life,* 56 (13 March), 15.

Review of *Strangelove* with a brief discussion of the special effects used in filming.

185 Walsh, Moira. "Films: *Dr. Strangelove*." *America*, 110 (28 March), 462.
Analysis of the film and its use of satire. Concludes that the reviewer has "no strong feelings on film pro or con."

1965

186 Bernstein, Jeremy. "Beyond the Stars." *New Yorker*, 41 (24 April), 38-39.
Interview with Clarke and Kubrick dealing with their new film and book to be called *Journey Beyond the Stars* [later titled *2001: A Space Odyssey*]. Includes a discussion of the technical research and study that has gone into making the film. Both Clarke and Kubrick "hoped their film would give people a real understanding of the facts and of the overwhelming implications that the facts have for the human race." They hope to release the film in December 1966.

187 Cowie, Peter. *International Film Guide for 1965*. Vol. 2. New York: A. S. Barnes, pp. 26-29.
Review of *Dr. Strangelove* with credits, biography, and analysis of film. Compares the film to Welles' *The Trial*, saying: "*Dr. Strangelove* is an artist's crystal clear reflection of the distorted modern world and its terrifying systemization." Kubrick was named Director of the Year for his film *Dr. Strangelove*.

188 Hanson, Curtis Lee. "War: James B. Harris." *Cinema*, 3, no. 1 (December), 28-31.
Interview with James Harris who produced three films with Kubrick. Discusses the filming of *Lolita, The Killing* and *Paths of Glory*. Talks about the split between them and Harris's new film *The Bedford Incident*. Illustrated.

189 Hudson, Roger. "Three Designers." *Sight and Sound*, 34 (Winter), 15.
Discussion of the film designer's function and an interview with Ken Adams, whose credits in film design include working with Kubrick on *Dr. Strangelove*.

190 Macklin, F. Anthony. "Sex and *Dr. Strangelove*." *Film Comment*, 3, no. 3 (Summer), 55-57.
Study of *Dr. Strangelove* as a sex allegory from "foreplay to explosion in a mechanized world." Discusses the names of the characters: Jack D. Ripper, Lionel Mandrake, Premier Kissoff, and Dr. Strangelove, as suggestive of sexual deviations in humans. All of the characters in the film have names that represent various aspects of sex. In addition many of the settings, including the womb-like war room, take on added significance when examined in the context of the subtitle of the film, "How I Learned to Stop Worrying and Love the Bomb." Film ends in orgiastic purgation with screen filled with mushrooming clouds of the bomb going off.

191 Thomas, John. Review of *Lolita. Film Society Review* (October), pp. 14-15.
Compares the novel and film versions of *Lolita*.

1966

192 Anon. "To Prepare a Man for the Extraordinary." *Esquire*, 65 (May), 117.
Discusses the plans for *2001: A Space Odyssey*.

193 Anon. "Kubrick, Further Out." *Newsweek,* 68 (12 September), 106-106B.
Discusses the preparations for and filming of Stanley Kubrick's new film *2001: A Space Odyssey*. The film has involved a great deal of research for the special effects sequences that recreate space travel in the film. Kubrick says: "*2001* is not a fantasy though a portion of it is speculative." Elaborate sets and special techniques have been used to create effects never before used in cinema. Kubrick's motto is: "If you can describe it, I can film it."

194 Alpert, Hollis. "Offbeat Director in Outer Space." *New York Times Magazine* (16 January), p. 14.
Interview with Kubrick about the filming of the soon to be released film *2001: A Space Odyssey*. Discusses the writing of the screenplay for *2001* with Arthur Clarke. Presents a biography of Kubrick and an analysis of the special effects used in filming *2001*. Cites Kubrick's experience as a second unit director on the *Omnibus* series on television and the fact that his early film *The Killing* was named one of the ten best films of 1956 for *Time* and *Saturday Review* magazines.

195 Barr, Charles. "Cinemascope: Before and After," in *Film: A Montage of Theories.* Edited by Richard Dyer McCann. New York: Dutton, p. 12.
See entry 132.

196 Bernstein, Jeremy. "Profiles: How About a Little Game?" *New Yorker,* 42 (12 November), 70-110.
Detailed biography of Stanley Kubrick with a survey of his films. Bernstein had a friend who used to play chess with Kubrick in Washington Square and the friend introduced Bernstein to Kubrick while he was on location shooting his film *2001* in Boreham Wood, England. Details the early life of Kubrick growing up in New York City, attending Taft High School, working for *Look* magazine, and producing his first short film *Day of the Fight*. Follows Kubrick's career from *Fear and Desire* through *Dr. Strangelove,* with detailed information about Kubrick not otherwise available. Offers insight into Kubrick's fascination with the game of chess and the elaborate research and study that has gone into his current work on the film *2001: A Space Odyssey*. Discusses Kubrick's work with Marlon Brando on the film *One-Eyed Jacks,* which Kubrick was going to direct but finally withdrew from. Contains excerpts from Arthur Clarke's short story *The Sentinel,* the basis for *2001*.

197 Bontemps, Jacques. "Le Cahier des Autres." *Cahiers du Cinema,* no. 179 (June), p. 78.
Discussion of David Robinson's article in *Sight and Sound*. *See* entry 201. Announces the collaboration of Stanley Kubrick and Arthur Clarke for a new film, *2001*. Compares Kubrick to director Orson Welles. In French.

198 Hudson, Roger. "Putting the Magic in It." *Sight and Sound,* 35 (Spring), 78-83.
Films are a product of many fine technicians and directors, the most important of whom is the film editor. Several editors describe their working relationships with some of the best known directors. Anthony Harvey talks about working with Stanley Kubrick on *Dr. Strangelove*.

199 Kael, Pauline. *I Lost It At The Movies.* New York: Bantam Books, p. 184.
Brief reference to comedy in *Lolita.* Essay–analysis of the film.

200 Kauffmann, Stanley. *A World on Film.* New York: Harper and Row, p. 17.
Discussion of *Dr. Strangelove.* "Kubrick's precise use of camera angles, his uncanny sense of lighting, his punctuation with closeups, and occasionally with zoom shots, all galvanize the picture into macabre yet witty reality."

201 Robinson, David. "Two for the Sci-Fi." *Sight and Sound,* 35, no. 2 (Spring), 57-60.
Review and discussion of the films *2001* and *Fahrenheit 451.* Discusses the collaboration of Kubrick and Arthur Clarke and the superior special effects in Kubrick's film. Both films are currently being made in England.

202 Spinrad, Norman. "Stanley Kubrick in the 21st Century." *Cinema,* 3, no. 4 (December), 4-6, 10.
A pre-release analysis of the cinerama spectacle, *2001: A Space Odyssey* and a theory concerning its relationship to science fiction films of the past and future.

203 Walker, Alexander. *The Celluloid Sacrifice: Aspects of Sex in the Movies.* London: Michael Joseph, pp. 158-160.
Discussion of Kubrick's filming of *Lolita.* Kubrick and Nabokov turned the eroticism of the novel into visual comedy that never for an instant lost its undertones of irony or pity.

1967

204 Dempewolff, R. F. "*2001*: Backstage Magic for a Trip to Saturn." *Popular Mechanics,* 127 (April), 106-109.
Analysis of some of the special effects used in filming Kubrick's *2001,* including the elaborate creation of sets and film equipment used to create the image of outer space. Reprint: *See* entry 225.

205 MacFadden, Patrick. "Dr. Strangelove." *Film Society Review,* 2 (January), 22-24.
Analysis of the film and the use of satire in developing a critique of nuclear war.

206 Thomson, David. *Movie Man.* New York: Stein and Day, pp. 29-31, 100, 207.
Discussion of Kubrick's film *The Killing* and analysis of film sequences.

1968

207 Anon. Review of *2001: A Space Odyssey. Monthly Film Bulletin,* 35 (June), 88-89.
2001 is unquestionably the most ambitious and generally successful science fiction film ever made. The script, photography, and direction are all superb. In particular, the special effects sequences deserve a great deal of credit for its success. "Kubrick has provided a new mythology for space age man." Compares the effect of the film *2001* to Homer's *Odyssey.*

208 Anon. "2001: The First Space Ship Introduced Out of a Flying Thighbone." *New York Free Press* (11 April), pp. 9-10.

Analysis of some of the special effects used in the film *2001: A Space Odyssey.*

209 Anon. Review of *2001: A Space Odyssey. Filmfacts,* 11, no. 7 (1 May), 95-99.

Includes credits, plot summary, and excerpts from major reviews of Kubrick's *2001: A Space Odyssey.* Critiques of the film from *Variety, New York Times, Time, New York* magazine, and *Saturday Review* are included. Illustrated with photographs from film.

210 Anon. Review of *2001. Positif,* 99 (November), 54-56.

Further analysis of *2001* as a film and the very special techniques used in making the film. *See* entry 243. In French.

211 Adler, Renata. Review of *2001: A Space Odyssey. New York Times* (4 April), p. 58.

Discussion of the unusual quality of the film and the audience reaction to it. It is a long film that seems to need additional scripting and dialogue.

212 Adler, Renata. "Astronauts, Maoists—and Girls." *New York Times* (21 April), Section 4, 1D, 28D.

Negative review of *2001: A Space Odyssey* in a review of Godard's *La Chinoise* and Jacques Demy's *The Young Girls of Rochefort.*

213 Allen, John. "High Voltage on Four Circuits." *Christian Science Monitor* (10 May), Section 2, p. 9.

"It is part of the genius of *2001* that it must be approached on several levels at once. There are in a sense four films on the screen at all times, three of them available to all viewers and a fourth one perhaps unique to each viewer." Discusses the different levels of *2001:* (1) the science fiction film level, (2) the kinesthetic or psychological effect of the film, (3) the gift of myth to man, and (4) the level of subjective response involving the introspection of the viewer. Concludes that the film is like space travel itself and man's encounter with the unknown. Presents detailed analysis of each level. Still photos from the film.

214 Austen, David. Review of *2001: A Space Odyssey. Films and Filming,* 14, no. 10 (July), 24-27.

Analysis of *2001: A Space Odyssey* as a film dealing with faith beyond rational proof and "as such it must be a personal experience for each individual spectator."

215 Barker, Cliff. "Is *2001* Worth Seeing Twice?" *Cineaste,* 2, no. 1 (Summer), 15-16.

Describes *2001* as a dramatized documentary and takes issue with Andrew Sarris, who said that the film was a failure. (*See* entry 250). The fault lies not with the film but with those who have preconceived notions about it. Kubrick uses poetry, surrealistic and abstract images to engage audience interest. The strongest and most important element in the film is the theme Kubrick emphasizes. Kubrick believes that man will encounter a more advanced form of life existing in the universe. The film should be seen twice.

216 Becker, Michael. "2004." *Cineaste,* 2, no. 1 (Summer), 17.

Brief article explaining the cuts made in the original version of *2001: A Space Odyssey.* The new version is 19 minutes shorter than the original 160 minute version. A total of 30 cuts were made by Kubrick in the film from the following areas: (1) computer requesting permission to repeat the message for mission control telling of its own malfunction, (2) parts of the scene in which Keir Dullea replaces the faulty transmitter in the Jupiter-bound craft, and (3) Hal's turning off the pod radio before killing Lockwood. Complains about differences between the original and cut versions of *2001.*

217 Bernstein, Jeremy. "Books: Chain Reaction." *New Yorker,* 44 (21 September), 180-184.

Discussion of both the film and the book *2001: A Space Odyssey.* The book is a novel version of the screenplay for Kubrick's new film. Presents a plot summary of both film and story. Discusses many of the techniques that went into making the film and the collaboration between Stanley Kubrick and Arthur Clarke. Both film and book are outstanding.

218 Ciment, Michel. "L'Odyssee de Stanley Kubrick." *Positif,* no. 98 (October), pp. 1-22.

Detailed discussion of Kubrick's career from *Killer's Kiss* to *2001.* With Jerry Lewis and Arthur Penn, Kubrick is without doubt one of the last of the great directors of the American cinema. The world of Kubrick is always one of destruction. Presents biography and filmography of Kubrick along with extensive discussion and analysis of *2001: A Space Odyssey.* In French. *See* 342 for English version.

219 Clark, Paul Sargent. "2001: A Design Preview." *Industrial Design,* 15 (May), 34-41.

Presents a detailed review of the technology displayed in Stanley Kubrick's *2001: A Space Odyssey.* Outlines the numerous agencies and corporations that supplied designs and data for the production of the film. Concludes with an appraisal of the future of technology as presented in the film.

220 Clarke, Arthur Charles. *2001: A Space Odyssey.* New York: New American Library. 222 pp.

Novel version of the screenplay written by Kubrick and Clarke for film. *See* entry 593.

221 Crowdus, Gary. "A Tentative for the Viewing of *2001.*" *Cineaste,* 2, no. 1 (Summer), 12-14.

Discusses the reaction of the major film critics to *2001* and their complaints about the film. Reactions include: (1) the film has no story line, no plot; (2) the film is badly structured, the four major sequences have no relation to each other; (3) the film has bad acting, particularly some very wooden performances; (4) the film is confusing and/or ambiguous. The generation gap seems to play a significant role in the polarization of critical and general audience reaction to the film. "It is the difference between those who are able to comprehend the purely visually narrative sequences of the film and those who are confused by them." Answers each of the four main objections.

222 Daniels, Don. "Letter to the Editor." *Film Heritage,* 3, no. 2 (Winter), 31-32.
Discussion of the particular excellence of *2001.* Part of the work's real originality is in its "accession of philosophic, scientific concepts; its restructuring of those ideas, and their expression in visual metaphors of great beauty." Among the points noted in the film are: (1) Hal is among other things a critic, (2) Bowman dies (the human Bowman), (3) Kubrick uses a wasteland at the opening to suggest timelessness, (4) when Poole and the hibernauts die they are already almost dead, (5) a pattern of deceit runs through *2001,* (6) Clarke's theory of Hal's malfunction is omitted from the film, and (7) Kubrick added an extra inset shot (of the African monolith) to the 141 minute version of the film. Daniels thinks this last insertion is a flaw in the film.

223 ______. "2001: A New Myth." *Film Heritage,* 3, no. 4 (Summer), 1-9.
Both Kubrick and Clarke want us to see *2001* as a new myth. The narrative is to be taken on more than a literal plane, and the characters must be seen "as serving an allegorical argument, as generalized personifications of abstract ideas." *2001* also celebrates change. "Ape is transformed into man. Man learns to leave the earth to voyage in space—an evolutionary step that Clarke has equated with the progress of animal life from sea to land." One of the basic themes in *2001* is that "the price of survival in the atomic age has been the death of the emotions."

224 Del Ray, Lester. "2001: A Space Odyssey." *Galaxy Magazine,* 26 (July), 193-194.
Negative review of *2001: A Space Odyssey,* claiming that Kubrick's film is not really a science fiction film at all in the true sense of the genre.

225 Dempewolff, R. F. "2001: Backstage Magic for A Trip to Saturn." *Science Digest,* 63 (May), 34-39.
See entry 204.

226 Didion, Joan. Review of *Dr. Strangelove,* in *Slouching Toward Bethlehem.* New York: Dell, pp. 154-155.
Brief analysis of the film, concluding "rarely have we seen so much over so little."

227 French, Philip. "Plans That Go Wrong." *London Magazine,* new series, 8, no. 4 (July), 68-71.
Review of *2001.* The film is remarkable on a number of accounts. It is perhaps the "first multi-million dollar work since D. W. Griffith's *Intolerance* which can genuinely be regarded as the work of one man." It can be regarded as the highwater mark of science fiction movie-making. More importantly, it marks a significant point in the career of Stanley Kubrick, a "fastidious director of small output." Analyzes *2001* and compares it to all of Kubrick's pictures in which plans go wrong. While *2001* is an outstanding film, there are problems in the "time ride" sequence and in the ending.

228 Fritscher, John J. "Stanley Kubrick's *2001: A Space Odyssey:* A Sleep and A Forgetting." *Journal of Popular Culture,* 2, no. 1 (Summer), 167-171.
Review essay on *2001.* "Kubrick takes age-old humanistic questions of life and death in space and time and re-asks them, well aware of what many do not yet perceive, that we are evolved beyond industrialization into technology."

Discusses the implications of Kubrick's film and its meaning for today's audience. "Kubrick and crew are almost the perfect marriage of the new technology with the age old values of humanism."

229 Gasser, Mark. "2001: A Space Odyssey." *Cineaste,* 2, no. 1 (Summer), 10-11.
Discusses the relationship of the beginning and ending of *2001* and the way in which there is a definite continuity between the "Dawn of Man" sequence and the "Jupiter and Beyond" sequence. Kubrick wastes too much time on the 50-minute center sequence to point out the noncommunication theme. It would have been better to explain the black slab movements or develop some inter-being conflict or confrontation. The film lacks enough of a human element and the music at times is a bit bothersome. Nonetheless one must acknowledge Kubrick's "opening and closing as the most exciting film moments of quite a while."

230 Geduld, Harry M. "Return to Méliès: Reflections on the Science Fiction Film." *Humanist,* 28 (November-December), 23-24, 28.
Discussion of *2001: A Space Odyssey* as a science fiction film in the tradition of Méliès, who saw man as a pawn in the network of larger forces. *See* entry 357.

231 Gelmis, Joseph. "The Message of Kubrick." *Newsday* (6 April), p. 63.
Review of *2001: A Space Odyssey.*

232 Gentleman, Wally. "Inside *2001*: *Take One* Talks to Wally Gentleman." *Take One,* 1, no. 11 (May-June), 18-22.
Interview with Gentleman, who worked on special effects sequences with Stanley Kubrick for *2001.* Feels that many of the special effects sequences were not needed in the film, particularly the centrifuge scene. Special effects should exist for the film story and not as special effects in themselves. Explains how various scenes in *2001* were made. The film did not turn out as well as he expected. The story is exceedingly weak, very spotty, and irritatingly episodic. Concludes that "no one works with Kubrick, one works for him."

233 Gilliatt, Penelope. "The Current Cinema: After Man." *New Yorker,* 44 (13 April), 150-152.
Review of *2001.* "I think Stanley Kubrick's *2001* is some sort of great film, and an unforgettable endeavor. . . . It is as eloquent about what is missing from the people of 2001 as about what is there." Discusses different types of people's reaction to film. "It is also a uniquely poetic piece of sci-fi, made by a man who truly possesses the drives of both science and fiction."

234 Hartung, Philip T. Review of *2001. Commonweal,* 88, no. 7 (3 May), 207-208.
Analysis of the film concluding that its length is a problem. Kubrick needs to provide more explanation of the meaning of the black slab.

235 Hofsess, John. Review of *2001: A Space Odyssey. Take One,* 1, no. 11 (May-June), 29.
Analysis of *2001* and comparison with *Dr. Strangelove.* In both films Kubrick suggests "the possibility that man is as much at the mercy of his own artifacts as ever he was of the forces of nature." Most of the critics who have "rhapsodized about the film (and falsified it) have overlooked the salient fact

that it clearly depicts an early death for modern man." Kubrick offers two futures for man and both are funerals: in *Dr. Strangelove,* man dies in nuclear war unconscious of what drives him or his war machines; in *2001,* man "gains sufficient self awareness to unplug his machines and phase himself out of existence." An inarticulate rave is not a substitute for understanding."

236 Hunter, Tim. Review of *2001: A Space Odyssey. Film Heritage,* 3, no. 4 (Summer), 12-20.

"Much of *2001*'s conceptual originality derives from its being both anti-Christian and anti-evolutionary in its theme of man's progress controlled by an ambiguous extra-terrestrial force, possibly both capricious and destructive." In the final transfiguration both Kubrick and Clarke may be suggesting that evolutionary progress "may in fact be cyclical, perhaps in the shape of a helix formation. Man progresses to a certain point of evolution, then begins again from scratch on a higher level." Discusses the film's technqiue and the meaning of the ending.

237 Kael, Pauline. *Kiss Kiss, Bang Bang.* Boston: Little Brown, p. 16.

Discussion of Kubrick's film *The Killing.* The film is "an expert suspense film, with fast incisive cutting, a nervous edged style, and furtive little touches of character."

238 Klieb, Werner. "2001 Odyssee in Weltraum." *Film,* 9, no. 6 (September).

Positive review of *2001* as one of the best films of the year. In German.

239 Kloman, William. "In 2001, Will Love be a Seven Letter Word?" *New York Times,* (14 April), Section 2, p. 15.

Interview with Kubrick about his new film *2001.* Discusses the unusual nature of the film and the fact that the film only contains 46 minutes of dialogue in three hours. Essentially the film is a mythological statement. Its meaning is to be found at a sort of visceral psychological level rather than in a specific literal explanation.

240 Kohler, Charlie. "Stanley Kubrick Raps." *Eye* (August), pp. 84-86.

Stanley Kubrick answers questions about the scientific accuracy of *2001,* costumes in the film, his collaboration with Arthur Clarke and the making of the film. He also talks about his earlier films, the centrifuge in *2001,* and how to learn film making. Concludes with a discussion of the ending of *2001.*

241 Kubrick, Stanley. "Quotesmanship." *Action,* 3, no. 3 (May-June), 20.

Quotation from Kubrick about his intentions in making *2001: A Space Odyssey*: "I wanted to make a non verbal statement one that would affect people on the visceral emotional and psychological levels. People over 40 aren't used to breaking out of the strait-jacket of words and literal concepts, but the response so far from younger people has been terrific."

242 ______. "Kubrick Reveals All." *Cineaste,* 2, no. 1 (Summer), 17.

Presents Kubrick's response to a *New York Times* query about the ending of *2001*: "But what is there has visceral clarity. . . . He (Keir Dullea) sees himself in a time mirror. His entire life passes in what appears to him as a matter of moments. He dies and is reborn, transfigured, an enhanced being, a star child. The ascent from ape to angel is complete." *See* entry 239.

243 Lightman, Herb A. "Filming *2001: A Space Odyssey.*" *American Cinematographer,* 49, no. 6 (June), 412–414, 442–447.

Discussion with Douglas Trumbull about the filming and special photographic effects for *2001.* Contains a biography of Kubrick. Discussion of specific techniques, including front projection, camera lenses, camera angles, and use of wires in the film. Contains numerous photographs and diagrams about specific scenes in *2001.* Trumbull was in charge of special effects for the film.

244 Madsen, Axel. Review of *2001: A Spacy Odyssey. Cinema,* 4, no. 2 (Summer), 59.

Analyzes the use of special effects sequences in the film and the scope of epic film.

245 Manvell, Roger. *New Cinema in the USA: The Feature Film Since 1946.* New York: Dutton, pp. 6, 23, 41.

Contains brief references to Kubrick as a film director.

246 Milne, Tom. "A Visionary En Voyage." *Observer Review* (5 May), p. 29.

Review of *2001: A Space Odyssey.* Discusses the use of special effects and music.

247 Morgenstern, Joseph. "Kubrick's Cosmos." *Newsweek* (15 April), 97, 100.

Favorable review of *2001: A Space Odyssey* and the ideas of extra-terrestrial life in the film.

248 Norden, Eric. "Interview with Stanley Kubrick." *Playboy,* 15, no. 9 (September), 85.

Kubrick discusses his film career and his latest film *2001: A Space Odyssey. See* entry 239. Reprinted 1970. 284.

249 Rosenfeld, Alfred. "Fanciful Leap Across the Ages." *Life,* 64 (6 April), 24–35.

Photographic essay showing an elaborate planning session for making *2001: A Space Odyssey.* Outlines the research and work Kubrick did to complete the film.

250 Sarris, Andrew. Review of *2001: A Space Odyssey. Village Voice,* 13, no. 26 (11 April), 45.

"*2001* is a thoroughly uninteresting failure and the most damning demonstration yet of Stanley Kubrick's inability to tell a story coherently and with a consistent point of view." The film has little acting or writing to speak of and makes little sense. Kubrick seems both fascinated and frightened by the implications of machinery.

251 ______. *The American Cinema: Directors and Directions: 1929–1968.* New York: Dutton, pp. 195–196.

Brief discussion of Kubrick's films and place in the American cinema.

252 ______. *The Film.* Indianapolis: Bobbs Merrill, *passim.*

Brief discussion of Stanley Kubrick and his particular type of film in *2001: A Space Odyssey.*

253 Schlesinger, Arthur, Jr. Review of *2001: A Space Odyssey. Vogue,* 155 (June), p. 76.

"But in *2001* one feels that this most deliberate of artists has lost control over his materials. It is morally pretentious, intellectually obscure, and inordinately long. . . . Mr. Kubrick has some nice satire about the squareness of interplanetary travel and travellers." Discussion of various weaknesses in the film.

254 Shatnoff, Judith. "A Gorilla to Remember." *Film Quarterly,* 22, no. 1 (Fall), 56-62.

Review of *2001: A Space Odyssey* and *Planet of the Apes.* Discusses the success of *2001* but finds problems with the plot and story line. Kubrick never tells us what the meaning of the slab is. *2001* explores life, death, and rebirth but we are left with puzzles and questions. *2001* is a spatial and visual achievement of the contemporary cinema. "The same ideas [as in *Planet of the Apes*] are the springboard for Kubrick's flight to the future, the origin of man, the force of evolution, the most contemporary speculations in paleontology, and primatology."

255 Shuldiner, Herbert. "How They Filmed *2001: A Space Odyssey.*" *Popular Science,* 192 (June), 62-79.

Analysis of the various special effects used in making *2001.* Discusses the use of the centrifuge and how Kubrick created the illusion of weightlessness in space. Also shows photographs from the film.

256 Spinrad, Norman. Review of *2001: A Space Odyssey. Cinema,* 4, no. 2 (Summer), 58.

Review and discussion of Kubrick's film *2001.* Includes photographs from the film.

257 Stine, Harry G. "2001: A Space Odyssey." *Analog Science Fiction/Science Fact,* 82 (November), 167-168.

Review analysis of *2001: A Space Odyssey* with discussion of the incredible costs of the special effects used to recreate space in the film. Compares the effort to the *Star Trek* television series.

258 Strick, Philip. Review of *2001: A Space Odyssey. Sight and Sound,* 37, no. 3 (Summer), 153-154.

"Whatever one's theory of evolution the Kubrick-Clarke screenplay doesn't bear analysis any too well." Praises the special effects sequences in a film with poor characterization. "Kubrick has always pushed men to extremes in his films, finding them in the last resort incapable, and on the immense canvas of *Space Odyssey* he again appears to be expressing that vote of no confidence, which has been, after all, the constant theme of most written science-fiction." Kubrick has won the ultimate "technical triumph in that his film is beautiful to watch from start to finish." His greatest achievement has been to persuade us to believe him.

259 Trumbull, Douglas. "Creating Special Effects for *2001: A Space Odyssey.*" *American Cinematographer,* 49, no. 6 (June), 416-422, 451, 454, 459, 461.

Comments on the filming of *2001* by one of the four special effects experts who worked with Stanley Kubrick. Discusses the spacecraft shots, use of plastic models, and the centrifuge used in making the film. Contains numerous photographs and diagrams illustrating the various methods (like front projection) that helped contribute to the illusion of space travel. Detailed analysis of the moon and Jupiter sequences.

260 Westover, Logan. Review of *2001: A Space Odyssey. Films in Review,* 19, no. 5 (May), 308-309.

All of the money spent by MGM for *2001* was wasted. The film is a failure, a "meaningless adolescent muddle" that ends up as a "159 minute bore." *2001* makes no sense at all and makes miraculous aspects of the universe seem uninteresting. Kubrick spent money on film "effectively in only one area, special effects." Film is incompetent in script writing because Kubrick has three stories "going at once, all dangling." Special effects go to waste "because Kubrick himself refused to admit that story is the *sine qua non* of effective film making."

261 Wolf, William. Review of *2001: A Space Odyssey. Cue* (13 April), p. 57.

Kubrick has to move at an ultra-slow pace to create his very special atmosphere in *2001*. "Unable to get the film out of my mind, I wanted a *second* look and found both experiences spellbinding. I believe the unique odyssey will grow in stature on the list of Kubrick's films, as we move towards the 21st century."

262 Youngblood, Gene. "Stanley Kubrick's '2001': A Masterpiece." *Los Angeles Free Press* (19 April), reprinted in *Village Voice* (2 May), p. 44.

Review of Kubrick's film praising the use of special effects and the story. Discusses the use of visual special effects along with music in the film.

1969

263 Alpert, Hollis. "2001: A Space Odyssey," in *Film 68/69*. Edited by Hollis Alpert and Andrew Sarris. New York: Simon and Schuster, pp. 57-60.

Presents Alpert's favorable reactions to *2001: A Space Odyssey,* including the discussions of special effects, color, and the use of classical music in film.

***264** Austen, David. *The Cinema of Stanley Kubrick.* London: Zwemmers.

Cited in *Renaissance of the Film,* edited by Julius Bellone, New York: Collier-Macmillan, 1970, p. 352. Unable to locate a copy of the book.

265 Clarke, Arthur. *2001: een ruimte odyssee.* Utrecht/Antwerpen: A. W. Bruna and Zoon. 190 pp.

Translation of *2001: A Space Odyssey*. In Flemish.

266 Cowie, Peter. Review of *2001: A Space Odyssey,* in *International Film Guide.* Edited by Peter Cowie. New York: A. S. Barnes, pp. 84-85.

Discussion of the outstanding cinematic quality of *2001*. The visual quality of the film helps illuminate the theme of man's subservience to nature.

267 ______. *Seventy Years of Cinema.* New York: A. S. Barnes, p. 222.

Brief discussion of Kubrick's use of camera angles in making film *Paths of Glory*.

268 Delaney, Samuel R. Review of *2001: A Space Odyssey,* in *Best SF: 1968.* Edited by Harry Harrison. New York: G. P. Putnam's Sons, pp. 26-31.

Discusses the use of visual effects in the film and the theme of *2001: A Space Odyssey.*

269 Eisenschitz, Bernard. "La Marge" *Cahiers du Cinema,* no. 209 (February), pp. 56-57.
Analysis of Kubrick's *2001: A Space Odyssey* praising the film for its important advances. In French.

270 Flatto, Elie. "2001: A Space Odyssey: The Eternal Renewal." *Film Comment,* 5, no. 4 (Winter), 6-10.
2001 represents man's eternal quest for spiritual meaning and self-renewal. Man has come to the end of a long journey that began with his inception as a species on earth.

271 Holland, Norman. "*2001*: A Psychosocial Explication." *Hartford Studies in Literature,* 1 (Fall), 20-25.
Examines the theme of *2001: A Space Odyssey* and the dominant use of myth in the film.

272 James, Clive. "2001: Kubrick vs. Clarke." *Cinema* [London], 2 (March), 18-21.
Raises questions about the story line in the film and the combination of Kubrick and Clarke as director and writer. The spirit of the film's story was not the same as Clarke's *The Sentinel.* "Why does Kubrick arrange his film so that Clarke's foremost narrative gift, plausibility of effect, is employed less and less as the film goes forward?" The orchestration of visual effects is important "but above all, there is a level of sympathy that can accept the film as truly great." *See* entries 295, 343.

273 Johnson, William. "Face the Music." *Film Quarterly,* 22, no. 4 (Summer), 3-18.
In a lengthy article about music in film, there is a brief mention (p. 8) of Kubrick's use of classical music in *2001.* Discussion of the Adagio from Kachaturian's *Gayne* ballet and the cinematic use of it in the Jupiter spacecraft scenes of *2001.*

274 Macklin, F. Anthony. "The Comic Sense of 2001." *Film Comment,* 5, no. 4 (Winter), 10-14.
An examination of the tone of *2001* leads one to recognize the fun, the satire, and the wild imagery Kubrick used in the film. "There is a comic sense subjective and often unobtrusive which permeates *2001* and gives it a dimension that must be realized for a full awareness of the richness of the film." Discussion of the comic treatment of men and machines.

275 McKee, Mel. "2001: Out of the Silent Planet." *Sight and Sound,* 38, no. 4 (Autumn), 204-207.
Discusses the similarities between *2001* and a trilogy by C. S. Lewis, *The Ransom Trilogy* (*Out of the Silent Planet, Perelandra,* and *That Hideous Strength*). Points out seeming parallels between the books and the film. "These works are not just a journey of physical discovery and characterization like Homer's but also are journeys of psychic and spiritual discovery. . . . In Kubrick and Clarke's work, with its analogies in Lewis' trilogy and the Christian myth, man can't get to God, God gets to man."

276 Michelson, Annette. "Bodies in Space: Film as Carnal Knowledge." *Artforum,* 6 (February), 54-63.

Stanley Kubrick's *2001: A Space Odyssey* is a paradigm of filmic experience. The emphasis in the film is on phenomenology and epistemology.

277 O'Meara, Robert. Review of *2001: A Space Odyssey. Screen,* 10, no. 1 (January-February), 104-112.

Discusses the unique contributions of Kubrick in *2001: A Space Odyssey.*

278 Rapf, Maurice. "A Talk with Stanley Kubrick." *Action,* 4, no. 1 (January-February), 16-18.

Interview with Kubrick about *2001* and popular reaction to the film. Those who did not respond to *Space Odyssey* were verbally oriented people. It is a visually oriented film. Kubrick talks about the cool reaction of the New York film critics and his decision to tighten up the film by deleting nineteen minutes from the original two hours and forty-one minutes. Discusses the stylistic beauty of *Alexander Nevsky* as "possible one of the most beautiful movies ever made." In *2001* the mood hitting you is the visual imagery. Includes still shots from *2001.*

279 Sarris, Andrew. "Films." *Village Voice,* 14, no. 19 (20 February), 47.

"The critical fallout from *2001* from around the country has not shaken my initial intuitive reaction to the boredom it induced in me." Comments on the renewed interest in the film and the fact that younger people are supposed to like it more than older people.

280 Sineux, Michel. "Echecs et Maths." *Positif,* no. 104 (April), pp. 59-63.

Review of *2001* that analyses various aspects of film, including special effects. Compares the themes of *Dr. Strangelove* and *2001: A Space Odyssey.* Kubrick's achievement is unique and ranks him as one of the outstanding directors of his age along with Roman Polanski. In French.

281 Stover, Leon E. "Apeman, Superman—Or *2001*'s Answer to the World's Riddle." *Amazing Stories* (March), 137-141.

Analysis of the theme of good and evil in the universe and the way in which this is presented in Kubrick's film *2001: A Space Odyssey.*

282 Trumbull, Douglas. "The Slit-Scan Process as Used in *2001: A Space Odyssey* and Beyond." *American Cinematographer,* 50, no. 10 (October), 998-1005.

Details explanation of an exciting new light in space technique for filming in the space age. Discusses Kubrick's suggestion for the process and explains how the psychedelic space ride effect was filmed. Discusses the principles of animated streak photography as a method of producing and exposing a controlled image movement onto motion picture film one frame at a time. Contains photographs from *2001: A Space Odyssey.*

283 Walter, Renaud. "Entretien avec Stanely Kubrick." *Positif,* no. 100 (December-January), pp. 19-39.

Extensive interview with Kubrick dealing with his films from *Fear and Desire* to his work on *A Clockwork Orange*. The main emphasis is on the technique of *Dr. Strangelove* and *2001: A Space Odyssey*. Kubrick discusses his work with film actors Peter Sellers, Kirk Douglas, and Sterling Hayden. Presents insights into Kubrick's film career and his development as a director. In French.

1970

284 Agel, Jerome. *The Making of Kubrick's 2001.* New York: New American Library, 367 pp.

Presents a detailed analysis of every aspect of the production of Kubrick's *2001: A Space Odyssey*. Includes the complete text of *The Sentinel*, by Arthur Clarke, and reprints of many of the early reviews of the film. Analyzes the various technical crafts used in filming and shows how some of the scenes were created. Also contains the text of the *Playboy* interview with Kubrick. *See* entry 248. Contains a complete list of credits for *2001: A Space Odyssey* and several new essays not printed before. Includes many still photographs from *2001* as well as many photographs showing Kubrick during the production of the film. Offers the most complete information on filming of *2001: A Space Odyssey* and a substantial body of criticism of the film.

285 Baxter, John. *Science Fiction in the Cinema.* New York: A. S. Barnes, *passim.*

Contains an entry on *2001: A Space Odyssey* with credits and plot summary. Also bibliography and filmography.

286 Brustein, Robert. "Out of this World." in *Renaissance of the Film.* Edited by Julius Bellone. London: Collier-Macmillan, pp. 71-78.

See entry 152.

287 Canby, Vincent. "Spaced Out by Stanley." *New York Times* (3 May), Section 2, pp. 1, 21.

Discussion of the controversial reaction to *2001: A Space Odyssey* and what the film really means.

288 Ciment, Michel and Bertrand Tavernier. "Propos de Kirk Douglas." *Positif,* no. 112 (January), pp. 12-18.

Profile of Kirk Douglas during which he discusses his career and his two films with Stanley Kubrick, *Paths of Glory* and *Spartacus.* Brief comments about the importance of *Paths of Glory* in Douglas's career. Discussion of working with Kubrick. In French.

289 Cluny, Michel Claude. *2001: l'Odyssee de l'Espace. Dossiers du Cinema, Film I.* Edited by Jean-Louis Bory and Claude Michel Cluny. Paris: Casterman, 4 pp.

Pamphlet presentation of biography, analysis of *2001: A Space Odyssey,* credits, and synopsis of the film. In French.

290 Dumont, Jean Paul and Jean Monod. *Le Foetus Astral.* Paris: Editions Christian Bourgeois, 197 pp.

A study of *2001: A Space Odyssey* from a structuralist's point of view. Compares the sequences of transformation in the "space ride" of *2001* to the movements in a chess game. The disappearance of piece after piece is similar to

Kubrick's film. Discusses the four major sequences in the film and presents illustrations and diagrams explaining the complex structure of the film. In French.

291 Durgnat, Raymond. *The Crazy Mirror: Hollywood Comedy and the American Image*. New York: Horizon Press, pp. 138, 199, 220.
References to Kubrick's use of comedy in *Dr. Strangelove* and *Lolita*.

292 Freeland, Nat. "Special Effects Expert Doug Trumbull: A Cinematic Peter Max." *Show* (23 July), pp. 44–45.
Discussion of Trumbull's work with Kubrick in making *2001: A Space Odyssey*. Explanation of the process used for the "star gate" sequence in the film.

293 Gelmis, Joseph. *The Film Director as Superstar*. New York: Doubleday, pp. 293-316.
Discussion of *2001*. In this film the process becomes more important than the plot. "It was a film not about space travel: it was space travel." Kubrick traces some of his fascination with the fluid camera back to Max Ophuls. Kubrick's films, with the single exception of the optimistic transfiguration in *2001*, are examples of "bleak skepticism and fatalism."

294 Jacobs, Lewis. *The Movies as Medium*. New York: Farrar, Straus and Giroux, p. 3.
Contains a quotation from Kubrick on the importance of not thinking of the camera too soon in making films.

295 James, Clive. "*2001*: Kubrick vs. Clarke." *Film Society Review*, 5, no. 5 (January), 27-35.
Discusses Kubrick's concern for formal beauty and lack of interest in a strictly narrative science fiction film. Arthur Clarke's contribution to the story *2001* is more concerned with maintaining a thematic and linear continuity in the story line. Contains illustrations from the film. *See* entry 343.

296 Kozloff, Max. "2001." *Film Culture*. 48–49 (Winter-Spring), 53-56.
Review analysis of *2001: A Space Odyssey*. "One senses through it all that something important has happened in the cinema." Discussion of lighting, plot, action, and theme in the film. The worth of the film is not in its narrative elusiveness as much as in the skill of its cinematic equalities, qualities of scale, light, and color. "Everywhere Kubrick has realized his material with such kinesthetic allies that he seems to cast us into a new dimension." Compares the film with Godard's *Alphaville*.

297 Nabokov, Vladimir. *The Annotated Lolita*. Edited by Alfred Appel Jr. New York: McGraw Hill.
Novel version from which Kubrick's film *Lolita* was adapted.

298 Pohl, Frederick. Review of *2001: A Space Odyssey*. *Film Society Review*, 5, no. 6 (February), 23-27.
Analysis of the film and the use of special effects sequences and music in *2001: A Space Odyssey*.

299 Romi, Yvette. "Deux Hommes et Deux Femmes: 4) Kubrick: 2001." *Midi/Minuit Fantastique,* no. 22 (Summer), pp. 72-73.
Interview with Arthur C. Clarke dealing with *2001: A Space Odyssey* and the various meanings in the film. In French.

300 Sragow, Michael. Review of *2001: A Space Odyssey. Film Society Review,* 5, no. 5 (January), 23-26.
Discussion of the film's theme and the various special effects used in depicting space travel.

301 Youngblood, Gene. "The New Nostalgia," in his *Expanded Cinema.* New York: E. P. Dutton, pp. 139-156.
Discussion of the philosophical meanings and the themes suggested in *2001: A Space Odyssey.*

1971

302 Alpert, Hollis. "Milk-Plus and Ultra Violence." *Saturday Review,* 54, no. 52 (25 December), 40-41.
Discussion of *A Clockwork Orange* as a fine adaptation of Burgess's novel. Kubrick builds upon tendencies already existing in our society. "It is doubtful that *any* novel has ever been adapted for the screen as brilliantly as this one." Each scene and shot is seasoned with "touches of satire" and Kubrick makes extensive use of almost every type of camera and sound technique.

303 Canby, Vincent. "*A Clockwork Orange* Dazzles the Senses and Mind." *New York Times* (20 December), p. 44.
Review of *A Clockwork Orange* focusing on the acting of Malcolm McDowell and the wide angle lens photography of Kubrick. "It is brilliant, a tour de force of extraordinary images, music, and words, and feelings, a much more original achievement for commercial films than the Burgess novel is for literature."

304 Cocks, Jay. "Kubrick: Degrees of Madness." *Time,* 98, no. 25 (20 December), 80-85.
Review of *A Clockwork Orange* praising Kubrick as "our most audacious film maker." Presents a biography of Kubrick and a note on his work habits in his home in England. "There is something about it [*A Clockwork Orange*] a little too neat and too cold. The wit is there and the ironic perception: it is funny and frightening, partly because of the world it presents but also because of the dispassionate attitude it adopts toward that world." Calls the film almost "flawless."

305 Cowie, Peter. *A Concise History of the Cinema. Volume 2, Since 1940.* London: A. Zwemmer, pp. 54-55.
Brief survey of Kubrick's films from *Fear and Desire* to *2001: A Space Odyssey.* Credits Kubrick with making "The greatest science fiction film ever made."

306 Crist, Judith. "A Feast, and About Time." *New York* (20 December), p. 90.
Praises *A Clockwork Orange* as an outstanding film and discusses the context of the film.

307 Daniels, Don. "A Skeleton Key to *2001*." *Sight and Sound,* 40, no. 1 (Winter), 28-33.

Argues that it is possible to praise and admire Kubrick's film *2001: A Space Odyssey* apart from the "cult" reaction to him. "The new *Odyssey*'s theme is epic, serious, worthy of its extended development and Kubrick has elevated the melodramatic didacticism of most science fiction to a filmic poetry that justifies its pretension with an Olympian spectacle." The film should be examined in different ways: (1) its visual beauty, (2) the ambivalent attitude toward technology in the film, (3) superterrestrial life and the power of machines theme, (4) the meaning of the monolith, (5) analysis of the film and the nature of HAL. "Kubrick's film is a study of various capacities for consciousness, an attempt to suggest through spectacle the possibilities and limitations of the powers of the mind for perception, intellection, and feeling."

308 Fitzgerald, John E. Review of *A Clockwork Orange. Catholic News* (30 December), p. 4.

Discussion of the film's theme of man being "more than a product of heredity." Instead of enhancing human life, technology in *A Clockwork Orange* annihilates it.

309 Gifford, Denis. *Science Fiction Film.* London: Studio Vista/Dutton Picture Book, pp. 107, 126, 127.

Includes references to *2001: A Space Odyssey* as the modern classic of science fiction, with photographs and a brief summary of the Arthur Clarke story.

310 Hoch, David G. "Mythic Patterns in *2001: A Space Odyssey*." *Journal of Popular Culture,* 4 (Spring), 961-965.

While the film is primarily a visual experience "the narrative pattern as the title indicates follows that of the oldest stories known to mankind and hence invites the kind of interpretation that myth is subject to." *2001* follows the pattern of the monomyth with mankind as its hero. "The *Space Odyssey* is a modern myth which in structure follows the pattern of all myths." Discusses the use of music and visuals in film.

311 Hofsess, John. "Mind's Eye." *Take One,* 3, no. 5 (May-June), 28-29.

Report of a luncheon with Kubrick at his Boreham Wood Studio in England and the six-hour conversation between them. Kubrick dislikes all critics and feels that he has not profited by them at all. It is absurd to see a film once (as a critic does) and feel one knows it. Kubrick makes his films so they can be enjoyed superficially or in depth. In doing this he broadens the spectrum of viewers who can like something in his work. Discussing *A Clockwork Orange,* Kubrick says: "as in a dream, the film demands a suspension of moral judgment," and later "a satirist is someone who has a very skeptical, pessimistic view of human nature but who still has the optimism to make some sort of joke out of it, however brutal that joke might be." Kubrick's films present life as constant struggle between creative and destructive impulses.

312 Houston, Penelope. "Kubrick Country." *Saturday Review,* 54, no. 52 (25 December), 42-44.

Discussion of Kubrick's films and his most recent production of *A Clockwork Orange* at the British MGM studios at Boreham Wood. Interview with

Kubrick about his films and the philosophy of life he presents. Kubrick says: "I have always enjoyed dealing with a slightly surrealistic situation and presenting it in a realistic manner." Discussing the adaptation of novels for film, Kubrick says: "A great narrative is a kind of miracle. It's not something that can be forced. At the same time, I trust that I shall never be tempted to become an alchemist and believe that I can turn lead into gold."

313 Hughes, Robert. "The Decor of Tomorrow's Hell." *Time,* 98, no. 26 (27 December), 59.

Analysis of the use of mise-en-scène in the film, *A Clockwork Orange.* The film is a brilliant cultural satire on the world of tomorrow. "No movie in the last decade (perhaps in the history of film) has made such exquisitely chilling predictions about the future role of cultural artifacts: paintings, buildings, sculptures, music,–in society or extrapolated them from so undeceived a view of our present culture." Analyzes the geography of Kubrick's landscape. Art has no ethical purpose in the world of *A Clockwork Orange.*

314 Kriegsman, Alan. "*A Clockwork Orange.*" *Filmfacts,* 14. 649-655.

Presents a synopsis of the film and offers the major reviews of *A Clockwork Orange* from newspapers, film journals, and magazines.

315 Kubrick, Stanley. "What Directors are Saying." *Action,* 6, no. 1 (January-February), 30.

Quotation by Kubrick from *The Film Director as Superstar* (*See* entry 293). "A Director is kind of an idea and taste machine."

316 ______. "What Directors are Saying." *Action,* 6, no. 6 (November-December), 23.

Quotation by Kubrick on the subject of editing and creating main titles. Kubrick says that he never worries about main titles.

317 McCarty, Clifford. *Published Screenplays: A Checklist.* Kent, Ohio: The Kent State University Press, p. 100.

Reference to the published screenplay of *2001: A Space Odyssey* by Stanley Kubrick and Arthur Clarke.

318 Pechter, William. *24 Times a Second.* New York: Harper and Row, p. 8.

Reference to Kubrick in a discussion of film development in America.

319 Robinson, W. R. "The Movies are a Revolutionary Moral Force." *Contempora,* 1, no. 6 (April-May), 15.

Review of *2001: A Space Odyssey.*

320 Sarris, Andrew. "Films in Focus." *Village Voice,* 16, no. 52 (30 December), 49-50.

Review of *A Clockwork Orange.* "The film manifests itself on the screen as a painless, bloodless, and ultimately pointless futuristic fantasy." Sees the major difference between book and novel not so much "in narrative line as in the disturbing implication of Kubrick's decor and mise-en-scène." Concludes that "What we have here is simply a pretentious fake. . . . Don't take my word for it. See *A Clockwork Orange* for yourself and suffer the damnation of boredom."

321 Simon, John. *Movies into Film.* New York: The Dial Press, pp. 18-19, 52-53, 311-313.

Reprints of reviews originally published in *New Leader,* including discussions of *Lolita* and *Dr. Strangelove, or How I Learned to Stop Worrying and Love the Bomb.* Also includes a review of *2001: A Space Odyssey,* calling it a "regrettable failure."

322 Verrill, Addison. "London Junkets for Kubrick Fans." *Variety* (22 December), p. 13.

Discusses ways in which Warner Brothers promoted Kubrick's film *A Clockwork Orange.*

323 Walker, Alexander. *Stanley Kubrick Directs.* New York: Harcourt Brace Jovanovich, 272 pp.

Presents the first extended book-length discussion of Kubrick as a director. Analyzes Kubrick's development as a director from his earliest film *Day of the Fight* through *A Clockwork Orange.* Includes an extended interview with Kubrick discussing his films and his intentions as a director. Compares Kubrick's moves as a director to the skillful moves of a chess player. Detailed analysis of *Paths of Glory, Dr. Strangelove, or How I Learned to Stop Worrying and Love the Bomb, 2001: A Space Odyssey, The Killing* and *Killer's Kiss.* Discusses in detail the use of shot composition in Kubrick's films with still photographs from the original films. Traces some of Kubrick's themes in films and relates them to the directors who have most influenced him. Contains whole sections of still photographs from Kubrick's films along with captioned explanations of their importance in the development of theme and plot. Contains filmography with complete credits for all of Kubrick's films from *Day of the Fight* through *2001: A Space Odyssey.* Reviewed in *Sight and Sound,* 41, no. 1 (Winter, 1971-72), 54. *See* entry 355. Expanded edition 1972. *See* entry 403.

324 Weiler, A. H. "*Clockwork Orange* Wins Critics Prize." *New York Times* (29 December), p. 22.

News release on voting of the New York critics award for *A Clockwork Orange* as Best Motion Picture of the Year and the award of Best Director of the Year to Stanley Kubrick. Reference to Kubrick's award for *Dr. Strangelove* in 1964. Kubrick received 38 votes on the second ballot for *A Clockwork Orange.*

1972

325 Abet, A. "Une vision de la relativité." *Cahiers de la Cinémathèque* [Perpignan], 7 (Summer), 21.

Review analysis of *2001: A Space Odyssey.* In French.

326 Anon. "*Detroit News* Submits a Jog to Conscience." *Journal of the Producers Guild of America* [Los Angeles], 14, no. 3 (September) 14, 16.

Presents the arguments of the *Detroit News* against printing any ads for the film *A Clockwork Orange* because of its X rating and pornographic content.

327 Anon. "A Clockwork Orange." *Playboy* (January), 205.

Photographic essay with color still shots from *A Clockwork Orange.*

328 Anon. Review of *A Clockwork Orange. Playboy* (March), p. 36.
Analysis of the film and discussion of raciness in the story. *A Clockwork Orange* should maintain more of the pace of the first half of the film without the boredom of the second half.

329 Austin, Charles M. "Stirring the Guttywuts." *Christian Century,* 89, no. 7 (16 February), 207.
Review analysis of *A Clockwork Orange.* "Kubrick's cry for a sane society goes beyond his own amazing creativity." Discusses the similarities between *A Clockwork Orange* and *2001: A Space Odyssey*; both being essentially visual and auditory experiences. "Here his film art is so well developed that a quick scene, a terse phrase, a twanged nerve convey what for some directors would require an entire characterization . . . this is a beautiful film. Beautiful in the way Fellini films are beautiful, except for Kubrick the grotesque is found not in man's ugliness but in the society which man's ugliness creates."

330 Bangs, Lester. "Welcome to the Future (on 35mm Celluloid, where it belongs)." *Creem,* (March), pp. 35-37.
Analysis of *A Clockwork Orange* as a film that presents a "moral and a chillingly accurate prognostication of where we're headed in the last half of this century."

331 Barr, C. "*Straw Dogs, A Clockwork Orange,* and the Critics." *Screen,* 13, no. 2 (Summer), 17-31.
A comparison of the use of violence in the films *A Clockwork Orange* and *Straw Dogs.* Discusses the nature of the reaction of the critics to this violence and how both films have been received.

332 Benayoun, Robert. "Stanley Kubrick le libertin (Sur *A Clockwork Orange*)." *Positif,* no. 139 (June), pp. 34-44.
Discussion review of Kubrick's treatment of violence in *A Clockwork Orange.* Presents an analysis of Alex and his treatment at the hands of society. Discussion of the plot of the film and the various critical reactions to the film's allegedly excessive use of violence. In French.

333 Bourget, Jean-Loup. "Les avatars du cercle." *Positif,* no. 136 (March), pp. 22-27.
Discusses the use of a circular plotting in *A Clockwork Orange.* Analyzes the five different aspects of the plot: (1) sequences at the milk bar, (2) destruction at Alex's home, (3) Alex in his parents' apartment, (4) the battle of Alex and Dim, (5) the return of Alex after prison. Draws a comparison between *A Clockwork Orange* and Kubrick's earlier films like *The Killing, Spartacus,* and *2001: A Space Odyssey.* Discussion of the differences between Kubrick's film and Burgess's book. In French.

334 Boyers, Robert. "Kubrick's *A Clockwork Orange*: Some Observations." *Film Heritage,* 7, no. 4 (Summer), 1-6.
Comparison of Kubrick's film and Burgess's novel. "I think we shall do better to describe Kubrick's vision less definitely, to speak of it more as a series of tensions than as something rigorous and final. . . . In this respect the film serves the conventional purposes of art and of human beings who find themselves living through a largely intolerable period: it shows us what we need to know

and allows us yet to go home marveling at the wizardry of the spectacle without dwelling to excess on ills about which little can be done." Kubrick's vision is "not of the permanently irremediable, like tragedy, but of the temporarily inevitable . . ." What is so striking about this vision, though, is that "where it is most deeply felt, it is both moral and religious." Examines the "Home sequence" as the central focus in the story.

335 Burgess, Anthony. "Clockwork Marmalade." *Listener,* 87, no. 2238 (17 February), 197-199.

Presents Burgess's response to attacks on the film by critics who deplore the violence in the book and the film. Burgess explains the origin of his own book and the term "clockwork orange" as a term he heard originally from an eighty-year-old Cockney man. Burgess is concerned that people are taking his book and Kubrick's films as: "a gratuitous indulgence in violence which turns an intended homiletic work into a pornographic one." Attempts to clarify the meaning of film and story. Concludes that: "It looks as though I [Burgess] must go through life as the fountain and origin of a great film, and as a man who has to insist against all opposition, that he is the most unviolent creature alive. Just like Stanley Kubrick."

336 ______. "Sur *A Clockwork Orange.*" *Positif,* no. 139 (June), pp. 32-33. Translated by Jeannine Cement.

Presents Burgess's letter to the *Los Angeles Times* drawing out the distinctions between his book and Stanley Kubrick's film of the same name. He does not defend or attack Kubrick for what he includes or fails to include in his version of the film. In French.

337 ______. "Juice From a Clockwork Orange." *Rolling Stone* (8 June), pp. 52-53.

Defends the film version of his novel and the ideas on violence in both book and film. Presents discussion of the last chapter of the book *A Clockwork Orange* (English edition) which was not used by Kubrick in the film adaptation.

338 Burgess, Jackson. Review of *A Clockwork Orange. Film Quarterly,* 25, no. 3 (Spring), 33-36.

Finds problems in Kubrick's film. What the film really boils down to is forty minutes of Alex torturing people and forty minutes of Alex being tortured. Alex is somewhat of a comic hero operating in the almost "dreamlike quality" of Kubrick's films sets. "Kubrick has long shown a horrified fascination with dehumanization: the vision of machinelike people, or manlike machines which mock our humanity. . . . *Clockwork Orange* simply pulls the levels of fear which is a different thing." Discusses the brainwashing technique of the film. "It's a spook show. If it weren't the work of a serious artist, and if it weren't so painful, it would be trivial." The film manipulates the "most visceral level of feeling."

339 Burke, Tom. "Malcolm McDowell: The Liberals, They Hate *Clockwork.*" *New York Times* (30 January), p. 13.

Interview with Malcolm McDowell, star of Kubrick's film *A Clockwork Orange,* in which he talks about making the film and Kubrick's ideas for many of the sequences in the film, including the use of "Singing in the Rain" as the closing song in the film. Describes Kubrick's genius as "his ability to somehow create the atmosphere that you as an actor need to do the performances he wants. Without words!"

340 Canby, Vincent. "Orange, Disorienting, but Human Comedy." *New York Times* (9 January), Section 2, p. 1.

Review analysis of *A Clockwork Orange* focusing on the visual effects in the film and the use of the song "Singing in the Rain" to add an ironic dimension to the theme. Praises the film and Kubrick's abilities as a director.

341 Ciment, Michel. "Entretien avec Stanley Kubrick (Sur "A Clockwork Orange)." *Positif,* no. 139 (June), pp. 23-31.

Interview with Kubrick about his newest film *A Clockwork Orange* and the changes that he made from the Burgess book. Kubrick says the film speaks about the choices man has between good and evil. Examines various scenes in the early part of the film, including the milk bar and "home" sequences. The milk bar idea was Kubrick's own. He selected music after filming a particular scene. Discussion of the ending of the film. In French.

342 ______. "The Odyssey of Stanley Kubrick: Part 3: Toward the Infinite—*2001*," in *Focus on the Science Fiction Film.* Edited by William Johnson. Englewood Cliff,s New Jersey: Prentice-Hall, pp. 134-141.

See entry 218.

343 Clarke, Arthur C. *The Lost Worlds of 2001.* New York: New American Library, 240 pp., 40 illustrations.

Presents the texts of *2001: A Space Odyssey* and *The Sentinel,* and the different versions of the film as it evolved.

344 Cluny, C. M. "Orange Mécanique. Un pessimisme éblouissant." *Cinema* [Paris], 166 (May), 128-130.

Review of *A Clockwork Orange* with illustrations from the film. In French.

345 Colaciello, R. "A Clockwork Orange." *Inter/View,* 19 (February), 39.

Review analysis of *A Clockwork Orange.* In Italian.

346 Connelly, Wayne. "Optimism in Burgess's *A Clockwork Orange*." *Extrapolation,* 14. 25-29.

Discussion of Anthony Burgess's novel *A Clockwork Orange* and the different endings in the American and English editions of the novel. Brief mention of the film adaptation of Stanley Kubrick.

347 Corbucci, G. "Arancia Meccanica." *Cinema Nuovo,* 21, no. 219 (September-October), 377-378.

Review of Kubrick's film *A Clockwork Orange.* In Italian.

348 Costello, Donald. "From Counter-Culture to Anti-Culture." *Commonweal,* 96, no. 16 (14 July), 383-386.

Comparative study of the films *A Clockwork Orange, Woodstock,* and *Easy Rider* as cultural events in themselves. "Stanley Kubrick takes the values of *Woodstock,* the prophetic warning of *Easy Rider,* and reduces them to the ashes of the future."

349 Cullinan, John. "Anthony Burgess's *A Clockwork Orange*: Two Versions." *English Language Notes,* 9, no. 4 (June), 287-292.

Discusses the distinct difference between the English version of *A Clockwork Orange* and the American versions published by Norton and Ballantine Books. Both of the American editions omit the 21st chapter as it appears in the original by Anthony Burgess. When Stanley Kubrick made the film version, he based it on the shortened American version that did not include Chapter 21. Questions the effectiveness of the novel in each version.

350 Daniels, Don. "A Clockwork Orange." *Sight and Sound,* 42, no. 1 (Winter), 44-46.

Review analysis of the film. "Kubrick's adaptation of Burgess's novel makes us privy to Alex's vision to show us its seductive beauty while carefully keeping all hands clean." Compares the development of theme in both novel and film. "Kubrick's film refashions the materials of the novel, and the rigour of the reworking gives the film a poetic compression and resonance that the novel lacks despite its disturbing narrator, intricate structure, and brilliant language."

351 Denby, David. "Pop Nihilism at the Movies." *Atlantic,* 229, no. 3 (March), 100-104.

Analysis of Kubrick's film *A Clockwork Orange.* "A powerful part of the mass media has settled on this movie as the best our cinema has to offer; and given the subject of *A Clockwork Orange,* the ironic triumph of a sadistic young thug—the choice is a landmark in the history of American mass culture." Discusses the source of Kubrick's greatness in the Burgess novel of the same title. Kubrick's last three films have been marked by a progressive reduction of human feeling and solidarity. *A Clockwork Orange* "simply gives rise to feelings of repulsion and dismay." Discussion of Kubrick's manipulation of his audience in the film and the decadence and nihilism of the film.

352 Dimeo, Steven. "The Ticking of an Orange." *Riverside Quarterly,* 5, no. 4 (Fall), 318-321.

Analysis of how Kubrick faithfully adapted Burgess's novel for the screen. Discusses various sequences in the film *A Clockwork Orange.*

353 Faltysova, H. "Interview with Stanley Kubrick." *Filma Doba,* 18, no. 8 (August), 442-444.

Discussion with Kubrick about the film *A Clockwork Orange.* Contains illustrations from the film. In Czech.

354 Fisher, J. "Too Bad Lois Lane: The End of Sex in '2001'." *Film Journal,* 2, no. 1 (September), 65.

Suggests that in the world of *2001: A Space Odyssey* sex is actually alien to the needs of the humans of the future.

355 French, Philip. "Review of *Stanley Kubrick Directs.*" *Sight and Sound,* 41, no. 1 (Winter), 54.

Review of Alexander Walker's book *Stanley Kubrick Directs.* Cites two problems in Walker's book: (1) it lacks an historical placement of Kubrick in the development of film directors, (2) it lacks a bibliography. Great value in the book is the account of the "relationship between Kubrick's mind and its cinematic expression." *See* entry 323.

356 Geber, N. and H. and T. Manns. "En Urvershapelsien." *Chaplin,* 14, no. 3, (114), 100-105.

Discussion of Kubrick's view of human nature with specific reference to *A Clockwork Orange.* In Danish.

357 Geduld, Harry M. "Return to Méliès: Reflections on the Science Fiction Film," in *Focus on the Science Fiction Film.* Edited by William Johnson. Englewood Cliffs, New Jersey: Prentice-Hall, pp. 142-147.

See entry 230.

358 Gow, Gordon. Review of *A Clockwork Orange. Films and Filming,* 18, no. 5 (February), 43-49.

Analysis of *A Clockwork Orange.*

359 Gress, E. "Kosmorama Essay. Apropos Virkeligheden." *Kosmorama,* 19, no. 111 (October), 28-31.

Discusses the new sense of realism in Western cinema as represented by *A Clockwork Orange, Carnal Knowledge, Catch-22,* and *Sunday, Bloody Sunday.* Analyzes Kubrick's film in this context. In Danish.

360 Gumenik, Arthur. "*A Clockwork Orange*: Novel into Film." *Film Heritage,* 7, no. 4 (Summer), 7-18, 28.

Discussion of Kubrick's adaptation of the novel. "Turning Alex into a Machiavellian is Kubrick's ultimate sin," according to Gumenik. The film differs from the novel in showing the effect of treatment on Alex. "Kubrick makes Alex's victims far more repulsive than Burgess's. . . . Kubrick greatly increases the importance of the libido. To a large degree Kubrick has Alex's energy emanate from between his legs." The major fault lies in undercutting Alex's awareness and his role as a Christ figure. Discusses the repetition of various pieces of classical music during scenes of violence and rape.

361 Hart, Henry. Review of *A Clockwork Orange. Films in Review,* 23, no. 1 (January), 51.

Negative review of *A Clockwork Orange.* Refers to the film as an evil motion picture. "The way Kubrick shot and edited all this makes it obvious he is truckling to today's alienated young, and promotes the kind of nihilism that has political purposes, not all of which the young perceive." The use of music in *A Clockwork Orange* deserves extended analysis but the script is "adolescent."

362 Hyman, Stanley Edgar. "Afterword," in *A Clockwork Orange* by Anthony Burgess. New York: Ballantine Books, 326 pp.

Discussion of the effect of Burgess's book and the treatment of the individual. Refers briefly to Kubrick's film.

363 Johnson, William, ed. *Focus on the Science Fiction Film.* Englewood Cliffs, New Jersey: Prentice-Hall, pp. 126-133, 134-141, 142-147.

Contains several references to *2001: A Space Odyssey* in the development of the science fiction film. Reprints of articles by Lightman, Ciment, and Geduld. *See* entries 218, 230, 243, 342, 357.

364 Kael, Pauline. "The Current Cinema: Stanley Strangelove." *New Yorker,* 48 (1 January), 50-51.

Negative review of *A Clockwork Orange.* Sees the film as a dangerous influence on the audience and questions the motives of Kubrick in the emphasis on violence so obvious in the film. Finds no motivating emotion in the film and is disgusted by the beatings and rapes. "Kubrick tries to work up kicky violent scenes, carefully estranging you from the victims so that you can enjoy the rapes and beatings." Moves to a general discussion of violence in the cinema. Kubrick is appealing to the worst aspects in his audience. Reprinted 1973. *See* entry 428.

365 Kagan, Norman. *The Cinema of Stanley Kubrick.* New York: Holt, Rinehart, and Winston, 204 pp.

Presents full-length chapter studies of each of Kubrick's films from *Fear and Desire* to *A Clockwork Orange.* Each chapter contains an insight into the making of the film, a plot summary of the action, and a summary of the major critical reactions to the film. In addition, Kagan traces each of the following themes as they appear in Kubrick's films: (1) the use of an imaginary world, (2) the futility of intelligence and the errors of emotion, (3) the journeys to freedom, (4) the triumph of an obsessional dedicated hero, and (5) homicides and suicides. Analyzes the thematic development of ideas in each of Kubrick's films and relates these to his treatment of mankind in films. Includes a biography of Kubrick and full filmography of all films including *Day of the Fight* and *The Flying Padre.* Partial bibliography included in the notes to each chapter. Contains an extensive selection of still shots from each of the films discussed.

366 Kauffmann, Stanley. "Stanley Kauffman on Films." *New Republic,* 158 (14 January), 22-23.

Review of *A Clockwork Orange.* Finds the film boring and ultimately morally dangerous.

367 Kinder, Marsha, and Beverle Houston. *Close-Up: A Critical Perspective on Film.* New York: Harcourt Brace Jovanovich, pp. 85-92, 93.

Discussion of *2001: A Space Odyssey* as an example of the use of special effects in film making. Explains how the film was made and examines the use of camera angles in the film sequences. Examines the three-part structure of *2001* and shows how it is a combination of old and new techniques. Includes still photos from the film.

368 Kolker, Robert Philip. "Oranges, Dogs, and Ultraviolence." *Journal of Popular Film,* 1, no. 3 (Summer), 159-172.

Discussion of the use of violence in *Straw Dogs* and *A Clockwork Orange. Dirty Harry* is a violent film, *Straw Dogs* and *A Clockwork Orange* are films *about* violence. In *A Clockwork Orange,* "it is difficult to find Kubrick's point. Is he praising destructive activity, over programmed passivity? . . . . This lack of thematic focus is a major flaw of the film, otherwise, whatever he is saying Kubrick is having a great deal of fun saying it." Kubrick's examination of the violent nature of man seems an extension of the idea suggested in the "Dawn of Man" sequence in the film *2001: A Space Odyssey.*

369 Krassner, P., J. Burks, and S. Feldman. "A Clockwork Orange." *Take One,* 3, no. 3 (April), 20-21.

Presents three separate reviews of *A Clockwork Orange.* Krassner writes a comic review of the film, complaining that too many people find the violence in the film bothersome. Burks presents a negative review, saying that the film does little more than catalogue the daily horror of news events. Feldman praises the film and points out that there is nothing in *A Clockwork Orange* that was not fully developed in Kubrick's earlier films.

370 Lee, Walt and Bill Warren. Editors. *Reference Guide to Fantastic Films, Science Fiction, Fantasy and Horror.* Los Angeles: Chelsea House. 3 vols. *passim.*

Refers to Kubrick's films, *Dr. Strangelove* and *2001: A Space Odyssey.*

371 Lefebvre, Jean Pierre. "Les stock-shots du futur présent." *Cinéma Québec,* 1, no. 8 (March-April), 28-30.

Analysis review of *A Clockwork Orange.* All of Kubrick's films, including *Clockwork,* are essentially about the moral order. In French.

372 Lefevre, R. "Orange Mécanique." *Image et Son,* 262 (June-July), 93-95.

Review analysis of *A Clockwork Orange.* In French.

373 Leroux, André. "Une Mystification." *Cinéma Québec,* 8 (March-April), 31-33.

Analysis of the structure of *A Clockwork Orange* as a film. Considers the two different parts of the film: Alex and society, and Alex after prison. In French.

374 Lightman, Herb A. "Filming 2001: A Space Odyssey," in *Focus on the Science Fiction Film.* Edited by William Johnson. Englewood Cliffs, New Jersey: Prentice-Hall, pp. 126-133.

See entries 243, 363.

375 McGregor, Craig. "Nice Boy from the Bronx?" *New York Times* (30 January), Section 2, p. 1, 13.

Interview with Kubrick about his latest film *A Clockwork Orange* and the various reactions to it. Kubrick feels he is satirizing both man and society in the film: "Man isn't a noble savage, he's an ignoble savage. . . . I'm interested in the brutal and violent nature of man." Kubrick gives his feelings about *A Clockwork Orange*: "I'm very pleased with *Clockwork Orange.* I think it is the most skillful movie I have ever made. I can see almost nothing wrong with it." Kubrick arrived at this pessimistic view of man by "observation knowing what has happened in the world seeing the people around me." Kubrick's concept of man as essentially evil is straight Manichean, one of the most perverse yet persistent of Christian heresies. Contains a cartoon drawing of Kubrick.

376 Martin, M. "Orange méchanique." *Ecran,* 6 (June), 58-59.

Review analysis of *A Clockwork Orange* with photographs from the film. In French.

377 Mengershausen, J. Von. "Uhrwerk Orange." *Filmkritik,* 16, no. 6 (June), 322-323.

Review analysis of *A Clockwork Orange.* In German.

378 Millar, Gavin. "Treatment and Ill Treatment." *Listener,* 87, no. 2234 (20 January), 93, 95.

Describes Burgess's book as a one-idea book and therefore Kubrick has had to push hard to make *A Clockwork Orange* into the absorbing film that it is here. Kubrick has done an outstanding job in set design and the creation of a world in film that is harshly realistic. Describes some of Kubrick's techniques in film.

379 O'Konor, L. "Hjarnans Mekanik, Valdet och den Fria Viljan." *Filmrutan,* 15, no. 2 (1972), 54-55.
An analysis of *A Clockwork Orange.* In Swedish.

380 Oms, M. "L'homme est encore à vivre!" *Cahiers de la Cinémathèque* [Perpignan], 7, (Summer), 22-23.
A review analysis of *2001: A Space Odyssey.* In French.

381 Pechter, William. "Peckinpah and Kubrick: Fire and Ice." *Commentary,* 33, no. 3 (March), 79-82.
Negative review of *A Clockwork Orange.* Argues that *A Clockwork Orange* "only marks the further progress of Stanley Kubrick's art into that of interior decoration." Kubrick's best film was *The Killing* but in *Clockwork Orange* there is no feeling at all, just a desire to be photogenic. Compares Kubrick and Peckinpah (*Straw Dogs*) as similar in the treatment of violence in films.

382 Phillips, Gene. "Kubrick." *Film Comment,* 7, no. 4 (Winter), 30-35.
Interview with Kubrick containing a biography and filmography. Discusses the independent philosophy of Kubrick as a director. Kubrick analyzes the role of the director in making a film. Considers the background of *A Clockwork Orange* and why Kubrick was interested in making a film of Burgess's novel. Includes still photographs from each of Kubrick's films through *A Clockwork Orange.*

383 Rice, Susan. "Stanley Klockwork's Cubrick Orange." *Media and Methods* (March), pp. 39-43.
Analysis of *A Clockwork Orange* and the question of adaptation of Burgess's novel. Considers the film version successful and examines the book and film versions.

384 Ricks, Christopher. "Horror Show." *New York Review of Books* (6 April), pp. 28-31.
Negative review of Kubrick's *A Clockwork Orange.* Praises Burgess's novel but finds too much removed in the film version by Kubrick.

385 Riley, Clayton. "Or, a Dangerous, Criminally Irresponsible Horror Show." *New York Times* (9 January), Section 2, p. 1.
Negative review of *A Clockwork Orange.* "The film is finally a monumental bore, a fitful parade of those technical bonbons that characterize our television commercials . . . a menage à trois." The film deals with perverse thrills and "in the name of free will, all self expression becomes highly valued—even the freedom to commit atrocities." Charges Kubrick with being "both criminally irresponsible and stupidly naive" in making *A Clockwork Orange.* As a hero Alex is a "one dimensional cretin."

386 Robinson, William R. and Mary McDermott. "*2001* and the Literary Sensibility." *Georgia Review,* 26, no. 1 (Spring), 21-37.
Discussion of the visual experience of viewing *2001: A Space Odyssey.* "What puzzles us—and is the metaphysical issue of our time—is how the physical senses can transcend themselves, how the 'physical' can metamorphose into another

life beyond the 'physical.' That is the mysterious creative problem Kubrick addresses himself to and works out in '2001' . . ." Kubrick's story is a new one that looks beyond exhausted verbal sources and values. "It takes as its province purely visual relations, connections too subtle for verbal articulation."

387 Sadoul, Georges. *Dictionary of Films.* Translated, edited and updated by Peter Morris. Berkeley and Los Angeles: Univeristy of California Press, pp. 87-88, 278, 386-87.

Includes summaries and credits for Kubrick's films *Paths of Glory, Dr. Strangelove, Or How I Learned To Stop Worrying and Love the Bomb,* and *2001: A Space Odyssey.* Also includes a brief analysis of critical reaction to the films and comments by Kubrick on the films.

388 Samuel, Charles Thomas. "The context of *A Clockwork Orange.*" *American Scholar,* 41, no. 3 (Summer), 439-443.

Study of Kubrick's career as a film maker and his success with *A Clockwork Orange.* "Nevertheless, flawed as Kubrick's first films are, they clearly establish him as more than an entertainer willing to adorn any project offered him with the standard quality of kinetic thrills. . . ." Sets Kubrick's work within the context of other American film makers. Kubrick's fascination with man reminds us that he is a "master visualizer" and that his latest film (*A Clockwork Orange*) is "sensational in both senses of the term: 'outstanding' and also a work dependent on 'exaggerated or lurid details.'" Sees Kubrick's best film as *Dr. Strangelove, Or I How I Learned to Stop Worrying and Love the Bomb.*

389 Schepelern, P. "A Clockwork Orange." *Kosmorama,* 18, no. 109 (June), 233-234.

Review analysis of *A Clockwork Orange.* In Danish.

390 Shickel, Richard. "Future Shock and Family Affairs." *Life* (4 February), p. 14.

Review of *A Clockwork Orange.* Kubrick fails to translate Burgess's book to the screen. "It is a viciously rigged game. We are never for a moment allowed even a fleeting suggestion of sympathy for anyone else, never permitted to glimpse any other character of personal magnetism, wit or sexual attractiveness comparable to Alex's." Discusses some of the changes between book and film.

391 Shrader, Paul. "Notes on Film Noir." *Film Comment,* 8 (Spring), *passim.*

Brief references to examples of *film noir* in works of Stanley Kubrick: *Fear and Desire* and *Killer's Kiss.*

392 Silber, Irwin. "*A Clockwork Orange.*" *Guardian* (5 January), pp. 13-14.

Marxist analysis of *A Clockwork Orange.* Finds the film lacking in a number of areas. Calls into question the decaying system in the film: "When such art consciously addresses itself, however, to social questions, then the lack of a revolutionary world view inevitably cripples both its political and aesthetic worth."

393 Solomon, Stanley J. *The Film Idea.* New York: Harcourt Brace Jovanovich, pp. 55, 77, 210, 232, 240.

Brief references to Kubrick and his contributions as a film director. Includes photographs from *2001: A Space Odyssey.*

394 Steinbrunner, Chris and Burt Goldblatt. *Cinema of the Fantastic.* New York: Saturday Review Press, p. 282.

Brief discussion of the film *2001: A Space Odyssey* and Kubrick's contribution to the science fiction film.

395 Strick, Phillip. "Kubrick's Horrorshow." *Sight and Sound,* 41, no. 1 (Winter), 44-46.

Positive review of Kubrick's *A Clockwork Orange,* comparing the film to the novel and pointing out Kubrick's additions. Considers each of the following topics (1) the beginning and ending of the film, (2) the acting (3) the technical shots in the film, (4) the action in the film itself, the language in the film. Compares *A Clockwork Orange* with Kubrick's earlier film *2001: A Space Odyssey* in its innovative use of music. "At the centre of Kubrick's films is an endurance test and *A Clockwork Orange* continues the pattern." Praises the use of music, hand held cameras, and the general quality of outstanding acting that is at the heart of most of Kubrick's other films. Relates *Clockwork Orange* to earlier Kubrick films in theme, technique, and achievement. Singles out the superb acting of Malcolm McDowell and Patrick Magee. "Kubrick justly deserves his reputation as the cinema's greatest perfectionist."

396 ______ and Penelope Houston. "Interview with Stanley Kubrick." *Sight and Sound,* 41, no. 2 (Spring), 62-66.

Discussion with Kubrick about his newest film, *A Clockwork Orange* and his development as a film maker. Considers several topics including (1) the importance of editing, (2) acting, (3) camera techniques, (4) shot selection, (5) use of music in his films. Kubrick compares Alex with Richard III and discusses the importance of choice for free will. Comments by Kubrick on the film: "The danger of everything that you do in a film is that it may not work, it may be boring, or bland, or stupid." And "the thing film does best is to use pictures with music and I think these are the moments you remember." Concludes with Kubrick's reaction to the critics of *A Clockwork Orange.*

397 Talvat, H. "*2001,* une odyssée de l'espace." *Cahiers de la Cinémathèque,* 7 (Summer), 17-20.

Review analysis of *2001: A Space Odyssey.* In French.

398 Tournes, A. "Orange mécanique." *Jeune Cinéma,* 63 (May-June), 39-40.

Review of *A Clockwork Orange* with photographs from the film. In French.

399 Versens, Pierre. *Encyclopédie de l'utopie, des voyages extraordinaries, et de la science fiction.* Lausanne: Editions L'Age d'Homme, *passim.*

References to *2001: A Space Odyssey.* In French.

400 Verstappen, Wim. "Kubrick i.v. m. A Clockwork Orange." *Skoop,* 8, no. 2, 4-6.

Review of *A Clockwork Orange* and refutation of the glorifying reviews written about the film. In Dutch.

401 Vitoux, Frederic, "Un film daté." *Positif,* no. 143 (October), pp. 73-75.

Analysis of the timeless value of Kubrick's film *Paths of Glory.* Although the film is dated and does have flaws, its qualities stand out above its defects. Examines the ending of the film and suggests that it shows the optimism of

Kubrick much as *A Clockwork Orange* reflects his pessimism. The film is more interesting today, now that we can see the direction of Kubrick's later work in cinema. In French.

402 V[rhovec], B. "2001: Odiseja v Vesolju." *Ekran,* 10, no. 92-93 (1972), 135-136.

Review of *2001: A Space Odyssey.* In Serbo-Croatian.

403 Walker, Alexander. *Stanley Kubrick Directs.* Expanded edition. New York: Harcourt Brace Jovanovich, 304 pp.

Includes an expanded discussion of *A Clockwork Orange,* pp. 268-299. Does not include chapter-length discussions of *Lolita* and *Spartacus.* Includes biography, filmography, and numerous still photos from Kubrick's films. *See* entry 323.

404 Walker, Beverly. "From Novel to Film: Kubrick's *A Clockwork Orange.*" *Women and Film,* 2. 4+.

Analysis of Kubrick's adaptation of Burgess's novel and the treatment of women in both novel and film.

405 Walz, Eugene P. "Dr. Strangelove, Or How I Learned To Stop Worrying and Love the Bomb," in *Frames of Reference.* Edited by Eugene Walz, John Harrington, and Vincent DiMarco. Dubuque, Iowa: Kendall-Hunt Publishing, pp. 69-81.

Analysis of the film and survey of the critical reaction to *Dr. Strangelove.* Includes discussion of the visual and verbal satire in the film and the various special effects techniques used in filming. Also includes a series of questions for discussion about the film and the wide diversity of critical response to it. Contains credits for *Dr. Strangelove* and listing of Kubrick's other films.

406 Weinraub, Bernard. "Kubrick Tells What Makes *Clockwork Orange* Tick." New York Times (4 January), p. 26.

Review analysis of *A Clockwork Orange.* Discusses the various levels of understanding in the film, including political, psychological, sociological, and symbolic. Discusses Kubrick's lifestyle in his mansion at Boreham Wood, outside of London. Concludes "as an artist Mr. Kubrick has a point of view that is undeniably bleak." Kubrick discusses his early life growing up in New York and attending the RKO Fordham theater.

407 Westerbeck, Colin L. Jr. Review of *A Clockwork Orange. Commonweal,* 95, no. 15 (14 January), 351-352.

Discusses the treatment of women in *A Clockwork Orange* and *Lolita.* Compares the film with Kubrick's earler work in *Dr. Strangelove* and *2001: A Space Odyssey.* These earlier films represent Kubrick's best effort.

408 Willis, Donald C. *Horror and Science Fiction Films: A Checklist.* Metuchen, New Jersey: Scarecrow Press, pp. 134-135, 495.

References to Kubrick's films *Dr. Strangelove, Or How I Learned to Stop Worrying and Love the Bomb,* and *2001: A Space Odyssey.* Includes cast and credits for each film.

409 Zimmerman, Paul D. "Kubrick's Brilliant Vision." *Newsweek,* 79, no. 1 (3 January), 28-33.

Discusses the use of unconventional techniques in making *A Clockwork Orange.* "Stanley Kubrick's unique contribution to contemporary film is this capacity to tackle essential and awesome questions that intimidate film makers of lesser nerve and intellect." Includes biography of Kubrick and analysis of Kubrick's other films. Examines how Kubrick "has grown into an artist with a deep concern for the fate of a species increasingly caught between the sweet orange of humanity and the cold clockwork of technology." *A Clockwork Orange* presents an "ironic galvanizing vision of those aspects of modern life that frighten us all." Includes Kubrick's comments to his earlier producer, James Harris: "If there's some shortcoming in a film that was brought about by your failure to face a problem—you didn't want to hurt somebody's feelings or you wanted to avoid conflict—it's still your film to live with the rest of your life."

1973

410 Anon. "The Refiner's Fire." *Christianity Today* (6 July), pp. 20-21.

Negative review of Kubrick's *A Clockwork Orange.* Concludes that the implication of the film is "everyone is corrupt; one has only to choose his corruption."

411 Anon. "Burgess, Originator of 'Clockwork' says, 'Let Kubrick Defend Himself.'" *Variety,* 272, no. 2 (22 August), 2, 40.

Burgess talks about the film and his admiration for Kubrick. He refuses to take the blame for what people are saying about the filmed version of the novel and insists that Kubrick made the film and let him take any blame for it. Cites a teenage attack in London that may have been inspired by the film.

412 Appel, Alfred Jr. "Nabokov's Dark Cinema: A Diptych." *Triquarterly* (Spring), pp. 267-273.

Brief discussion of the adaptation of Nabokov's novel by Kubrick. Analysis of some of the scenes that Kubrick retained in the film.

413 ______. "The Eyehole of Knowledge: Voyeuristic Games in Film and Literature." *Film Comment,* 9, no. 3 (May-June), 20-26.

Discussion of the original screenplay for *Lolita* written by Nabokov. This screenplay would have resulted in a seven-hour film. Kubrick had Nabokov rewrite a shorter version of the screenplay and then used only about 20 percent of this. Praises the acting of James Mason and Peter Sellers in the film by Kubrick. Compares the book and film versions.

414 Casty, Alan. *Development of the Film: An Interpretative History.* New York: Harcourt Brace Jovanovich, pp. 315-316.

Discussion of the treatment of violence in Kubrick and Peckinpah. Includes an analysis of *A Clockwork Orange.*

415 Ciglic, M. "Mechanicna Oranza." *Ekran,* 11, no. 104/105, pp. 158-167.

Review analysis of *A Clockwork Orange.* In Serbo-Croatian.

416 Codelli, Lorenzo. "Review of the *Lost Worlds of 2001.*" *Positif,* no. 148 (March), pp. 85-86.

Review of Arthur Clarke's book *The Lost Worlds of 2001,* dealing with the making of the Kubrick film. Kubrick fans will particularly enjoy the several passages from Clarke's journal talking about various aspects of the production of *2001: A Space Odyssey.* Clarke's book contains the script from the film and the original story written by Kubrick and Clarke. Detailed discussion in Clarke's book of the minute care that went into making the film. In French.

417 Comuzio, E. "Ludwig e gli Altri." *Cineforum,* 13, no. 119 (January), 75-78.
Discussion of the soundtrack of *A Clockwork Orange* and Kubrick's use of classical music. In Italian.

418 Cullinan, John. "Anthony Burgess: Interview." *Paris Review* (Spring), pp. 119-163.
Discussion with Burgess about the last chapter missing from the American version of *A Clockwork Orange* and how Kubrick obtained the films rights for Burgess's novel.

419 Denby, David. "Has Film Violence Gone Too Far?", in *Film72/73: An Anthology by the National Society of Film Critics.* Edited by David Denby. Indianapolis: Bobbs-Merrill, pp. 121-124.
Discussion of the treatment of violence in a number of the more popular films, including Stanley Kubrick's *A Clockwork Orange.*

420 Devries, Daniel. *The Films of Stanley Kubrick.* Grand Rapids, Michigan: William B. Eerdmans Publishing, 75 pp.
Contains summary and discussion of all of Kubrick's films from *Fear and Desire* through *A Clockwork Orange.* Discusses Kubrick's films as visual works of art as well as works that deal with ideas. The world of Kubrick's films is not a pleasant place to be. Many of his films are marked by a belief in the badness of mankind. Kubrick seems to be on a downhill trend with his latest film *A Clockwork Orange.* He must rid himself of the bad habits in his present film in order to regain his former greatness. His best films are *Paths of Glory, Dr. Strangelove, Or How I Learned To Stop Worrying and Love the Bomb,* and *2001: A Space Odyssey.* Presents a brief biography of Kubrick and a limited study of his earliest films *Fear and Desire* and *Killer's Kiss.* Contains brief bibliography and filmography on Kubrick.

421 Frezzato, A. "Reproposta della Vita." *Cineforum,* 13, no. 119 (January), 66-74.
Review analysis of *A Clockwork Orange.* In Italian.

422 Gambetti, G. "Due Tipi di Violenza." *Cineforum,* 13, no. 119 (January), 54-65.
Analysis of the linguistic elements in *A Clockwork Orange.* In Italian.

423 Geduld, Carolyn. *Filmguide to 2001: A Space Odyssey.* Bloomington and London: Indiana University Press, 87 pp.
Presents a complete analysis of Kubrick's film and the various aspects associated with the production of the film. This volume includes: biography of Kubrick, plot summary of *2001: A Space Odyssey,* analysis of major critical reactions to the film, production notes about special effects used in the film, placement of *2001: A Space Odyssey* in the context of science fiction films, filmography and an annotated bibliography of articles and books on Kubrick. Also contains complete film credits and production calendar for *2001.*

424 Goshgarian, Gary and Charles O'Neill. "The Future is Not What it Used to Be," in *Order and Diversity: The Craft of Prose.* Edited by Robert B. Parker and Peter L. Sandberg. New York: Wiley, pp. 132-139.

Discusses the process of evolution in *2001: A Space Odyssey* and some of the basic themes in the film that can be traced back to Melies' *A Trip to the Moon:* (1) alien invaders, (2) bastard offspring of the nuclear age, (3) man's creations, and (4) man leaves his own world to face the unknown.

425 Hanjutin, J. "Koshmar t na b Desheto." *Kinoizkustvo,* 28 (September), 50-63.

Analysis of anti-utopian films and Kubrick's *A Clockwork Orange.* In Bulgarian.

426 Hiltunen, E. "Kenelle Kellopeli soi." *Filmhillu,* no. 4, pp. 20-22.

Analysis of *A Clockwork Orange.* In Finnish.

427 Isaac, Neil D. "Unstuck in Time: *Clockwork Orange* and *Slaughterhouse Five.*" *Literature/Film Quarterly,* 1, no. 2 (Spring), 122-131.

Examination of the adaptation of Burgess's novel in Kubrick's film *A Clockwork Orange.* Focuses on the language used in book and film. Kubrick talks about his satirical view as Hobbesian, a cold hard look at humanity through a technology fiction. Kubrick's film "argues the need for peaceful coexistence within each of us and with all of us together."

428 Kael, Pauline. *Deeper Into Movies.* Boston and Toronto: Atlantic Monthly Press, pp. 99, 131, 373, 378, 426.

References to Kubrick's films: *2001: A Space Odyssey* and *A Clockwork Orange.* Reprint of "Stanley Strangelove" pp. 373-378. *See* entry 364.

429 Karkosch, K. "Stanley Kubrick." *Film & Ton Magazin,* 19 (December), 39-42.

Review analysis of *A Clockwork Orange.* In German.

430 McCracken, Samuel. "Novel Into Film; Novelist into Critic: *A Clockwork Orange* . . . Again." *Antioch Review,* 32, no. 3, 427-436.

Reaction to Burgess's comment on the intention of the screenplay of *A Clockwork Orange.* Discusses the distinct difference between the schema of the book and the film regarding such topics as free will and Kubrick's deeper exploration of it. Presents detailed discussion of the screenplay (pp. 434-436) and notes that the minor alterations in plot and characters are very important to understanding both novel and film.

431 Mamber, Stephen. "A Clockwork Orange." *Cinema* [Los Angeles], 7, no. 3 (Winter), 48-57.

Detailed analysis of *A Clockwork Orange* by sequences. In Kubrick's earlier films the pattern of ironic cyclical rebirth has been presented. In *Clockwork Orange,* Kubrick employs a similar theme that is strongly linked to symmetrical relationships on several levels. Discusses the function of parody in the film and surveys the general critical reaction to the film by the critics. Offers a detailed examination of *A Clockwork Orange* in relation to Kubrick's earlier work. Includes a useful bibliography on the film.

432 Marszalek, R. "Help!" *Kino,* 8 (June), 42-49.
Review analysis of *A Clockwork Orange.* In Polish.

433 Mast, Gerald. *The Comic Mind: Comedy and the Movies.* Indianapolis: Bobbs-Merrill, pp. 25, 208, 239, 316-319.
Offers a detailed examination of the different types of comedy in *Dr. Strangelove, Or How I Learned To Stop Worrying and Love the Bomb.* Includes references to the use of games, sight gags, puns, and sexual symbols in *Strangelove.* Point of view in film is critical to Kubrick's success in this dark comedy. "Kubrick's film is a warning to unfreeze us, to (in Bergson's terms) replace the mechanical with flexible life. For Kubrick's farce depicts a mechanical society in which everyone is frozen—perhaps to death." Also includes passing references to Lubitsch and Renoir techniques in Kubrick.

434 Monaco, James. "The Films of Stanley Kubrick." *New School Bulletin* (Summer), pp. 75-76.
Analysis of Kubrick's films and his themes. "Ever since his earliest films, Kubrick's worldview has been informed by the proposition that contemporary alienation is best seen as the result of a dialectical tension between human beings and their inventions." Kubrick's films comprise an important body of work which may be "best described as contemporary anthropology."

435 Phillips, Gene D. "Stanley Kubrick," in *The Movie Makers: Artists in Industry.* Chicago: Nelson-Hall, pp. 114-131.
Analysis of Kubrick's films from *Fear and Desire* through *A Clockwork Orange.* Discusses Kubrick's background as an independent film maker who learned much of the technical aspects of making a film on his own. When he finally made a motion picture for a major studio he was ready to understand all of the aspects related to putting a film together: editing, direction, production, script, casting, and sound. Each of Kubrick's films is summarized along with comments about the production of the film and some of the critical reactions to it. Includes many still photographs from each of the major films, a brief bibliography and filmography.

436 Roffé, A. "La naranja mecanica." *Cine al Dia,* 16 (April), 32-33.
Review of Kubrick's *A Clockwork Orange.* In Spanish.

437 Sar"ivanova, M. "Konfrontatssia-Varshava" *Kiniozkustvo,* 28 (August), 69-75.
Review of *A Clockwork Orange.* In Bulgarian.

438 Sarris, Andrew. *The Primal Screen: Essays on Film and Related Subjects.* New York: Simon and Schuster, pp. 95, 115, 130, 154, 200, 201, 202, 203, 233.
Contains passing references to Kubrick and his films.

439 Schuster, Mel. *Motion Picture Directors: A Bibliography of Magazine and Periodical Articles, 1900-1972.* Metuchen, New Jersey: Scarecrow Press, pp. 226-228.
Contains a reference list of articles about director Stanley Kubrick.

440 Simonelli, G. "Arancia Meccanica." *Cschedario,* no. 62 (February), pp. 53-63.
Critical review of *A Clockwork Orange.* In Italian.

441 Sishel, G. "Intervja med Stanley Kubrick." *Fant VII,* 1, no. 24, 49-53.
Interview with Kubrick about his film *A Clockwork Orange.* In Swedish.

442 Solomon, Stanley J. *The Classic Cinema: Essays in Criticism.* New York: Harcourt Brace Jovanovich, pp. 148, 196.
Brief reference to Kubrick and Welles and the use of music in their films. Includes a reference to the influence of Fritz Lang on Kubrick.

1974

443 Anon. Review of *2001: A Space Odyssey. Cue,* 43, no. 30 (23 September), 28.
Discusses the important contributions of the film to the science fiction film genre.

444 Anon. "A Clockwork Orange." *Cue,* 43, no. 1 (7 January), 39.
Analysis of the violence and special effects in the film.

445 Anon. "2001: A Space Odyssey." *Media Methods,* 11, no. 4 (December), 38.
Review of Kubrick's film and the use of special effects in it.

446 Anon. "Test Revival of '2001' a Smash." *Variety,* 275 (7 August), 5, 22.
Article on the revival of Kubrick's film *2001: A Space Odyssey* at the Cinerama Dome in Hollywood. With the cost of the film at $10,400,000, it has already exceeded $20,347,000 in domestic rentals alone. The film has done better the second time around than anybody at MGM expected.

447 Anon. "*Glory,* 17 Year Old Pacifist Film, May Finally Play French Dates." *Variety,* 276, no. 8 (2 October), 36.
News item about the removal of the censorship ban on Kubrick's film *Paths of Glory* in France. Kubrick insisted on the original version of the film without cuts. The film will be released in a dubbed version for the first time since its completion in 1957. The film will premiere in Paris.

448 Appel, Alfred Jr. *Nabokov's Dark Cinema.* New York: Oxford University Press, *passim.*
References throughout the volume to the collaboration of Kubrick and Nabokov on script of *Lolita.* Includes details on the relationship between the two in writing the screenplay of the novel.

449 Bobker, Lee R. *Elements of Film.* New York: Harcourt Brace Jovanovich, pp. 17, 130, 148, 149-150, 153, 156, 189-192.
Discussion of Kubrick as a director with specific reference to *A Clockwork Orange.* Identifies the characteristic traits of Kubrick's films: (1) intense humanistic interest in broad philosophical questions, (2) carefully planned meticulous scripts, (3) highly imaginative visual design and use of special effects, (4) mobile complex camera work, (5) intelligent acting performances that reflect the director's ability to communicate to his cast, and (6) effective use of many styles of music. Includes photographs from *A Clockwork Orange* and of Kubrick.

450 Bauche, Freddy. *Le Cinéma Américain, 1955-1970.* Lausanne: Editions L'Age D'Homme, pp. 461-466.

Discusses Kubrick as one of the best young American directors. Includes reviews and analysis of *Killer's Kiss, Lolita, Paths of Glory, Spartacus,* and *Dr. Strangelove,* plus Kubrick filmography. In French.

451 Carringer, Robert. "Kubrick's *Dr. Strangelove*: A Guide to Study." *Journal of Aesthetic Education,* 8, no. 1 (January), 43-53.

Presents suggestions for teaching the film in class. Includes: biography of Kubrick, film credits, discussion of major sequences in the film, study questions, and bibliography of materials on *Dr. Strangelove.* Explains that Kubrick's preoccupation in the later films is "with what Jonathan Swift called 'that damned animal man' and his most despicable traits." The point of many Kubrick films is that he takes "a rational position and strings it out to an absurd conclusion."

452 Chin, K. "2001: A Space Odyssey." *Photon,* no. 24, p. 25.

Analysis of the theme of the film and the development of plot interest.

453 Cooper, Duncan. "A Second Look: *Spartacus.*" *Cineaste,* 6, no. 3, 30-31.

Analysis of the distinct differences in approach to the film by Kubrick and Dalton Trumbo. "But whereas Trumbo wanted to emphasize the essentially pacifist, humane and reformist aspects of Spartacus's rebellion, Kubrick wished to portray with stark realism the darker more brutal aspects of the revolt." Since all final decisions were made by the executive producer and star, Kirk Douglas, the film failed to bring together the triumph and tragedy of Spartacus.

454 Deer, Harriet and Irving. "Kubrick and the Structures of Popular Culture." *Journal of Popular Films,* 3, no. 3 (Summer), 233-244.

Analysis of *Paths of Glory, Dr. Strangelove,* and *A Clockwork Orange.* "Stanley Kubrick's major films reveal his search for an unrestricted form through which he can communicate with his audience without coercing them into mistaking his particular structures for reality. Increasingly, he has come to use the popular arts as his central means for expressing that search. He does this by showing us the contradictory meanings and implications of the popular arts, their escapist as well as life asserting implications, the ways in which they reveal the contemporary tendencies to run away from the complex. . . ." Illustrates this by extensive analysis of *A Clockwork Orange.* Concludes that Kubrick "achieves the paradoxical McLuhanesque mystery of transforming his medium, film, a popular art itself, into his message." *A Clockwork Orange* reduces life to two basic impulses: sex and survival.

455 Delrogh, Dennis. "Lolita, the Songs I've Been Making for You." *Village Voice,* 19 (13 June), 99, 104.

The publication of *Lolita: A Screenplay* by Vladimir Nabokov (McGraw-Hill, 1974), has done Kubrick a service because it is a sounder testament to Kubrick's ingenuity than are his screenplays for his films *2001: A Space Odyssey* and *A Clockwork Orange.* "There is a solidarity to the script that the movie lacks." Discusses the various changes that Kubrick made in the screenplay in making the film version of *Lolita.* Somewhere in the middle of the screenplay the story of *Lolita* begins to work.

456 Evans, W. "Violence and Film: The Thesis of Kubrick's *A Clockwork Orange.*" *Velvet Light Trap,* no. 13 (Fall), pp. 11-12.

Analysis of Kubrick's *A Clockwork Orange* and the theme of violent action.

457 Gerlach, John C. and Lana. *A Bibliography of Articles on Film in English, 1946-1973, Arranged by Names and Topics.* New York: Teachers College Press, Columbia University, pp. 154-157.

Contains annotated listings on criticism of Kubrick's films up through *A Clockwork Orange.*

458 Gow, Gordon. "Novel into Film," in *Film Review,* 1974-75. Edited by Maurice Speed. London: W. H. Allen, pp. 33-42.

Analysis of differences between Anthony Burgess's novel *A Clockwork Orange* and Kubrick's film. While Burgess toned down the violence in his novel, Kubrick illustrated it on the screen. It is important to note that the printed version of the film script calls attention to the difference by its title: *Stanley Kubrick's A Clockwork Orange.* Suggests the difference in the language of the novel and the film.

459 Haskell, Molly. *From Reverence to Rape.* New York: Holt, Rinehart, and Winston, pp. 204, 323, 326, 330, 361-362.

Discussion of the treatment of women in Kubrick's films with special attention to *A Clockwork Orange.* Contends that Kubrick dislikes women and his "strongest emotion is a slight aversion to the human race."

460 Helman, A. "Stanley Kubrick, albo Synteza Rudzajow." *Kino,* 9 (December), 61-63.

Analysis of *2001: A Space Odyssey.* In Russian.

461 Hochman, Stanley. *A Library of Film Criticism, American Film Directors, with Filmographies and Index of Critics and Films.* New York: Frederick Ungar, pp. 231-239, 548.

Reference guide to articles about Kubrick's films and reference to his supposed next film *Napoleon.* Includes all of Kubrick's feature length films through *A Clockwork Orange.*

462 Houston, Penelope. "Barry Lyndon." *Sight and Sound,* 43, no. 2 (Spring), 88-89.

Report on the current film now in production in Ireland under Kubrick's direction. The film is called *Barry Lyndon* and is based on a novel by Thackeray entitled *The Luck of Barry Lyndon.* Summarizes the plot of the novel and suggests that Kubrick is exploring the opposite side of the coin from his most recent film *A Clockwork Orange.* "It seemed a little startling when one reads that Kubrick was retreating from the future into a nineteenth century novel about an eighteenth century rogue." Concludes that Kubrick, as usual, knows what he is doing.

463 Hutchinson, Tom. *Horror and Fantasy in the Cinema.* London: Studio Vista, pp. 19, 35, 47, 90, 106, 110, 111, 118, 149, 153.

References to Kubrick's films *A Clockwork Orange, Dr. Strangelove,* and *2001: A Space Odyssey.*

464 Jennings, Robert. "*Playboy* Interview: Anthony Burgess." *Playboy* (September), pp. 69-71.

Discussion of the adaptation of the novel with Anthony Burgess. Burgess expresses some dislike of the results of Kubrick's adaptation.

465 Kagan, Norman. *The War Film.* New York: Pyramid Publications, pp. 140-141.
Analysis of the treatment of war in Kubrick's film *Paths of Glory* and the use of realism in the film. Minor reference to *Dr. Strangelove,* p. 54.

466 Kaminsky, Stuart. *American Film Genres: Approaches to a Critical Theory of Popular Film.* Dayton, Ohio: Pflaum, pp. 63, 76, 87-88.
Brief analysis of the use of lighting techniques in Kubrick's film *The Killing.*

467 MacDowall, D. "2001: A Critique." *Photon,* no. 24, pp. 24-36.
Extensive analysis of the theme of *2001: A Space Odyssey.*

468 Nabokov, Vladimir. *Lolita: A Screenplay.* New York: McGraw-Hill, 213 pp.
This is the original screenplay that Nabokov wrote for Kubrick's film adaptation. According to the "Introduction" by Nabokov, Kubrick used about 20 percent of the material in the film *Lolita.* Presents background information on working with Kubrick and Nabokov's own reaction to the film.

469 Scheugl, Hans. *Sexualität und Neurose im Film: Die Kinomythen von Griffith bis Warhol.* München: Carl Hansen Verlag, pp. 141, 381.
Discussion of the treatment of sexuality in Kubrick's film *A Clockwork Orange.* In German.

470 [Sobolev]. "Apokalipsis po Stenli Kubriku." *Iskusstvo Kino,* no. 9, pp. 145-164.
Analysis of Stanley Kubrick and *A Clockwork Orange* in relation to the general problems of modern times. In Russian.

1975

471 Anon. Review of *Barry Lyndon. Catholic Film Newsletter,* 40, no. 24 (30 December), 112.
Analysis of the film story and the problems of the length of the film.

472 Anon. "Stanley Kubrick's *'Barry Lyndon.'*" *Films and Filming,* 22 (December), 25-28.
Photos and dialogue from Kubrick's new film *Barry Lyndon.* Also includes a brief description of the story and partial film credits.

473 Blesch, E.J. "2001: A Space Odyssey." *Media and Methods,* 12, no. 4 (December), 49.
Discussion of the film and the use of special effects to create an illusion of space.

474 Cameron, Ian. *A Pictorial History of Crime Films.* New York and London: Hamlyn, pp. 32, 115, 128, 135.
Brief analysis of Kubrick's films *Killer's Kiss* and *The Killing* as examples of crime stories.

475 Canby, Vincent. "Kubrick's Latest has Brains and Beauty." *New York Times* (21 December), Section 2, pp. 1, 17.
"*Barry Lyndon* is unlike any other period—or feather—film I can remember

seeing though it has close associations to both *A Clockwork Orange* and *2001*." Film is a "leisurely, serious, witty, inordinately beautiful premium length screen adaptation."

476 Carducci, Mark. "In Search of Stanley Kubrick." *Millimeter*, 3 (December), 32-37, 49-53.

Biography of Kubrick and his elusive relations with the press in maintaining his privacy. Offers anecdotes about Kubrick's early life in New York and his present work on the film *Barry Lyndon.* In connection with this article, Carducci ran ads asking for any information on Kubrick's life. Many of the responses to that ad are included in the article. Kubrick is a difficult person to get to and only if he wants to see you will you gain entrance to his estate in Boreham Wood.

477 Cluny, Claude M. "Le long chemin des sentiers de la gloire." *Cinema* [Paris], 194 (January), 28-30.

Review analysis of *Paths of Glory* after its release in Paris following a seventeen-year censorship. In French.

478 Coleman, John. "Films: Copping It." *New Statesman*, 90 (25 July), 123-124.

Review of *Paths of Glory*. This is a well made film excellently cast and performed. The photography is quite stunning in presenting the contrast between the grandeur of the chateaus and the misery of the trenches. Excellent casting with Kirk Douglas but the final scenes evoke mixed reactions. This review was written about a recent revival of Kubrick's 1957 film.

479 ______. "Films: In-Fighting." *New Statesman*, 90 (12 December), 766.

Negative review of *Barry Lyndon.* "Why Stanley Kubrick would choose this 'hush of a hush' sub Fielding to film rests beyond my conjecture. Over two years in the making, Kubrick knows how many dollars in the casting, certainly a mountain of research and devotion: from which a three hour molehill. . . ." Discusses the problem of the film's length and lack of plot that "bored me into bewilderment."

480 Debiesse, F. "Les sentiers de la gloire." *Cinematographe*, no. 13 (May-June), p. 6.

Review of *Paths of Glory.* In French.

481 Deglin, P. "Spartacus." *Cine Revue*, 55 (10 July), 14.

Photographic essay on Stanley Kubrick's 1960 film, *Spartacus.*

482 De Nitto, Dennis and William Herman. *Film and the Critical Eye.* New York: Macmillan, pp. 207, 325.

References to Kubrick as director of *Dr. Strangelove* and *2001: A Space Odyssey.*

483 Duarte, F. "O Genial Stanley Kubrick." *Celuloide*, 18 (February), 11-16.

Review analysis of *A Clockwork Orange.*

484 Duffy, Martha and Richard Schickel. "Kubrick's Grandest Gamble." *Time*, 106, no. 24 (15 December), 72-78.

In-depth analysis of Kubrick's production of *Barry Lyndon.* Discusses the background of the filming of *Barry Lyndon* and Kubrick's work habits at his home outside London. Includes notices about the stars Ryan O'Neal and Marisa Berenson. Extensive interview with Kubrick and his ideas on film making: "From start to finish on a film, the only limitations I observe are those imposed on me by the amount of money I have to spend and the amount of sleep I need. You either care or you don't and I simply don't know where to draw the line between those two points." In *Barry Lyndon,* Kubrick relies more on images than words to tell his story. Includes photographs from the film and on location shots of Kubrick and the cast.

485 Dyment, Alan R. *The Literature of the Film: A Bibliographic Guide to the Film as Art and Entertainment, 1936-1975.* London: White Lion, *passim.*
Brief references to Kubrick and the books by Alexander Walker, *Stanley Kubrick Directs,* and Jerome Agel, *The Making of Kubrick's 2001. See* entries 323, 284.

486 Eames, John Douglas. *The MGM Story: The Complete History of Fifty Roaring Years.* London: Octopus Books, pp. 306, 316, 342.
References to films made by Kubrick with MGM, including *Lolita, Dr. Strangelove,* and *2001: A Space Odyssey,* with photographs.

487 Enser, A. G. S. *Filmed Books and Plays: A List of Books and Plays From which Films Have Been Made, 1928-1974.* Revised edition. London: Andre Deutsch, *passim.*
Includes references to the novels on which Kubrick's films have been based: *Paths of Glory* by Humphrey Cobb, *Spartacus* by Howard Fast, *Lolita* by Vladimir Nabokov, *Red Alert* by Peter Bryan George, *The Sentinel* by Arthur C. Clarke, and *A Clockwork Orange* by Anthony Burgess. Includes information on title of book, publication data, date of film, and distributor.

488 Evans, P. "The Heat from 1000 Candles." *New York,* 8 (15 September), 42-43.
Advance story on *Barry Lyndon* and Kubrick's special effects techniques in the film.

489 Fell, John. *Film: An Introduction.* New York: Praeger, pp. 96-97, 100-101, 131, 230.
References to *A Clockwork Orange, Dr. Strangelove,* and *2001: A Space Odyssey.* Discussion of Kubrick's use of popular songs in his films, of color and costumes, and of the special effects in *2001: A Space Odyssey.*

490 Ferrari, A. "Les sentiers de la gloire." *Telecine,* no. 198 (April), pp. 17-18.
Review of *Paths of Glory* after the ban against the film in France was lifted. In French.

491 Ferro, M. "Les sentiers de la gloire." *Jeune Cinema,* 86 (April), 29-31.
Review analysis of *Paths of Glory.* In French.

492 Gaulier, P. "Les sentiers de la gloire." *Revue de Cinema,* 299 (October), 324-325.
Analysis of *Paths of Glory.* In French.

493 Gow, Gordon. "Something More." *Films and Filming,* 22, no. 1 (October), 10-16.

Interview with Malcolm McDowell, star of Kubrick's film *A Clockwork Orange.* Discussion of working with Kubrick and his ability to develop a close working relationship with actors. Kubrick has an ability to experiment and try out new techniques and devices with his actors. Kubrick's ideas for music in *A Clockwork Orange* were suggested during filming.

494 Gray, J. "Barry Lyndon." *Cine Review,* 55 (23 October), 12-13.
Review of Kubrick's new film based on the novel by William Makepeace Thackeray.

495 Green, Benny. "Another fine Mess You've Got us Into, Stanley." *Punch* (17 December), p. 1168.
Review of *Barry Lyndon* in which the critic cannot "understand why Kubrick selected *Barry Lyndon* in the first place, at least give us Thackeray at his best not worst." Describes the film as a failure, an "escapade in an otherwise distinguished career."

496 Kael, Pauline. "Kubrick's Gilded Age." *New Yorker,* 51 (29 December), 49-51.
Negative review of *Barry Lyndon.* "He [Kubrick] has written his own screenplay, and the film lacks the tensions and conflicting temperaments that energized some of his earlier work and gave it jazzy undercurrents." Kubrick has controlled the film so much that he has squeezed the life out of his characters. "He won't let Barry come to life, because he's reaching for a truth that he thinks lies beyond dramatization and he thinks he can get it by photographing externals." Concludes that "we might as well be at a three-hour slide show for art-history majors" and observes that the narrator constantly tells you what is going to happen before it happens.

497 Klain, S. "Barry Lyndon." *Independent Film Journal,* 77 (24 December), 35.
Review of *Barry Lyndon.*

498 Kroll, Jack. "Rogue Male." *Newsweek,* 86, no. 25 (22 December), 49-50.
Review analysis of *Barry Lyndon.* "Seeking the sources of our alienation in the explosively random energies of the eighteenth century, Kubrick has created an epic of esthetic self-indulgence, beautiful but empty. He needs to come back to earth from the outer spaces of past and future." Partial success of the film is due to Kubrick's set pieces and the cinematography of John Alcott. "In *Barry Lyndon* the energy has slowed to a near-stasis and his beautiful images stalk themselves into a giant $11 million picture book to be brooded over for three hours by the audience."

499 Lefevre, R. "Les sentiers de la gloire." *Revue de Cinema,* 295 (April), 59-78.
Review of Kubrick's film *Paths of Glory.* Includes credits for the film and still photos. In French.

500 Martin, M. "Les sentiers de la gloire." *Ecran,* 36 (May), 64-65.
Analysis of Kubrick's *Paths of Glory* following the lifting of the French ban on the film. In French.

501 Marton, T. "'2001': Film Poetry." *Cinefantastique,* 4, no. 1, 44-45.
Discussion of the intention and achievement of Kubrick's *2001: A Space Odyssey.* In French.

502 Michael, Paul. *The Academy Awards: A Pictorial History.* New York: Crown, pp. 326-327, 380.

Reference to the Academy of Motion Pictures Award (1968) for Special Visual Effects for *2001: A Space Odyssey,* and brief reference to *Dr. Strangelove* and *A Clockwork Orange.*

503 Monaco, James. "Why Still Photographers Make Great Directors." *Village Voice,* 20 (22 December), 85-86.

Kubrick's cinema is a lab in which the contrasting elements of still and movie aesthetics are rigorously tested. Compares Kubrick's work in films with still photographers Gordon Parks and Jerry Shatzber. In his latest film *Barry Lyndon,* Kubrick shows us "the images photographers of the 1780's would have produced" if still photography had existed then. "Each of these zooms and tracks allows Kubrick to do what a still camera seldom can, direct our attention to details while at the same time giving us the broad scope of environment." Kubrick learned many of these skills as a still photographer for *Look* magazine.

504 Monserrat, Ann. "Thackeray and Barry Lyndon." *Times* [London], *Saturday Review* (6 December), p. 7.

Story of the background of the novel and how Thackeray got his idea for the book. Includes photographs from Kubrick's film production of *Barry Lyndon.*

505 Murf [A. D. Murphy]. "Barry Lyndon." *Variety,* 281 (17 December), 23.

Review of *Barry Lyndon* following the premiere at Burbank Studios of Warner Brothers. Calls the film a "stylish elegant Stanley Kubrick filmization of Thackeray novel." Points to problems in the length and the low key drama that could stall public interest in it. "The film therefore has theatrical importance without compelling significance. Put another way could anyone else have pulled this off? . . . all associated craftsmen have done outstanding work."

506 Murray, Edward. *Nine American Film Critics.* New York: Ungar, p. 212.

Discussion of the film review of *Lolita* by Dwight MacDonald. *See* entry 125.

507 Phelps, Guy. *Film Censorship.* London: Victor Gollancz, pp. 80-83 and *passim.*

References to the treatment of the question of pornography in *Clockwork* by various critics. Includes numerous references to the treatment of sex and violence in the film *A Clockwork Orange.*

508 Phillips, Gene D. *Stanley Kubrick: A Film Odyssey.* New York: Popular Library Film Series, 189 pp.

Detailed discussion and analysis of Stanley Kubrick's career as a film director, including *The Seafarers,* a short documentary that Kubrick produced. Chapter-length discussion of each of Kubrick's works (except *Day of the Fight, The Seafarers* and *The Flying Padre,* grouped in the first chapter). Analysis of Kubrick's films is augmented by a personal interview with him at his home in Boreham Wood, England. Includes extensive bibliography and filmography complete through *A Clockwork Orange,* with partial credits for *Barry Lyndon.* Volume includes many photographs from each of the feature films. Expanded edition 1977, *see* Entry 604.

509 Pitman, Jack. "Irish Band Hypo via Kubrick Film." *Variety,* 280 (15 October), 1, 76.

Stanley Kubrick's film *Barry Lyndon* helped to advertise the Chieftains, a musical group that provided about forty minutes of background music in the film. Group has become more popular since the release of the film.

510 Powell, Dilys. "Barry Lyndon." *Times* [London] (14 December), p. 10.
Review of Kubrick's film *Barry Lyndon.*

511 Rabourdin, D. "Les sentiers de la gloire." *Cinema 75,* no. 198 (May), pp. 101-103.
Review of *Paths of Glory* after its first screening in France since the original release in 1957. In French.

512 Rich, Frank. Review of *Barry Lyndon. New York Post* (19 December), p. 22.
Discusses the use of special effects and elaborate costumes and scenery in the film.

513 Robinson, David. "Stanley Kubrick Retreats to Thackeray." *Times* [London] (12 December), p. 1.
Negative review of *Barry Lyndon.* "Plastically, certainly the film is marvellous, but not quite enough to hold your patience for upwards of three hours or to stop wondering what Kubrick was going to substitute for the brutality of Thackery he took out." Bewildering aspect is that Kubrick had so much to choose from but that so much is muted in the film. "He has turned to a little read nineteenth century failed classic and filmed it in a way that leaves his intentions totally enigmatic."

514 Rovin, Jeff. *A Pictorial History of Science Fiction Films.* Secaucus, New Jersey: Citadel Press, pp. 116-123, 164-165, 188-190.
Discussion of the kinds of science fiction in Kubrick's *Dr. Strangelove, 2001: A Space Odyssey,* and *A Clockwork Orange.* Included in this volume are numerous photographs from each of Kubrick's films, especially *2001: A Space Odyssey.*

515 Sarris, Andrew. "What Makes Barry Run?" *Village Voice,* 20 (29 December), 111-112.
"Stanley Kubrick's *Barry Lyndon* is clearly the most expensive meditation on melancholy every financed by a Hollywood studio." Thackeray's novel serves only as a pretext "for the projection of Kubrick's utter despair." Expresses doubts about the value of the film and the problem of plot. "Neither escapist or scapegoatish in his approach, he seems to be telling us that Past and Future, Here and There, I and Thou, are equally arid domains of the doomed ego. Indeed the film of *Barry Lyndon* is over for all dramatic and psychological purposes almost as soon as it begins. It will all end badly, of that we are sure."

516 Scott, James F. *Film: The Medium and the Maker.* New York: Holt, Rinehart, and Winston, p. 115.
Describes the visual effects used in *2001: A Space Odyssey.*

517 Simon, John. "Million Dollar Blimps." *New York,* 9, no. 1 (29 December-5 January), 84-87.
Negative review of *Barry Lyndon.* Praises the technical use of candlelight sequences in the film and the magnificent use of landscape and color. "But how does one attrack crowds with a humdrum story about unprepossessing

characters played by mostly undistinguished actors? No stars, no sex, no violence, no rollicking *Tom Jones* humor. Are the masses to be brought in by their interest in neo-classical architecture?" Simon observes, "Watching the movie is like looking at illustrations for a work that has not been supplied."

518 Sklar, Robert. *Movie-Made America: A Social History of the American Movies.* New York: Random House, pp. 182, 184, 296.

Discussion of Stanley Kubrick as a director and the use of special effects in his films.

519 Sterritt, David. "A Breathtaking Mysterious Achievement." *Christian Science Monitor* (22 December), p. 22.

Review of *Barry Lyndon* focusing on the problems in the film with screenplay, musical score, and cinematography. "It is a flawed but often deeply moving epic . . . *Barry Lyndon* sometimes loses sight of the difference between the evocative and the trifling, and Kubrick too often gets infatuated with his own shots." Like *2001: A Space Odyssey, Barry Lyndon* is "a giant of a movie."

520 Taylor, John Russell. "Stanley Kubrick," in his *Directors and Directions: Cinema for the Seventies.* New York: Hill and Wang, pp. 100-135.

Detailed analysis of all of Kubrick's films through *A Clockwork Orange.* Examines Kubrick's films in light of the auteur theory of film direction. "And yet, for myself I find there is always something in Kubrick's films, brilliant though most of them are, that seems to stop short of the total creative involvement of the true *auteur.* Is it perhaps that he is keeping back something vital of himself, that the films seem in a way like so many masks assumed by their maker rather than various aspects of his own face? Possibly. Anyway, a sense of slight disquiet persists. I find it easier to bring the films in focus one by one, as isolated phenomena, than to get a unified picture of them all together." Kubrick's best films are: *Paths of Glory, A Clockwork Orange, Lolita,* and with reservations *2001: A Space Odyssey.* "In his finest films his ambition is matched only by his achievement; and there is not one of the nine features he has made in the last twenty years which does not have some strong virtues and some critics to expound them enthusiastically."

Reviewed in *American Film,* a (October, 1975), pp. 77+.

521 Wagner, Geoffrey. *The Novel and the Cinema.* Madison, New Jersey: Fairleigh Dickinson University Press, pp. 307-313.

Discussion of the adaptation of Anthony Burgess's novel *A Clockwork Orange* and Kubrick's film. Includes references to Kubrick's other films: *Dr. Strangelove, Lolita, The Killing,* and *2001: A Space Odyssey.*

522 Walz, Eugene Paul. "The Light-Mare World of Recent Film Satire." Ph.D. dissertation, University of Massachusetts.

Chapter Four offers a detailed scene-by-scene analysis of *Dr. Strangelove, Or How I Learned to Stop Worrying and Love the Bomb,* and the use of satire in the film. "What *Dr. Strangelove* proposes is that the improvement of the earth is best accomplished by the elimination of mankind. In a confrontation between uncooperative, incompetent and silly human beings versus potent and fool-proof machines, not only *will* man be obliterated and replaced, the film says that he *should* be. For this reason there is no eschatological fury, no apocalyptic desperation or hysteria in the film. Nuclear cataclysm is not something lamentable or maddening or even very important. One can 'stop worrying and love the bomb' much the way one can love DDT: it exterminates an amusing but pesky colony of vermin. In this sense *Dr. Strangelove* is a satire in the tradition of Swift and Rochester, the only difference being the film's tone of grim facetiousness and nightmare inescapability."

523 Wolf, William. "A Woman Who Has Everything But Is Searching For More." *Cue* (13 December), pp. 27-28.

Offers an interview with Marisa Berenson, star of Kubrick's new film *Barry Lyndon.* Discusses the film and Kubrick's ability as a director. Kubrick is a perfectionist who takes a scene over and over until he gets what he wants. Includes photographs and background information about the film *Barry Lyndon* as a period film set in the eighteenth century dealing with love, war, and adventure.

524 ______. "Barry Lyndon." *Cue* (26 December), p. 26.

Review of the film praising it as "one of the most beautiful films ever made." Describes Kubrick's special visual effects in the film, concluding: "This may be the film that comes closest to reading a novel. It radiates as another master work of astonishing beauty and intelligence."

525 Wood, Michael. *America in the Movies, or Santa Maria, It Had Slipped My Mind.* New York: Basic Books, p. 149.

Brief reference to *A Clockwork Orange* and the use of popular music in Kubrick's film.

1976

526 Anon. Review of *Barry Lyndon. Modern Photography,* 40 (August), 41-42.

Analysis of the special effects in the film and the use of color photography.

527 Anon. "Clockwork Orange Pulls All Time High in Spain." *Boxoffice,* 109 (23 August), 10.

Report of the all time popularity of *A Clockwork Orange* as the best moneymaking film in the history of commercial cinema in Spain.

528 Anon. "Clockwork Orange May be Spain's Biggest Hit Ever." *Boxoffice,* 109 (13 September), E1.

Stanley Kubrick's film *A Clockwork Orange* continues to break all box office records for attendance at a commercial film in Spain.

529 Anon. "All Time Film Rental Champs." *Variety,* 281 (7 January), 20, 44.

Three of Kubrick's films appear in the listings of the top moneymaking films of all time. These films are: *2001: A Space Odyssey* ($23,077,000 gross), *Spartacus* ($14,600,000 gross), and *A Clockwork Orange* ($14,400,000 gross). This list is limited to all feature films yielding distributors $4,000,000 and upwards in profits.

530 Anon. "Confident Re: 'Barry L'." *Variety,* 281 (14 January), 6.

Warner Brothers vice-president and sales manager Terry Semel predicted that *Barry Lyndon* will be "the big picture of 1976." Picture is doing much better than okay and has received the Best Picture nod from the National Board of Review.

531 Anon. "Clockwork Orange Gross May Exceed $1 mil in Spain Run." *Variety,* 282 (21 April), 38.
Reports popularity of Stanley Kubrick's film, *A Clockwork Orange,* now touring Spain in an exclusive engagement. Attendance at the film will result in over $1 million in profits.

532 Anon. "Clockwork Cracks Records in Spain." *Variety,* 284 (8 September), 26.
Stanley Kubrick's film *A Clockwork Orange* has broken all box office records for film profits in Spain.

533 Atkins, Thomas R., ed. *Science Fiction Films.* New York: Monarch Press, Simon and Schuster, pp. 29–47.
Contains brief references to Kubrick's *2001: A Space Odyssey* in the history of the development of science fiction films. Contains several photographs from the film.

534 Aufhauser, Marcia Cavell. "The Genius of Kubrick." *New Leader,* 59, no. 2 (19 January), 23-25.
Review of *Barry Lyndon* with suggested comparisons to Kubrick's techniques in *A Clockwork Orange.* "Yet *Barry Lyndon* is as ambitious as Kubrick's other films and its picaresque style renders more poignant its serious intentions." It is a movie about space, and time and consciousness. The barbarity of civilized society is a theme that is common to both *Barry Lyndon* and *A Clockwork Orange.* "In *Barry Lyndon* the point is expanded beyond the hypocrisy of social convention to the ambiguity of human nature." Includes analysis of Kubrick's use of space in the opening sequence of the film with Redmond Barry and Nora.

535 Barsacq, Leon. *Caligari's Cabinet and Other Grand Illusions: A History of Film Design.* Boston: New York Graphic Society, pp. 146, 152, 153, 191.
Includes discussion of the set designs for Stanley Kubrick's films *Dr. Strangelove, Or How I Learned To Stop Worrying and Love the Bomb* and *2001: A Space Odyssey.* Analysis of the front projection technique used in filming *2001: A Space Odyssey.*

536 Bawden, Liz-Anne. "Stanley Kubrick," in her *The Oxford Companion to Film.* New York and London: Oxford University Press, p. 398.
Includes a biographical sketch of Kubrick and brief comment on all of his films except *Barry Lyndon.* Kubrick demonstrates a dislike of modern society in his films.

537 Belmans, J. "Stanley Kubrick et 'Barry Lyndon.'" *Amis du Film & de la Television,* 244 (September), 6-7.
Review analysis of *Barry Lyndon* with film credits, filmography of Kubrick and portrait of Kubrick. In French.

538 Canham, C. "Barry Lyndon," *Audience,* 9 (August), 7.
Review of *Barry Lyndon* focusing on the scope and direction of the film.

539 Carey, J. "The Happy Squanderer." *Times Literary Supplement,* no. 3852 (9 January), p. 32.
Review of Stanley Kubrick's new film *Barry Lyndon.*

540 Casebier, Allan. *Film Appreciation.* New York: Harcourt Brace Jovanovich, pp. 106-110, 154-156.

Includes an analysis of Stanley Kubrick and his films: *Dr. Strangelove, 2001: A Space Odyssey,* and *A Clockwork Orange.* Discussion focuses on theme and technique in Kubrick's work and uses photographs from the films to illustrate its points.

541 Chappell, Fred. "The Science Fiction Film Image: A Trip to the Moon to 2001: A Space Odyssey," in *Science Fiction Films.* Edited by Thomas Atkins. New York: Monarch Press, pp. 29-47.

Presents a survey of the science fiction film and discusses the place of Kubrick's *2001: A Space Odyssey* as the most recent development of the form. Includes photographs from the film and a brief bibliography of articles and books on *2001: A Space Odyssey.*

542 Chown, Jeffrey. "The Adapted Novel as a Key to Film Understanding: Anthony Burgess's and Stanley Kubrick's *A Clockwork Orange.*" Master's thesis, University of Oklahoma, 1976.

Introduction, scene-by-scene analysis and review of scholarship on Kubrick's film *A Clockwork Orange.* Discussion of the film demonstrates the differences between novel and film and the reasons Kubrick chose certain scenes over others. Analyzes the various themes in both the Burgess novel and the Kubrick film. Includes information on production and the reaction to Kubrick's film by the major American and British film critics.

543 Clancy, J. "Barry Lyndon." *Cinema Papers,* 363 (March/April), 12-14.

Review analysis of *Barry Lyndon.*

544 Combs, Richard. "Barry Lyndon." *Monthly Film Bulletin* (January), pp. 3-4.

"The essential, and quite characteristic irony of *Barry Lyndon* is that one of Kubrick's most personal and complex films should also look one of his most blankly remote and unapproachable. . . . *Barry Lyndon* emerges as perhaps Kubrick's most intensely human spectacle comparable to *Paths of Glory* in its tragic confrontations that seem to throw whole worlds into the balance with individual lives and far from the too neatly closed circuits of personal anarchy and social repression in *A Clockwork Orange.*" Includes credits for *Barry Lyndon* and a summary of the plot.

545 Craven, Jenny. "Barry Lyndon." *Films and Filming,* 22 (February), 33-34.

Mixed review of *Barry Lyndon.* "Kubrick has created not just moving pictures but moving paintings." Cannot understand what attracted Kubrick to this "indifferent saga" because Kubrick has been known for style and subject while Thackeray is known more for style than for his choice of subject. Dislikes the performance of Ryan O'Neal in the lead role and feels indifferent toward Marisa Berenson.

546 Crist, Judith. "Kubrick as Novelist." *Saturday Review,* 3 (10 January), 61.

Review of *Barry Lyndon* commenting on the scope and brilliance of the film adaptation from Thackeray's novel. "*Barry Lyndon* is a consummate work of film art; a 'literary' period piece brought to cinema terms of remarkable intelligence and overwhelming beauty." Praises Ryan O'Neal's acting and Marisa Berenson's eyes. Sees *Barry Lyndon* as an historical film with "outstanding vistas, landscapes, and interior shots."

547 Cumbow, R.C. and P. F. Palau. "Barry Lyndon." *Movietone*, no. 48 (February), pp. 30-31.
Review analysis of *Barry Lyndon.*

548 Dempsey, Michael. "Barry Lyndon." *Film Quarterly*, 30, no. 1 (Fall), 49-54.
Discusses the use of ceremonies in the film and the changes from the Thackeray novel. The theme of death pervades the film and every aspect of the film is calculated, "the film is as formal as a minuet." "*Barry Lyndon* is not a drama or a character study or even a satire on the abundant human corruption which it portrays," but rather a "meditation of the transience of life."

549 Everson, William K. Review of *Barry Lyndon. Films in Review*, 27, no. 2 (February), 121-122.
"*Barry Lyndon* is a work of consummate craftsmanship and one with a notably civilized stance." Compares the film with Lewin's *The Picture of Dorian Gray* and Huston's *The Red Badge of Courage* in its treatment of a passive expressionless hero and the use of voice over narration. Thackeray's novel and Kubrick's film "are parallel in their manner of treating passionate events in a passionless manner." Disagress with other critics who have disliked the film. "The reason critics have felt so ill at ease with the film is because it so resolutely refuses to adhere to currently popular directorial photographic and editing styles."

550 Feldmann, Hans. "Kubrick and His Discontents." *Film Quarterly*, 30, no. 1 (Fall), 12-19.
Analysis of Kubrick's films and comparison of them with his most recent film *Barry Lyndon.* "Kubrick is not at all interested in faithfully reproducing another artist's interpretation of life. He has his own reading of life and he feels free to alter arbitrarily another artist's work in order to express his vision, his interpretation of his age." Includes photographs from the film *Barry Lyndon.*

551 Ferlita, Ernest and John R. May. *Film Odyssey: The Art of Film as Search for Meaning.* New York and Toronto: Paulist Press, pp. 140-145.
Detailed analysis of the religious meanings in Kubrick's film *2001: A Space Odyssey.*

552 Garel, A. "Sur deux films de Stanley Kubrick." *Revue de Cinema*, no. 308 (September), pp. 63-81.
Analysis of Kubrick's films *Paths of Glory* and *Barry Lyndon.* In French.

553 Gorman, M. J. "'Barry Lyndon' (W B) is NSC selection for January's Blue Ribbon Award." *Boxoffice*, 108 (1 March), 11.
Award to Kubrick's film *Barry Lyndon* for outstanding cinematography in the film. Includes credits for the film and several still shots.

554 Hatch, Robert. Review of *Barry Lyndon. Nation*, 222, no. 1 (10 January), 30.
Review of *Barry Lyndon* that finds problems with staging, acting, and sets, "animation of production killed by a striving for perfection." Kubrick "took up Thackeray's little-known book, I think it is evident, because it gave him the chance to marshal all the resources of confectionary drama in the service of a thoroughly corrupt, sadistic, and remorseless story. The effect intended, I believe, is that your senses should be delighted at the same time your feelings are

plunged into despair." Hatch concludes that "*Barry Lyndon* is a subduing three hours to impose on an audience innocently bent on pleasurable escape into a more colorful, if not happier, age than its own."

555 Hofsess, John. "How I Learned To Stop Worrying and Love 'Barry Lyndon.'" *New York Times* (11 January), Section 2, p. 13.

Discussion of the visual qualities of *Barry Lyndon* that offers comparison to *2001: A Space Odyssey.* "What I have found is that the more completely cinematic a film is, the less interesting the screenplay becomes. Because a screenplay isn't meant to be read, it's to be realized on film. . . . It may be only half true to say that the split over Kubrick's film is mainly between those people who are verbally oriented and those who are visually oriented. Instead, the basic division seems to be between people who are fixed in their notions of what a film should be and those of more flexible personality who are willing to experience an esthetic experiment."

556 Hollow, John. "2001 in Perspective: The Fiction of Arthur C. Clarke." *Southwest Review,* 61, no. 2, 113-129.

Examines *2001: A Space Odyssey* in light of the other work done by Clarke.

557 Houston, Penelope. "Barry Lyndon." *Sight and Sound,* 45, no. 2 (Spring), 77-80.

Review analysis of *Barry Lyndon.* Includes a detailed plot summary of the film and commentary on Kubrick's style and technique. Relates the film to Kubrick's earlier work and concludes that Kubrick does not think much of the human race.

558 Jowett, Garth. [For The American Film Institute]. *Film: The Democratic Art.* Boston and Toronto: Little, Brown, p. 419.

Includes a quotation from Stanley Kubrick on the subject of a motion picture code and censorship: ". . . the Code has become the loose suspenders that hold up the baggy pants of the circus clown. It allows the pants to slip dangerously, but never to fall."

559 Jungstedt, T. "Barry Lyndon." *Chaplin,* 18, no. 2 (143), 51-54.

Review analysis of Kubrick's film *Barry Lyndon.* In Danish.

560 Kauffmann, Stanley. Review of *Barry Lyndon. New Republic,* 174, nos. 1-2 (3/10 January), 22-23.

Negative review of *Barry Lyndon.* Finds the acting, pacing, and storyline boring and very uninterestingly told. Kauffman comments: "Many sequences begin with a close shot of an object or person, then the camera pulls back slowly to set the initial subject in a vast environment. Over and over again, this style is repeated. . . . Kubrick has opted strongly for context as subject possibly to create a tension between the heavenly serenity of the places and the intrigue-cum-butchery they contain . . ." Kubrick has produced "three hours and four minutes of pictures." Concludes that Kubrick's latter-day work is "solipsist and smug, isolated and sterile."

561 Kowalski, Rosemary R. *Women and Film: A Bibliography.* Metuchen, New Jersey: The Scarecrow Press, items 1994 and 2105.

Includes references to articles on Kubrick's treatment of women in his films.

562 Lewis, George H. "Culture, Kubrick, and *Barry Lyndon*." *Society*, 13 (July), 81-82.
One of the constants in Kubrick's films is the fact that his characters are flat and one-dimensional and that he fails to explore the individual psychological implications of the grand environments his films have become. "Kubrick is an artist who recognizes the importance and explores the implications of the political, technological and cultural structures of contemporary society." *Barry Lyndon* is an exploration of the power of pop culture in society.

563 Lunday, J. Review of *Barry Lyndon. Rolling Stone* (29 January), p. 12.
Examines *Barry Lyndon* as a spectacle with problems.

564 McBride, Joseph. *Kirk Douglas*. New York: Pyramid Books, *passim*.
Biography of Kirk Douglas that focuses briefly on his association with Stanley Kubrick in making *Paths of Glory* and *Spartacus*. Explains why Douglas selected Kubrick to direct *Spartacus*.

565 McCubbin, S. "Reader's Right: *Dr. Strangelove*." *Films Illustrated*, 5 (April), 316-317.
Discussion of the popularity of *Dr. Strangelove*.

566 Macklin, F. Anthony. "Review of *Barry Lyndon*." *Film Heritage*, 11, no. 3 (Spring), 30-33.
"*Barry Lyndon* is a lengthy, slow, grand film that uses its own time and way to tell its story. That would be its downfall, it is also its mastery." Focuses on use of lighting, scenery, photography, and acting in *Barry Lyndon*. Discusses weak performances by actors selected for their weaknesses. Compares the acting of Sue Lyon in *Lolita* and Ryan O'Neal in *Barry Lyndon*. Kubrick has gained for himself a freedom in the film industry that is startling. "*Barry Lyndon* is a crown in Stanley Kubrick's achievements."

567 Mast, Gerald. *A Short History of the Movies*. Indianapolis: Bobbs-Merrill, pp. 323, 417, 429, 487, 492-495.
References to Kubrick's films and his place in the development of the American cinema. "The essential Kubrick theme is man's love affair with death. Kubrick seems to be a social critic in that his films consistently rip apart the hypocrisies of polite society: the military society of World War I France, the pseudo-intellectual society of suburbia, the political society of the White House and the Pentagon, the scientific society that can develop rockets that fly to the moon but cannot keep nations from warring with one another, the sterilized banality of a society of the future. As with Renoir, Kubrick's social evils are human evils; men created society, not the other way around. Human society and humanness are antithetical and yet life is so constitued that human life is paradoxically impossible without human society and impossible with it." Includes detailed discussions of *Dr. Strangelove, Lolita, 2001: A Space Odyssey*, and *A Clockwork Orange*. Refers to Kubrick as perhaps the most important American film maker of the last decade.

568 Pechter, William S. "Kubrick and Peckinpah Revisited." *Commentary*, 61, no. 3 (March), 60-62.
Negative review of *Barry Lyndon* and Peckinpah's *Killer Elite*. "Kubrick seems to be looking down at mankind through the wrong end of a telescope, an

anthology of beautiful views of beautiful scenery that seems hermetically sealed and cut off from such truly and diversely beautiful looking films as *Breathless* or *French Cancan*." Kubrick seems to "depict the life of the protagonist and everyone else in the film as one of virtually unrelieved unhappiness." Does not see anything new in *Barry Lyndon* that is not implied in Kubrick's earlier films.

569 Petric, Vladimir. "Film Scholarship and Impressionistic Film Criticism." *Quarterly Review of Film Studies*, 1, no. 2, 141-154.
Brief mention of Kubrick in a survey of film criticism.

570 Phillips, Harvey E. "Stunning Emptiness." *National Review*, 28, no. 13 (16 April), 399-400.
"*Barry Lyndon* is an infinitely lavish movie but its richness serves very little purpose. Not a single scene is excitingly written or played for dramatic potential. Worse, no actor is given a chance to establish more than a facade of characterization." Concludes that *Barry Lyndon* "impresses as a curious, overripe unresonant puzzle."

571 Rainer, P. "Movies: *Barry Lyndon* and *The Man Who Would Be King*." *Mademoiselle*, 82 (March), 38.
Review of *Barry Lyndon* calling attention to Kubrick's lavish use of sets and costumes.

572 Reilly, Charles Phillips. "1975's Ten Best." *Films in Review*, 27 (February), 65-70.
Award given to *Barry Lyndon* and *Nashville* as best pictures of 1975. Stanley Kubrick was awarded the Best Director of 1975 because although *Barry Lyndon* has both lovers and haters, the editors were impressed with "Stanley Kubrick's daring to produce an almost silent film."

573 Rice, Julian. "Barry Lyndon: Like Father, Like Son." *Film Criticism*, 1, no. 2 (Summer), 9-14.
Comparison of elements in the first and second parts of *Barry Lyndon* and the use of parallel elements in the lives of Redmond Barry and his father.

574 Riquelme, K. "Hype, hype, Hurrah." *Audience*, 8 (March), 10-11.
Review of *Barry Lyndon*.

575 Ritterman, B. "You Must Remember Theses [sic]." *Audience*, 8 (April), 8-10.
Review of *Barry Lyndon*.

576 Rosenbaum, Jonathan. "The Pluck of 'Barry Lyndon.'" *Film Comment*, (March-April), pp. 26-28.
Discussion of the critical reaction to Kubrick's film *Barry Lyndon* and an analysis of why it fails. Sees the critics as not understanding Kubrick's intentions and attempting to force a preconceived idea on the film that does not fit. Considers the importance of the narration in the film and the theme of attraction-repulsion that is common to both *Barry Lyndon* and *A Clockwork Orange*.

577 Rosenberg, Harold. "Notes on Seeing *Barry Lyndon*." *New York Times* (26 February), Section 2, pp. 1, 15.

Review of *Barry Lyndon* by an art critic who sees Kubrick's attention to detail in the film as critical to understanding its point. "In short the movie is a valid substitute for Thackeray's narrative because it is a substitute for something which the audience today doesn't have anyway." Includes photographs from the film and from nineteenth century artists. "The adventures of Barry are delivered in a faultless esthetic package. I could have watched *Barry Lyndon* for another two hours without the slightest interest in what happens to the hero."

578 Schupp, P. "Barry Lyndon." *Sequences,* no. 84 (April), pp. 39–41.
Review of Stanley Kubrick's *Barry Lyndon* with film credits and photographs from the film.

579 Segond, J. "Le hasard et la nécessité." *Positif,* no. 179 (March), pp. 2-10.
Review analysis of Stanley Kubrick's film, *Barry Lyndon* with film credits and still shots from the film. In French.

580 Sinyard, Norman. "Barry Lyndon." *Films Illustrated,* 5 (March), 270.
Review of *Barry Lyndon* with photographs from the film.

581 Tarnowski, J. F. "Les voies du silence et le cinéma fantastique." *Positif,* no. 177 (January), pp. 27-33.
Review of *Barry Lyndon.* In French.

582 Teegarden, J. and R. A. Wilson Jr. "Aural Fixations: Sound Tracks in Key." *Audience,* 9 (September), 11-12.
Analysis of the soundtrack of *Barry Lyndon* and the use of different types of music in the film.

583 Westerbeck, Colin L. Jr. "The Screen: Light Comedy." *Commonweal,* 103 (26 March), 208-209.
Discussion of Kubrick's use of light in *Barry Lyndon* as an image to illustrate life. Kubrick has "understood that the subject of all photography is light. Because Kubrick recognizes this light is always a form of imagery in his films. It does not shine on some other imagery of things or compositions: it is an image itself." Discusses the use of sunlight and candlelight in the film *Barry Lyndon*; Westerbeck examines the "rake's progress" of Barry in terms of the indoor and outdoor scenes in the film. "All the key scenes [in part 2] henceforth occur like this, indoors with outdoor lighting, and it is typical of Kubrick's sense of irony that he should make his hero's decline and fall with such a glorious blaze of light."

584 ______. "The Screen." *Commonweal,* 103 (9 April), 243-245.
Continuation of his review of *Barry Lyndon. See* entry 583. The meaning and order in the film accrue from what we see. "The allegory of light with which Kubrick has surrounded these developments turns a Rake's Progress into a Pilgrim's Progress of an ironic, secular kind. The film becomes another of Kubrick's long, acerbic and dazzingly eloquent essays on civilization." Shows how Kubrick enlarges on Thackeray's novel in the film version. Thackeray offered Kubrick one invaluable thing: "the nineteenth century insight into the eighteenth."

585 Wolfe, G.K. "*Dr. Strangelove, Red Alert,* and Patterns of Paranoia in the 1950's." *Journal of Popular Film,* 5, no. 1 (Winter), 57-67.

Analysis of the paranoid thinking of the fifties and "how this movie [*Dr. Strangelove*] can be directly traced to the sensibilities of the fifties through its source, Peter George's 1958 novel *Red Alert*; and how it fits into the overall history of paranoid culture since the war."

586 Wood, M. "No, But I Read the Book." *New York Review of Books,* 23 (5 February), 3-4.

Review of *Barry Lyndon* comparing the film with the novel by Thackeray.

587 Wood, Robin. *Personal Views: Explorations in Film.* London: Gordon Fraser, p. 15.

Includes a brief reference to Kubrick's film *A Clockwork Orange* and the issue of the controversy surrounding film.

588 Wordsworth, A. "Tableaux Vivants." *Times Educational Supplement* [London], no. 165 (30 January), p. 86.

Review of Stanley Kubrick's new film *Barry Lyndon.*

1977

589 Aros, Andrew. *A Title Guide to the Talkies, 1964-1974: A Guide to the Literary Sources of Screenplays.* Metuchen, New Jersey: The Scarecrow Press, items 553, 803a, 3128.

Includes complete bibliographical information on the literary sources of Kubrick's *A Clockwork Orange, Dr. Strangelove, or How I Learned To Stop Worrying and Love the Bomb,* and *2001: A Space Odyssey.*

590 Braudy, Leo. *The World in a Frame: What We See in Films.* New York: Anchor Press/Doubleday, pp. 51, 55, 58, 63, 65, 124, 160.

Includes many brief references to Kubrick and the use of music and camera angles in his films. Includes a discussion of *Barry Lyndon*: "Stanley Kubrick in *Barry Lyndon* (1975) constantly pulls his camera back from his characters to subordinate them to the more inclusive vision of the director and the formal beauty of the landscape."

591 Brustein, Robert. "Out of this World," in *Language and Film: Essays in Criticism.* Edited by Wallace Coyle. Boston: Northeastern University Press, pp. 18-21.

See entry 152.

592 Byron, Stuart and Elisabeth Weis. *The National Society of Film Critics on Movie Comedy.* New York: Grossman, pp. 145, 177, 179-183, 193, 288.

Includes a section on comedy in *Dr. Strangelove* and a brief note on comedy in *A Clockwork Orange.*

593 Clarke, Arthur C. "Son of Dr. Strangelove; or How I Learned To Stop Worrying and Love Stanley Kubrick," in *Turning Point: Essays on the Art of Science Fiction.* Edited by Damon Knight. New York: Harper and Row, pp. 277-284.

Discussion by Clarke of working with Kubrick on the film *2001: A Space Odyssey.*

594 Derry, Charles. *Dark Dreams: A Psychological History of the Modern Horror Film.* New York: A. S. Barnes, pp. 47, 50-51, 124, 130.

Brief discussions of the horror element in Kubrick's films: *Dr. Strangelove, 2001: A Space Odyssey,* and *A Clockwork Orange.* Includes photographs from the films.

595 Halliwell, Leslie. *Halliwell's Film Guide: A Survey of 8000 English-Language Movies.* London: Granada, *passim.*

Presents credits, plot summaries, critiques, and details of all of Stanley Kubrick's films except *Fear and Desire* and *Barry Lyndon.*

596 Kauffman, Stanley. "Stanley Kauffman on Film." *New Republic,* 175 (10 December), 20-22.

In a review of the new science fiction film *Close Encounters of the Third Kind,* Kauffmann compares the film to Kubrick's *2001: A Space Odyssey* in its plot, theme, and use of special visual effects. Discusses how they are different kinds of films in the science fiction mode.

597 Koszarski, Richard. "Stanley Kubrick," in *Hollywood Directors, 1941-1976.* New York: Oxford University Press, p. 305.

Brief survey of Kubrick's film career as an introduction to his article on adapting *Lolita* for the films. *See* entry 95.

598 Leyda, Jay, ed. *Voices of Film Experience, 1894 to the Present.* New York: Macmillan, pp. 247-249, and *passim.*

Contains several quotations from Kubrick on the subject of making films, especially his ideas about *Dr. Strangelove, 2001: A Space Odyssey,* and *A Clockwork Orange.* This volume also includes the comments of various actors, actresses, and technicians who have worked with Kubrick on various films. These include: Wally Gentleman (*2001*), Anthony Harvey (*Dr. Strangelove*), Malcolm McDowell (*A Clockwork Orange*), and Shelley Winters (*Lolita*).

599 Mast, Gerald, *Film/Cinema/Movie.* New York: Harper and Row, pp. 59, 61, 99, 161, 223, 224-225.

Includes brief references to Kubrick in the development of the cinema and a section on his talents as an outstanding American film director.

600 Mellen, Joan. *Big Bad Wolves: Masculinity in the American Film.* New York: Pantheon Books, pp. 221, 251-252.

Includes a discussion of the masculine image in Kubrick's film *Dr. Strangelove.* Explains how the film offers a sick version of maleness and how Kubrick satirizes it.

601 Monaco, James. *How to Read a Film: The Art, Technology, Language, History, and Theory of Film and Media.* New York: Oxford Univeristy Press, pp. 109-113, 186-187, 268-269, and *passim.*

Includes numerous references to Kubrick and the use of technical and artistic devices in his films. Presents specific discussion of (1) Kubrick's use of Zeiss lens in filming *Barry Lyndon,* (2) use of the front projection technique in *2001: A Space Odyssey,* (3) use of matte shots in *2001: A Space Odyssey,* (4) the match cut effect in the beginning of *2001: A Space Odyssey* (5) brief discussion of Kubrick's career from his earliest films to *Barry Lyndon.* Includes numerous photographs illustrating the various technical accomplishments in Kubrick's films.

602 Moskowitz, Ken. "Clockwork Violence." *Sight and Sound,* 46, no. 1 (Winter), 22-23, 44.

Discussion of Kubrick's last three films and the theme of violence in *2001: A Space Odyssey, A Clockwork Orange,* and *Barry Lyndon.* "With each new film, Kubrick becomes more precise and definite about the central irrational urge for violence, the unpredictable threat to the complacent, and superficially stable social order." On the treatment of violence in the three films: "In each movie, irrational but fundamental human violence is juxtaposed with or encased in the most formal ritual or latest technological move." Kubrick's last three films "constitute a coherent imaginative vision" and also are increasingly pessimistic. Kubrick insists "that we must tame the ape in us if we are to attain an order that is not superficial, fleeting and illusory as coloured images flashing on a screen."

603 Parish, James Robert and Michael R. Pitts. *The Great Science Fiction Pictures.* Metuchen, New Jersey: The Scarecrow Press, pp. 63-65, 333-335.

Presents picture credits and summaries of *2001: A Space Odyssey* and *A Clockwork Orange.* Notes that the original voice of HAL was Martin Balsam but that his voice was redubbed by Douglas Rain in the release version of the film. Also includes a complete list of science fiction checklists and bibliographies.

604 Phillips, Gene D. *Stanley Kubrick: A Film Odyssey.* New York: Popular Library, 210 pp.

Expanded edition of an earlier book. Includes material on *Barry Lyndon* and complete credits. *See* entry 508.

605 Walker, Alexander. *Double Takes: Notes and Afterthoughts on the Movies, 1956-1976.* London: Elm Tree Books, pp. 122-125, 136-140, 152, 156, 161-162.

Includes original reviews of Kubrick's films *Barry Lyndon* and *A Clockwork Orange.* Discusses Kubrick's career and his contribution to the cinema.

606 Wiswell, Frank. "Barry Lyndon Revisited." *Films and Filming,* 24, no. 1 (October), 40-43.

Review of *Barry Lyndon.* "But as well as Kubrick captures or reflects the attitude of expatriate Americans in Europe toward the European environment in *Barry Lyndon,* he also captures a common European attitude toward the same elements in the environment." Discusses the relationship between art and life suggested by the film. In addition, music is the second element so noticeable in the film. "Barry Lyndon's ultimate fate haunts every expatriate American."

1978

607 Armes, Roy. *A Critical History of the British Cinema.* New York: Oxford University Press, pp. 293-299.

Presents a survey of Kubrick's films through *Barry Lyndon* concentrating on Kubrick's importance to the British cinema. Compares his work with Polanski and Losey. Includes detailed discussion of *Paths of Glory, 2001: A Space Odyssey,* and *Barry Lyndon.* Also includes selected bibliography on Kubrick as a director.

608 Boyd, David. "Mode and Meaning in *2001*." *Journal of Popular Film,* 6, no. 3 (Summer), 202-215.

Discusses the Homeric parallels in Stanley Kubrick's film *2001: A Space Odyssey* and surveys the critical reaction to the film on the occasion of its tenth anniversary. The importance of Kubrick's film is the central use of the mythic element in film. "And a recognition of the film's peculiar mixture of modes is perhaps even more vital because the film represents a fusion of two such *different,* perhaps even antithetical, modes: the satiric and the mythic . . . Myth represents fiction at the highest possible level of generality; whereas satire normally moves in the opposite direction focusing on the concrete particulars of life." Includes an analysis of myth and satire in the four major sequences of *2001: A Space Odyssey.*

609 Dick, Bernard F. *Anatomy of Film.* New York: St. Martin's Press, pp. 62, 76-77, 80.

Includes a discussion of Kubrick as a director and specific analysis of his direction in *Barry Lyndon* and use of music in *A Clockwork Orange.* Includes photographs showing the candelight sequences from *Barry Lyndon.*

610 D'Lugo, Marvin. "*Barry Lyndon*: Kubrick on the Rules of the Game." *Film Studies Annual 1977.* Pleasantville, New York: Redgrave Publishing Co.

Discussion of the use of games in Kubrick's film *Barry Lyndon.* "Stanley Kubrick's *Barry Lyndon* (1975) begins and ends with scenes of pistol duels. Though the sequences which carry us between these points are varied, all pervasively emphasize game elements: seductions, cardgames, a highwayman's tactics of ensnarement, battles and finally sword and pistol duels . . . unmistakably, the emblem of the game prevails throughout." Concludes with the observation: "The underlying philosophical question which the self-consciousness of games and artifice has raised is one which Kubrick has pondered in nearly all his films over the last fifteen years; simply stated it is this: What is Man? Kubrick's answer is posed necessarily in negatives. Man is neither the brute beast nor the rational god, although society insistently seeks to articulate the human essence as either one or the other."

611 King, Stephen. *The Shining.* New York: Signet Books, 448 pp.

This novel is reported to be the next film Kubrick plans to release. Advertisements from the novel proclaim: "soon to be a major new movie directed by Stanley Kubrick and starring Jack Nicholson!"

612 Knight, Arthur. *The Liveliest Art: A Panoramic History of the Movies.* New York: Macmillan, pp. 247, 253, 281.

Includes brief references to Kubrick's films: *Paths of Glory, 2001: A Space Odyssey,* and *A Clockwork Orange.*

612a Roth, Ellen Shamis. "The Rhetoric of First Person Point of View in the Novel and Film Forms: A Study of Anthony Burgess's *A Clockwork Orange* and Henry James's *Turn of the Screw* and Their Film Adaptations." Ph.D. dissertation, New York University, 1978.

A study of the adaptation of *A Clockwork Orange* by Kubrick and the role of Alex in both film and novel versions. Includes comparisons between similar scenes in the Burgess book and the Kubrick film.

1979

613 Bordwell, David and Kristin Thompson. *Film Art: An Introduction.* Reading, Massachusetts: Addison-Wesley, p. 173.

Brief reference to Kubrick's editing ability in *2001: A Space Odyssey.*

614 Ellis, Jack C. *A History of Film.* Englewood Cliffs, New Jersey: Prentice-Hall, pp. 338, 368–373.

Includes a discussion of Kubrick and Joseph Losey as examples of Hollywood directors who moved to Great Britain and who have produced much of their major work in England. "At his worst, or best, Kubrick brought a cold-blooded savagery to his analysis of the American scene; at the same time, and a mark of his consistency, it must be granted that the view *A Clockwork Orange* presents of modern English society is chilling and violent in the extreme." Offers a brief analysis of *Barry Lyndon* with discussion of the meticulous recreation of the eighteenth century world in it. Includes photography from *Barry Lyndon.*

1980

614a Hatch, Robert. "The Shining: Practice Makes Perfect," *Nation,* 230, no. 23 (14 June), 732-733.

Review of *The Shining* commenting that "the film is something of a sport because Kubrick is cavalier with his spookery; it is seldom clear where neurosis ends and haunting takes over."

614b Kauffmann, Stanley. "Films: The Dulling," *New Republic,* 182, no. 24 (14 June), 26-27.

Negative review of *The Shining.* Calls film "a grab bag of spook stuff, with no rhyme or reason of its own." Concludes that Kubrick fails because he "has flunked the elemental test for a horro film: *The Shining* doesn't scare. The only pang in it is that it's another step in Kubrick's descent."

614c Kroll, Jack. "Stanley Kubrick's Horrow Show," *Newsweek,* (26 May), 96-99.

Positive review of *The Shining* calling it "the first epic horror film." Contains analysis of the film, partial credits, and brief study of Kubrick's career and work habits. Includes photographs from film.

614d Maslin, Janet. "Flaws Don't Dim 'The Shining,'" *New York Times,* ii (8 June), pp. 1, 15.

Positive review of *The Shining* that draws comparisons between the film and *Lolita.* Includes plot summary of film and analysis of acting of Jack Nicholson and Shelley Duvall. Comments on some of the problems in the film but feels that some unexplained incidents in film do not detract from overall excellence of Kubrick effort.

614e Schickel, Richard. "Cinema: Red Herrings and Refusals," *Time* (2 June), 69.

Review of *The Shining*. Admires Kubrick for "flouting conventional expectations of his horror film just as he did those of the sci-fi tale in *2001*." Presents analysis of film and concludes: "By taking a book by an author who is at the center of the craze for the supernatural, and turning it into a refusal of and subtle comment on that loopy cultural phenomenon, Kubrick has made a movie that will have to be reckoned with on the highest level."

V Writings and Other Film Related Activity

WRITINGS

1961

615 "Words and Movies." *Sight and Sound,* 30 (Winter), 14.
Kubrick discusses the question of adapting novels, with specific reference to *Lolita. See* entry 95.

1963

616 "How I Learned To Stop Worrying and Love the Cinema." *Films and Filming,* 9 (June), 12-13.
Kubrick discusses his film career and his latest work on *Dr. Strangelove. See* entry 135.

1972

617 "Now Kubrick Fights Back," *New York Times* (27 February), Section 2, pp. 1, 11.
Response of Kubrick to a letter from Fred M. Hechinger attacking *A Clockwork Orange,* as a film "purveying the essence of fascism." Kubrick calls this reading an "irrelevant one" and concludes that "being a pessimist is not yet enough to qualify one to be regarded as a tyrant." Includes quotations from other reviews of the film.

618 *Stanley Kubrick's A Clockwork Orange, Based on the Novel by Anthony Burgess.* New York: Abelard-Schuman, 326 pp.
Presents a shot-by-shot script of the entire film with narration and dialogue. Includes full credits for film with beginning and end titles.

619 "What Directors are Saying" *Action,* 7, no. 1 (January-February), 37.
Includes comment by Kubrick on the subject of creative work on a film set. "Shooting is the part of film making I enjoy least. I don't particularly enjoy working with a lot of people. I'm just not an extrovert."

OTHER FILM RELATED ACTIVITY

620 *One-Eyed Jacks* (1961)

Kubrick worked on this film right up to the time production began on it. He was replaced by the main star in the film, Marlon Brando, who went on to direct his first film. Kubrick received $100,000 for his efforts on *One-Eyed Jacks.*

Produced by Frank P. Rosenberg
Directed by Marlon Brando
Executive Producer: George Glass and Walter Seltzer
A Paramount Production.

VI Archival Sources

UNITED STATES

CALIFORNIA

621 Margaret Herrick Library
Academy of Motion Picture Arts and Sciences
8949 Wilshire Boulevard
Beverly Hills, California 90211
(213) 278-8990, (213) 278-4313
Lisa Mosher, Assistant Librarian

9-5 Monday, Tuesday, Thursday, Friday
Open to public
Photograph duplication services available

Scripts:
2001: A Space Odyssey, A Clockwork Orange, Barry Lyndon

Production Files:
Fear and Desire, Killer's Kiss, The Killing, Paths of Glory, Spartacus, Lolita, Dr. Strangelove, 2001: A Space Odyssey, A Clockwork Orange, Barry Lyndon, The Shining.

Stills:
Killer's Kiss, The Killing, Paths of Glory, Spartacus, Dr. Strangelove, 2001: A Space Odyssey, A Clockwork Orange, Barry Lyndon.

Programs:
Spartacus, 2001: A Space Odyssey, Barry Lyndon

Pressbooks:
2001: A Space Odyssey, A Clockwork Orange, Barry Lyndon

Other
Dr. Strangelove, special effects material; *2001: A Space Odyssey,* program articles

622 Pacific Film Archive
University Art Museum
Berkeley, California 94720
(415) 642-1437

9-12, 1-5 Monday-Friday
"Non-circulating library, stills may not be copied, xerox available."

Stills:
Lolita, Dr. Strangelove

Pressbooks:
Spartacus, A Clockwork Orange, Barry Lyndon

Other:
Killer's Kiss (articles), *The Killing* (articles), *Dr. Strangelove* (articles), *A Clockwork Orange* (articles), *Barry Lyndon* (articles).

623 Theater Arts Library
University of California at Los Angeles
405 Hilgard Avenue
Los Angeles California 90024
Audree Malkin, Librarian

9-6 Monday-Friday
12-4 Saturday

Scripts:
Paths of Glory, Lolita (published screenplay), *Dr. Strangelove, 2001: A Space Odyssey, A Clockwork Orange* and published screenplay for *A Clockwork Orange.*

Stills:
Paths of Glory, Spartacus, Lolita, 2001: A Space Odyssey, A Clockwork Orange, Barry Lyndon

Programs:
Paths of Glory, Lolita, 2001: A Space Odyssey, Barry Lyndon

Other:
The Killing (clipping file, lobby card), *Paths of Glory* (articles, ads, and poster), *Spartacus* (souvenir book–illustrated story), *Lolita* (articles), *Dr. Strangelove* (articles), *2001: A Space Odyssey* (articles, pressbook, poster), *A Clockwork Orange* (articles and poster), *Barry Lyndon* (articles and photo of Kubrick on film set), Articles on Stanley Kubrick

MASSACHUSETTS

624 University Film Study Center
18 Vassar Street, 20B-120
Cambridge, Massachusetts 02139
(617) 776-8381

Restrictions: Reference only
Includes secondary materials on Kubrick and his films.
Limited to published books and some articles.

NEW YORK

625 Film Study Center
Museum of Modern Art
11 West 53rd Street
New York, New York 10019
(212) 956-4212
Charles Silver, Supervisor

1-5 Monday-Friday
Appointment necessary to use the facilities of the Film Study Center.
Appointments for viewing films must be made at least one week in advance.
Film stills are available through the Stills Archivist only. Telephone: (212) 956-4209.

"This material is made available only to qualified scholars working on specific research projects. Students who wish to view films must present a letter from their instructor requesting permission, stating the nature and validity of the project and listing the films required. Writers who obtain a similar letter from their editor or publisher may also obtain permission to view films. The Department of Film retains the right of approving all requests. Due to the limited facilities available, no projects requiring extensively detailed analysis (i.e. shot analysis) of individual films can be permitted."

35mm Prints:
The Killing, Paths of Glory, Spartacus.

16mm Prints:
Lolita, Dr. Strangelove

Other:
"Stills and clipping files on Kubrick and all films; other documentation."

626 Theater Collection
Library of the Performing Arts at Lincoln Center
New York Public Library
111 Amsterdam Avenue
New York, New York 10023
(212) 799-2200
Paul Myers, Curator

12-6 Monday-Saturday
12-8 Monday and Thursday

"The Theater Collection does not collect motion picture films, but we would have files of clipping material on Stanley Kubrick's films, as well as stills, pressbooks, and some of the scripts."

Other:
Collections of reviews of Kubrick's films; additional file on Kubrick himself (clippings).

WASHINGTON, D.C.

627 Motion Picture, Broadcasting, and Recorded Sound Division
Library of Congress
1046 Thomas Jefferson Building
Washington, D.C. 20540
(202) 426-5840
Barbara J. Humphrys, Reference Librarian

8:30-4:30 Monday-Friday

The Motion Picture Section maintains the Library's film collections for scholarly study and research. Public projection, preview, and loan services are not available. The Section staff answers written and telephone inquiries about the holdings and makes appointments for the use of the reference facilities by individual scholars.

The viewing facilities, which consist of several 16mm and 35mm viewing machines, may be used free of charge by serious researchers only; viewing times must be scheduled in advance. The facilities may not be used by high school students; undergraduate college students must provide a letter from their professor endorsing their project. The Section maintains a reading room with extensive card files describing the Library's motion picture holdings. The films include a shelf list, a dictionary catalog, a nitrate film file, a director's file, and chronological and production company files for silent films. Copies of film footage not restricted by copyright, by provisions of gift or transfer, or by physical condition may be ordered through the Section. The requestor is responsible for a search, either in person or by mail, of Copyright Office records to determine the copyright status of specific works.

Prints:
Paths of Glory, Spartacus, Lolita, Dr. Strangelove, 2001: A Space Odyssey, A Clockwork Orange, Barry Lyndon, Day of the Fight, Flying Padre, The Seafarers

Other:
Fear and Desire (synopsis), *Killer's Kiss* (pressbook, stills, lobby cards and poster), *The Killing* (pressbook, stills, lobby cards), *Paths of Glory* (pressbook), *Spartacus* ("description missing–probably a synopsis"), *Lolita* (cutting continuity–American version), *Dr. Strangelove* (picture continuity), *2001: A Space Odyssey* (cutting continuity, stills, pressbook, poster), *A Clockwork Orange* (synopsis, stills, pressbook, poster), *Barry Lyndon* (synopsis, pressbook, poster), *Day of the Fight* (cutting continuity), *Flying Padre* (cutting continuity)

WISCONSIN

628 Wisconsin Center for Film and Theater Research
816 State Street
Madison, Wisconsin 53706
(608) 262-0585, (608) 262-3338
Maxine Fleckner, Associate Film Archivist

8:30–4:30 Monday–Friday

Stills:
Killer's Kiss, The Killing, Paths of Glory, Spartacus, Lolita, Dr. Strangelove

Manuscript Material:
Paths of Glory (scripts, correspondence, miscellaneous publicity, financial records, production file, clippings, materials on Kirk Douglas), *Spartacus* (scripts, correspondence, dialogue, miscellaneous publicity, music, contracts, financial records, continuity, production file, materials on Kirk Douglas and Dalton Trumbo, tapes, book script), *Dr. Strangelove* (pressbook)

GREAT BRITAIN

629 British Film Institute
National Film Archive
81 Dean Street
London W1V 6AA
Telephone: 01-437-4355
David Francis, Curator

Prints:
The Killing, Paths of Glory, Spartacus, Lolita, Dr. Strangelove

Stills:
Killer's Kiss, The Killing, Paths of Glory, Spartacus, Lolita, Dr. Strangelove, 2001: A Space Odyssey, A Clockwork Orange, Barry Lyndon

Clippings, Posters, and Publicity Material:
Killer's Kiss, The Killing, Paths of Glory, Lolita, Spartacus, Dr. Strangelove, 2001: A Space Odyssey, Barry Lyndon, The Shining (clippings only)

Other:
Index listing of many articles on Kubrick and his films.

VII Film Distributors

630 Films Incorporated
440 Park Avenue South
New York, New York 10016

733 Greenbay Road
Wilmette, Illinois 60091

5589 New Peachtree Road
Atlanta, George 30341

5625 Hollywood Blvd.
Hollywood, California 90028

Lolita, 2001: A Space Odyssey

631 Swank Motion Pictures
201 South Jefferson
St. Louis, Missouri 63166

Barry Lyndon, A Clockwork Orange, Dr. Strangelove, Or How I Learned To Stop Worrying and Love the Bomb

632 Twyman Films
329 Salem Avenue
Dayton, Ohio 45401

Spartacus

633 United Artists 16
729 7th Avenue
New York, New York 10019

Killer's Kiss, Paths of Glory, The Killing

634 Universal Sixteen,
445 Park Avenue
New York, New York 10022

Spartacus

VIII Literary Works Adapted for the Cinema by Stanley Kubrick

Anthony Burgess, *A Clockwork Orange.* New York: W. W. Norton, 1962. 184 pp.

Arthur C. Clarke, "The Sentinel" in *The Making of Kubrick's 2001: A Space Odyssey.* New York, 1970.

Humphrey Cobb, *Paths of Glory.* New York: Grosset & Dunlap, 1953. 265 pp.

Howard Fast, *Spartacus.* New York: Modern Library, 1951.

Peter Bryan George, *Red Alert.* New York: Ace Books, 1958.

Stephen King, *The Shining.* New York: Signet Books, 1978. 448 pp.

Vladimir Nabokov, *Lolita.* New York: Putnam, 1955. 319 pp.

______. *Lolita: A Screenplay.* New York: McGraw-Hill, 1974. 213 pp.

William Makepeace Thackeray, *Barry Lyndon.*

Lionel White, *Clean Break.* New York: Gold Medal Books, 1950.

Author Index

Film Title Index